Speed Up Your Fren(

Speed Up Your French is a unique and innovative resource that identifies and explains the errors most commonly made by students of French.
From false friends to idiomatic expressions and the use of prepositions, each of the nine chapters focuses on an aspect of the language where English speakers typically make mistakes. Full explanations are provided throughout with clear, comprehensive examples, enabling students to acquire a surer grasp of French vocabulary and idiom, as well as grammar.

Key features:

- carefully selected grammar topics and examples based on the most commonly made errors
- extensive exercises and answer key to reinforce learning, link theory to practice and promote self-study
- use of mnemonic devices, including illustrations, to aid understanding
- supplementary exercises and answer key available at www.routledge.com/cw/jubb.

Suitable for either classroom use or self-study, *Speed Up Your French* is the ideal resource for all intermediate learners of French wishing to refine their language skills.

Margaret Jubb is Honorary Senior Lecturer in French at the University of Aberdeen.

Speed Up Your Language Skills

SERIES EDITOR: Javier Muñoz-Basols, *University of Oxford, UK*

The *Speed Up Your Language Skills* series publishes innovative, high-quality textbooks focusing on common errors as an effective tool to improve one's skills in a foreign language. Such errors are often either driven by linguistic transfer from English or caused by common misperceptions about the grammatical structure of a foreign language.

The primary objectives of the series are to explain and illustrate in context the most common errors made by English-speaking students in a foreign language and to classify them in easy-to-reference categories. Students can thus learn the appropriate usage of words and expressions and understand the reasons why they persistently make the same mistakes. The inclusion of exercises, shortcuts, mnemonic devices and much-needed strategies, not usually seen in conventional grammar books, facilitates vocabulary acquisition and mastery of essential grammatical elements.

Books in the series are intended as primary or supplementary texts at the intermediate and advanced levels. Due to its self-explanatory approach and user-friendly format, the series is also recommended for self-learners who wish to 'speed up' their language skills.

Available titles in the series:

Speed up your Arabic
Sebastian Maisel

Speed up your Chinese
Shin Yong Robson

Speed up your French
Margaret Jubb

Speed up your Korean
Lucien Brown and Jaehoon Yeon

Speed up your Spanish
Javier Muñoz-Basols, Marianne David and Olga Núñez Piñeiro

Speed Up Your French

Strategies to avoid common errors

Margaret Jubb

LONDON AND NEW YORK

First published 2016
by Routledge
2 Park Square, Milton Park, Abingdon, Oxon OX14 4RN

and by Routledge
711 Third Avenue, New York, NY 10017

Routledge is an imprint of the Taylor & Francis Group, an informa business

British Library Cataloguing-in-Publication Data
A catalogue record for this book is available from the British Library

Library of Congress Cataloging-in-Publication Data
Names: Jubb, Margaret A.
Title: Speed up your French : strategies to avoid common errors / Margaret Jubb.
Description: Milton Park, Abingdon, Oxon ; New York, NY : Routledge, [2016] | Series: Speed up your Language Skills | Includes bibliographical references and index.
Identifiers: LCCN 2015035056| ISBN 9781138849990 (hardback : alk. paper) | ISBN 9781138850002 (pbk. : alk. paper) | ISBN 9781315725062 (ebook)
Subjects: LCSH: French language—Grammar—Problems, exercises, etc. | French language--Errors in usage. | French language—Textbooks for foreign speakers—English.
Classification: LCC PC2460 .J83 2016 | DDC 448.2/421—dc23
LC record available at http://lccn.loc.gov/2015035056

ISBN: 978-1-138-84999-0 (hbk)
ISBN: 978-1-138-85000-2 (pbk)
ISBN: 978-1-315-72506-2 (ebk)

Typeset in Swiss 721 and Zapf Calligraphic
by Florence Production Ltd, Stoodleigh, Devon, UK

Contents

Introduction

This book is intended for English-speaking students, either at secondary school or at university, who have attained an intermediate level in French. It is designed primarily as a guide for self-learning, though it could also be used as a supplement to classroom materials, both for intermediate-level students and for more advanced students who need to revise particular areas of the language.

It focuses on the aspects of foreign language, such as false friends, idiomatic expressions, and the use of prepositions that typically cause English speakers difficulty in their production and understanding of French. The aim is to enable students to identify, understand and overcome their errors in order to become more competent and confident language users with a surer grasp of vocabulary and idiom, as well as grammar.

The illustrative examples that accompany the sections of explanation are as important as the explanations themselves in encouraging students to break old connections based on false analogies with English and form new connections and associations with other related French expressions. Students will develop their own learning strategies through active engagement with the material in the book, but at particular points mnemonic devices are suggested, both for immediate support and in the hope that they will encourage the creation of other self-tailored devices. Throughout the book, it is emphasised that the examples given can rarely be exhaustive, and students are advised, when appropriate, to consult a good bilingual dictionary or a reference grammar to further their independent learning.

Active learning is promoted by the extensive exercises and answer key for self-checking. In each chapter, the final exercise takes the form of a continuous text with gaps to be filled. Unlike the earlier sentence-based exercises, each of which relates to a particular section or sections of a chapter, this final exercise covers the whole chapter and serves as a revision tool.

It would be impossible to cover in a single book every type of common error, so a selection has necessarily had to be made. The author has deliberately decided not to write a revision grammar, but rather to follow the precedent set by the Spanish volume in the *Speed Up Your Language* series with a focus on vocabulary and idiom as much as on grammar. This book brings together a variety of material, accompanied by exercises, that is not readily available elsewhere in such a systematised form. We hope that it will enable students to improve their mastery of French not only by avoiding common errors but also by acquiring a deeper understanding of the language and a richer range of expression.

Chapter 1 deals with the gender and number of simple and compound nouns in French. The first part underlines how important it is for students to learn the gender of nouns so they can improve the accuracy of their spoken and written French. A list of general patterns helps to predict the gender of a noun, in some cases according to meaning, but more often according to ending. Notable exceptions are highlighted and attention is drawn to common problem nouns. Some subtleties of the language are then explored by discussing nouns that change meaning according to gender, e.g. *un crème* (a white coffee) as opposed to *la crème* (cream), or whose gender varies according to use, e.g. *tous les braves gens* (m.), but *toutes les vieilles gens* (f.). The second part of the chapter focuses on the formation of the plural of simple and compound nouns in French. It then highlights differences between the two languages in their treatment of the plural, discussing cases where a plural in French corresponds to a singular in English and vice versa. The final section of the chapter tackles common problems with adjective agreements, which arise as soon as matters of gender and number are considered.

Chapters 2, 3 and 4, though they deal respectively with verbs, nouns, and adjectives and adverbs, all focus on the phenomenon of 'false friends', which are a common cause of error for English-speaking students. These words look like English words, but they have a different meaning. In each chapter, there are two lists, the first consisting of 'false friends' proper and the second of words whose meaning overlaps partially with the assumed English equivalent. Example sentences are chosen to illustrate the meaning of the words in context and useful phrases are given to help fix them in the memory. Related words and synonyms are discussed, all with the aim of expanding students' vocabulary and accuracy of usage.

Chapter 5 deals with common phrases and idiomatic expressions used with the verbs *aller, avoir, donner, être, faire, mettre, prendre, tenir, tomber* and *venir*. If students are not aware of the variety of ways in which these verbs are used and how often their meaning is not a literal one, e.g. *venir de faire quelque chose* (to have just done something), common errors of misunderstanding may arise. This chapter encourages students to add these expressions to their active, as well as their passive, vocabulary.

Chapter 6 highlights pronominal verbs like *se débrouiller* (to manage). English-speaking students of French are sometimes surprised by the frequency with which these verbs occur when there is no reflexive or reciprocal meaning at issue. This chapter explains how and why they are used, and distinguishes between the pronominal and non-pronominal usage of verbs like *améliorer/s'améliorer* (to improve). It also discusses the use of a pronominal verb to translate an English passive and the distinction, often problematic for an English speaker, between action and state, as in *elle s'assied* (she sits down) and *elle est assise* (she is sitting).

Chapter 7 examines so-called problem pairs and other misused expressions. The problems discussed in the first part of the chapter arise from pairs or groups of French words that students sometimes find it difficult to choose between. These include: verbs such as *savoir* and *connaître*; nouns such as *le parti*, *la partie*, and *la part*; the pronouns *y* and *en*; and the adjective *meilleur* and the adverb *mieux* for 'better/best'. The next section of the chapter considers common French expressions that have more than one meaning, e.g. *arriver* (to arrive or to happen). The chapter concludes by highlighting some common French expressions that are sometimes misused, e.g. *il s'agit de* (it is a question of; it is about) or misunderstood, e.g. *tu me manques* (I miss you).

Chapter 8 deals with the use of prepositions. This is an area that can still cause difficulties even for quite advanced language learners, because usage is idiomatic and frequently different from English. The opening material is sub-divided into four categories (place, time, manner, measurement). Differences between the two languages in each category are then highlighted and mnemonic devices are provided to help reinforce the points. The remaining four sections of the chapter discuss: (i) common translation problems from English to French posed by particular prepositions; (ii) French verbs with two different usages, e.g. *penser à* and *penser de*; (iii) different constructions in English and French after a verb, e.g. *dépendre de* (to depend on); (iv) the translation of English phrasal verbs, e.g. 'to swim across', into French.

Chapter 9 presents spelling and more. It highlights key differences between French and English with regard to spelling, capitalisation and the presentation of numbers. It also focuses on particular features of French, such as the use of accents, elision and the notion of the aspirate 'h'. The exercises enable students to practise the various conventions and hence improve the professional appearance of their written French.

Appendix 1 is intended to complement Chapter 8 by providing students with more detailed information about the usage of prepositions with names of countries and islands. Experience has shown that although general guidance, as given in Chapter 8, is a good starting point, students often need more specific guidance and more information than they can find in a dictionary about a variety of place names.

Appendix 2 provides answers to the exercises contained in the chapters of the book.

Acknowledgements

First of all, I would like to thank Javier Muñoz-Basols, the creator and editor of the Routledge *Speed up your Language* series, for inviting me to submit a proposal for this French book and for his advice and encouragement in the early stages. I am grateful also to Samantha Vale Noya and Ruth Berry at Routledge for their guidance throughout the publication process. My particular thanks are due to my former colleague at the University of Aberdeen, Dr Roger Ravet, who has read the text carefully and given detailed feedback on it. Former students have also helped me, often unknowingly, by raising questions and so identifying problem areas for learners of French.

Website

Supplementary exercises for all the chapters are available on the companion website, www.routledge.com/cw/jubb.

Author

Margaret Jubb was Senior Lecturer in French at the University of Aberdeen until she retired in 2014. She has an MA in Modern and Medieval Languages (French and Spanish), a PhD in French from the University of Cambridge, and a PGCE from the University of Nottingham. Before becoming a university lecturer, she taught French and Spanish to A level in a sixth-form college. At the University of Aberdeen, she taught French at all levels from first-year beginners to final-year Honours students. She is the co-author with Annie Rouxeville of *French Grammar in Context*, 4th edition (Routledge, 2014) and the sole author of *Upgrade Your French*, 2nd edition (Routledge, 2007).

Gender and number

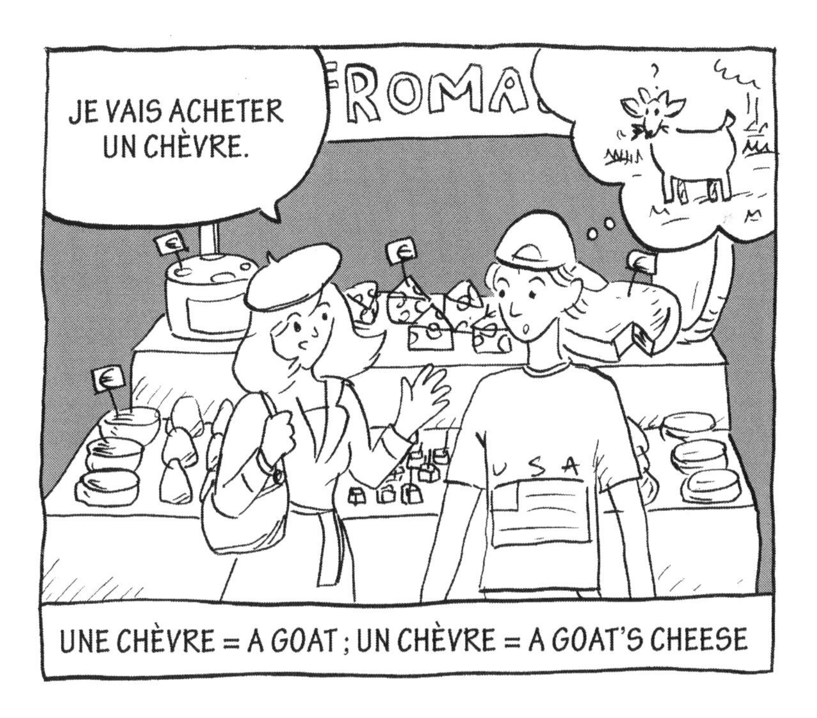

It is vital to learn the gender of nouns in French so that you can use the correct form of the article and make the necessary adjective and past participle agreements. The first part of this chapter outlines some general patterns that

can help you remember the gender of nouns and highlights common nouns that tend to cause problems. It also draws attention to nouns that change meaning according to their gender. The second part of the chapter discusses the formation of the plural and highlights cases where a plural noun in French corresponds to a singular noun in English and vice versa. It concludes by discussing common problems with adjective agreements.

Gender

Gender according to meaning

1 Gender and sex

In general terms, most nouns referring to males are masculine and most nouns referring to females are feminine, e.g. *un homme* (a man), *une femme* (a woman), *un garçon* (a boy), *une fille* (a girl).

In the past, nouns referring to professions predominantly occupied by men had only a masculine form, e.g. *un juge* (a judge), *un médecin* (a doctor), *un ministre* (a minister), *un professeur* (a teacher). A French government commission in the 1980s proposed feminine forms for such nouns, but it has taken time for some of these to be accepted into general usage. For instance, although *une médecine* for a female doctor is allowed, normal usage is *une femme médecin*. With some nouns, it is possible simply to change the determiner from masculine to feminine, e.g. *un / une maire* (a mayor), *un / une ministre* (a minister). In direct address to women, you will find either the masculine or the feminine article, e.g. *Madame le Ministre* or *Madame la Ministre*. If possible, it is advisable to ask the woman in question what she prefers. Usage varies according to register, user and country, so the abbreviated form, *la prof*, is quite common in familiar language, especially among young people, whereas *la professeure* has yet to gain widespread acceptance in metropolitan France, though it is accepted in Canadian French.

Some nouns are always feminine, even when they refer to a man, e.g. *une connaissance* (an acquaintance), *une personne* (a person), *une victime* (a victim).

Some nouns can be either masculine or feminine, depending on the sex of the person concerned, e.g. *un / une camarade* (a friend), *un / une collègue* (a colleague), *un / une élève* (a pupil). The same applies to all nouns ending in *-iste* that refer to people, e.g. *un / une touriste* (a tourist).

Some nouns change their form, as well as their gender, depending on the sex of the person concerned. Some examples of regular patterns are given below.

un ami	une amie	a friend
un employé	une employée	a worker
un candidat	une candidate	a candidate
un berger	une bergère	a shepherd / shepherdess
un paysan	une paysanne	a farmer
un hôte	une hôtesse	a host / hostess
un prince	une princesse	a prince / princess
un acteur	une actrice	an actor / actress
un lecteur	une lectrice	a reader; a language teaching assistant
un instituteur	une institutrice	a primary school teacher
un chanteur	une chanteuse	a singer
un voleur	une voleuse	a thief

Irregular patterns include the following:

un époux	une épouse	a husband / wife
un héros	une héroïne	a hero / heroine

2 Gender and other categories

Most nouns in the following categories are masculine.

- Names of trees and shrubs, e.g. *un chêne* (an oak tree), *un pommier* (an apple tree)
- Names of fruits and vegetables **not** ending in **-e**, e.g. *un ananas* (a pineapple), *un chou* (a cabbage)
- Names of languages, with no exceptions, e.g. *le français* (French), *le russe* (Russian)
- Names of colours, e.g. *le blanc* (white), *le bleu* (blue), *le rouge* (red). **Exception**: *l'écarlate* (scarlet) is feminine.
- Names of metric weights and measures, cardinal numbers and most fractions, e.g. *un gramme*, *un litre*, *un deux* (a two), *un tiers* (a third), *un dixième* (a tenth). **Exception**: *la moitié* (half). Note also *la livre* (pound; half a kilo) and the historical measure of distance, *la lieue* (league)
- Names of days of the week, months, seasons and points of the compass, e.g. *le dimanche* (Sunday), *janvier dernier* (last January), *un printemps tardif* (a late spring), *le nord* (North)

The names of most fruits and vegetables ending in **-e** are feminine, e.g. *une banane* (banana), *une pomme* (apple), *une courge* (vegetable marrow). **Exceptions**: *un pamplemousse* (grapefruit), *un concombre* (cucumber).

3 Gender of place names

As a general rule, the names of countries are feminine if they end in **-e** and masculine if they do not, e.g.

le Canada	la Belgique
le Danemark	la Chine
le Japon	la France
le Maroc	la Norvège
le Portugal	la Syrie

Exceptions: le Cambodge, le Mexique, le Mozambique, le Zimbabwe

Similarly, the names of most French regions, départements and rivers are feminine if they end in **-e** and masculine if they do not, e.g.

le Languedoc	la Normandie
le Jura	la Lozère
le Lot	la Loire

Exceptions: le Finistère, le Maine, le Rhône and the names of foreign rivers, many of which are masculine even though they end in **-e**, e.g. le Danube, le Gange, le Tage, le Tibre, le Tigre

The names of states and regions in other countries follow the general rule and are feminine if they end in **-e** and masculine if they do not, e.g.

le Massachusetts	la Californie
le Texas	la Floride

Exception: British counties are generally masculine, even if they end in **-e**, e.g.

le Sussex, le Lincolnshire, le Yorkshire

The names of towns are normally masculine.

Le grand Londres a une population de plus de 8 millions.
(Greater London has a population of more than 8 million.)

However, in formal written French, names that end in **-e** or **-es** are sometimes treated as feminine, e.g.

Bruxelles fut occupée par les Allemands en 1940.
(Brussels was occupied by the Germans in 1940.)

If the name of a town includes a definite article, any accompanying adjectives or participles must agree with the gender of the article, e.g.

Le Havre est situé en Normandie. La Baule est située en Loire-Atlantique.
(Le Havre is in Normandy. La Baule is in the Loire-Atlantique.)

4 Gender of cars, other vehicles and machines

Usually, the gender of makes of vehicles and machines is the same as the gender of the general noun.

Une voiture (a car) is feminine, so makes of car are feminine, e.g. *une Ford, une Renault, une Jaguar* (as distinct from *un jaguar*, which is an animal).

Un avion (a plane) is masculine, so types of plane are masculine, e.g. *un Boeing*.

Une cuisinière (a cooker) is feminine, so types of cooker are feminine, e.g. *une Belling*.

Gender shown by ending

It is impossible to predict with complete accuracy the gender of a particular noun according to its ending, but there are nevertheless some general patterns that can help. If in doubt, always check the gender of a noun in a dictionary.

1 Masculine

Many nouns whose singular written form ends in a vowel (excluding **-e** without an acute accent) are masculine and many nouns whose singular written form ends in a consonant are also masculine. However there are some important exceptions to this very broad generalisation.

The more detailed list of endings below will give you a better indication that a noun is likely to be masculine. In most cases, there are a few common exceptions to note.

- **-age**, e.g. *le chômage* (unemployment), *un stage* (a training course or work placement) **Exceptions**: *une cage* (a cage), *une image* (an image), *une page* (a page), *une plage* (a beach), *la rage* (rabies)
- **-ai**, -**oi**, e.g. *un délai* (a time limit), *un emploi* (job) **Exceptions**: *la foi* (faith), *une loi* (a law)
- **-ail**, -**eil**, -**ueil**, -**euil**, e.g. *un détail* (a detail), *un conseil* (a piece of advice), *un accueil* (a welcome), *un écureuil* (a squirrel)
- **-at**, e.g. *le chocolat* (chocolat), *un résultat* (a result)
- **-é (except -té and -tié)**, e.g. *un marché* (a market), *un thé* (a tea) **Exception**: *la clé* (key)

- **-eau**, e.g. *le couteau* (knife), *le gâteau* (cake), *le tableau* (picture), *le veau* (veal) **Exceptions**: *l'eau* (water), *la peau* (skin)
- **-ède**, **-ège**, **-ème**, e.g. *un remède* (a medicine, a cure), *un collège* (a secondary school), *un poème* (a poem), *un problème* (a problem), *un thème* (theme; prose translation) **Exception**: *la crème* (cream), but see section below on nouns that change meaning according to their gender for *un crème* (a white coffee)
- **-er**, whether pronounced or not, e.g. *un hiver* (a winter), *le dîner* (dinner) **Exceptions**: *une cuiller* (a spoon), *la mer* (the sea)
- **-ès**, whether pronounced or not, e.g. *un palmarès* (a list of winners), *un procès* (a trial), *un succès* (a success)
- **-et**, e.g. *un billet* (a ticket), *un secret* (a secret)
- **-i**, e.g. *un cri* (a shout), *un parti* (a political party), *le lundi*, *le mardi*, etc. (Monday, Tuesday, etc.) **Exceptions**: *une fourmi* (an ant), *la merci* (mercy), but see section below on nouns that change meaning according to their gender for *un merci* (a thank you)
- **-ier**, e.g. *un chevalier* (a knight), *un clavier* (a keyboard), *un peuplier* (a poplar tree)
- **-ing**, e.g. *un brushing* (a blow dry), *un parking* (a car park)
- **-isme**, e.g. *le christianisme* (Christianity). **Note in particular**: *le féminisme* (feminism)
- **-ment**, e.g. *un bâtiment* (a building), *un mouvement* (a movement) **Exception**: *une jument* (a mare)
- **-oir**, e.g. *un soir* (an evening), *le terroir* (land)
- **-ou**, e.g. *un bijou* (a jewel), *un voyou* (a yob)
- **the consonants -b, -c, -d, -g, -k, -p, -q or -z**, whether pronounced or not, e.g. *un club* (a club), *un sac* (a bag), *un regard* (a look), *un poing* (a fist), *un bifteck* (a steak), *un coup* (a blow), *un coq* (a cock), *un nez* (a nose)

2 Feminine

A common, but rather dangerous, generalisation is that many nouns whose singular written form ends in **-e** without an acute accent are feminine. There are numerous exceptions to this rule, in particular the masculine nouns ending in **-age**, **-ède**, **-ège**, **-ème**, **-isme** noted in the section above.

The more detailed list of endings below will give you a better indication that a noun is likely to be feminine. In most cases, there are a few common exceptions to note.

- **-ace**, e.g. *une menace* (a threat), *la race* (race) **Exception**: *un espace* (space), but see section below on nouns that change meaning according to their gender for *une espace* (a space in printing)
- **-ade**, e.g. *une promenade* (a walk), *une salade* (a salad) **Exceptions**: *un / une camarade* (a friend), *un / une malade* (a patient), *le grade* (rank), *un stade* (a stadium; stage) Note the phrase: *à ce stade* (at this stage)
- **-aie**, e.g. *la craie* (chalk), *la monnaie* (currency, change)
- **-aine**, **-eine**, **-oine**, e.g. *la haine* (hatred), *une semaine* (a week), *une douzaine* (a dozen), *la peine* (trouble), *l'avoine* (oats) **Exceptions**: *un capitaine* (a captain), *un chanoine* (a canon), *un moine* (a monk), *un domaine* (an estate, a field / domain), *le patrimoine* (heritage)
- **-aison**, e.g. *une comparaison* (a comparison), *une maison* (a house), *une raison* (a reason), *une saison* (a season)
- **-ance**, **-anse**, **-ence**, **-ense**, e.g. *une croyance* (a belief), *une danse* (a dance), *une influence* (an influence), *une dépense* (an expense) **Exceptions**: *le silence* (silence), *le suspense*
- **-èche**, **-èque**, **-èse**, **-ève**, e.g. *une crèche* (a crib, a creche), *une bibliothèque* (a library), *une thèse* (a thesis), *une grève* (a strike) **Exceptions**: *un chèque* (a cheque), *un / une élève* (a pupil)
- **-ée**, e.g. *la durée* (duration), *une idée* (an idea), *la marée* (tide), *une pensée* (a thought). **Exceptions**: *un athénée* (an athenaeum; a secondary school in Belgium), *un lycée*, *un musée* (a museum)
- **-euse**, e.g. *une religieuse* (a nun), *une mitrailleuse* (a machine gun), *une berceuse* (a lullaby)
- **-ie**, e.g. *la biologie* (biology), *une boulangerie* (a baker's), *une partie* (a part), *la pluie* (rain), *une vie* (a life) **Exceptions**: *un génie* (a genius), *un incendie* (a fire), *le Messie* (the Messiah), *un sosie* (a double, look-alike)
- **-ière**, e.g. *une bière* (a beer), *une lumière* (a light), *une manière* (a manner, way), *une rivière* (a river) **Exceptions**: *un cimetière* (a cemetery), *le derrière* (behind, rear)
- **-ine**, e.g. *une cuisine* (a kitchen), *une machine* (a machine), *une piscine* (a swimming pool), *une vitrine* (a shop window) **Exception**: *un magazine*

- **-ise**, e.g. *une brise* (a breeze), *une crise* (a crisis), *une église* (a church) **Exception**: *un pare-brise* (a windscreen) See section below on compound nouns
- **-sion**, **-tion**, e.g. *une occasion* (an opportunity), *une question* (a question), *une situation* (a situation) **Exception**: *un bastion*
- **-lle**, **-ille**, **-sse**, e.g. *une poubelle* (a dustbin), *une bulle* (a bubble, a balloon in a cartoon), *une feuille* (a leaf), *une famille* (a family), *une caresse* (a caress), *une hausse* (rise), *une tasse* (cup) **Exceptions**: *un intervalle* (an interval), *un violoncelle* (a cello), *un / une gosse* (kid)
- **-ette**, e.g. *une chaussette* (a sock), *une fourchette* (a fork) **Exception**: *un squelette* (a skeleton)
- **-ffe**, **-nne**, **-ppe**, e.g. *une truffe* (a truffle), *une personne* (a person), *une enveloppe* (an envelope) **Exception**: *un renne* (a reindeer)
- **-té** and **-tié**, e.g: *la bonté* (goodness), *la santé* (health), *la vérité* (truth), *une amitié* (a friendship), *la moitié* (half) **Exceptions**: *un arrêté* (an order, decree), *un comité* (a committee), *un côté* (a side), *l'été* (summer), *le pâté* (pâté; block of houses), *un traité* (a treaty)
- **-tte**, e.g. *une carotte* (a carrot), *une lutte* (a struggle)
- **-tude**, e.g. *une habitude* (a habit), *la solitude* (solitude)
- **-ure**, e.g. *une couverture* (a blanket), *une injure* (an insult), *la nature* (nature), *la nourriture* (food) **Exceptions**: chemical substances, e.g. *le mercure* (mercury) and *un murmure* (a murmur)

3 Some more **problematic endings** and some c**ommon mistakes** to avoid

-a
The common mistake is to assume that nouns with this ending are feminine, as you might expect them to be if you are familiar with Latin, Italian or Spanish. There are some feminines in French, e.g. *une cafétéria*, *une pizza*, *une villa*, but there are also many masculines, e.g. *un agenda* (a diary), *un cinéma*, *un panorama*, *un opéra*, *un visa*.

-mme, -rre
The common mistake is to assume that most nouns ending in **-e**, and particularly those ending in a double consonant + **-e** are feminine. In fact there are more masculine than feminine nouns that end in **-mme** and **-rre**. They include *un dilemme* (a dilemma), *un programme* (a programme), *le beurre* (butter), *le tonnerre* (thunder), *un verre* (a glass). Common feminine nouns include *une femme* (a woman), *une gamme* (a scale), *une guerre* (a war), *une pierre* (a stone), *la terre* (the earth).

-ère

Nouns ending in **-ère** that refer to male individuals are masculine, e.g. *un frère* (a brother) and nouns referring to females are feminine, e.g. *une étrangère* (a foreign woman).

However, other nouns may be masculine or feminine and just have to be learnt, e.g. *le caractère* (character), *un critère* (a criterion), *le ministère* (ministry), but *la colère* (anger), *la misère* (extreme poverty). The division is so arbitrary that *un hémisphère* is masculine, but *l'atmosphère* and *une sphère* are feminine!

-eur

The common mistake is to assume that all nouns with this ending are masculine.

Nouns referring to male individuals are masculine, e.g. *un acteur* (an actor), *un facteur* (a postman). *Un professeur* (a teacher) is masculine even if it refers to a woman.

Nouns referring to mechanical objects are also masculine, e.g. *un aspirateur* (a vacuum cleaner), *un moteur* (an engine), *un ordinateur* (a computer).

However, abstract nouns referring to colours, feelings or qualities are feminine, e.g. *une couleur* (a colour), *la douceur* (softness, sweetness), *une douleur* (a pain), *une humeur* (a mood), *la peur* (fear), *la saveur* (flavour). **Exceptions**: *le bonheur* (happiness), *le malheur* (misfortune), *l'honneur* (honour), *le déshonneur* (dishonour).

That leaves a miscellaneous group, some of which are masculine, e.g. *un cœur* (a heart), *l'extérieur* (outside), and some feminine, e.g. *une fleur* (a flower), *une lueur* (a glow), *la sueur* (sweat).

-o

Most of the small group of nouns ending in -o are masculine, e.g. *un numéro* (a number), *un piano* (a piano), *un studio* (a small flat). However, there are some important exceptions that are feminine, e.g. *une photo(graphie)* (a photo), *une radio* (radio, X-ray photo).

-oire

Nouns ending in -oire may be masculine or feminine and just have to be learnt, e.g. *un auditoire* (an audience) *un laboratoire* (a laboratory), *un territoire* (a territory), but *une baignoire* (a bathtub), *une histoire* (a history, story), *une victoire* (a victory).

4 Common problem nouns

Although they end in **-e** without an acute accent, the following nouns are all **masculine**: *le caractère* (character, temperament), *un cratère* (a crater), *un crime* (a crime), *le doute* (doubt), *un groupe* (a group), *un légume* (a vegetable), *le manque* (lack), *un siècle* (a century), *un questionnaire* (a questionnaire), *le salaire* (salary, wages), *le silence* (silence), *un site Internet* (an Internet site), *le vote* (voting, vote). But *une espèce* (a type, kind) is **feminine**.

Une idée (an idea), like most nouns ending in **-ée**, is **feminine**. The exceptions are *un athénéé*, *un lycée*, *un musée*.

Nouns ending in **-ème** are usually and nouns ending in **-isme** are always **masculine**. Note in particular: *un problème* (a problem), *un système* (a system), *le féminisme* (feminism).

The following nouns ending in a consonant are all **feminine**: *une croix* (a cross), *la fin* (the end), *une forêt* (a forest), *une noix* (a nut), *une vis* (a screw). But *un choix* (a choice) is masculine.

Mnemonic device

Everyone has their own way of remembering the gender of nouns. If you have a visual memory, you could keep a vocabulary book where you list masculine nouns in one colour and feminine ones in another. Alternatively, you could list masculine nouns on the left-hand page and feminine ones on the right.

If your memory is primarily aural, then you could learn each noun in association with an audibly masculine or feminine adjective, e.g. *il a mauvais caractère* (he is bad-tempered); *il y a eu un long silence* (there was a long silence); *des magazines féminins* (women's magazines); *l'espèce humaine* (humankind); *à cette fin* (to this end).

Ultimately, however, it is by listening attentively to and reading as much authentic French as possible that you will learn most effectively.

Gender of compound nouns

Strictly speaking, compound nouns consist of two elements linked by a hyphen. There are also some nouns that were originally compounds, but are now written as one word without hyphens, e.g. *un parapluie* (an umbrella), *un portefeuille* (a wallet). The latter will also be considered here.

1 Adjective + noun (or noun + adjective) compounds normally take the gender of the noun. In the following examples, the noun is highlighted in bold type.

un bas-**relief**	a low relief, bas relief
une basse-**cour**	a farmyard
une belle-**fille**	a daughter-in-law or a step-daughter
un **cerf**-volant	a kite
un rond-**point**	a roundabout

Exceptions: *un rouge-gorge* (a robin), *un rouge-queue* (a redstart). Remember that *un oiseau* (a bird) is masculine.

2 Noun + noun compounds take the gender of the principal noun, which is usually the first in French, though the second in English.

un camion-citerne	a tanker (-lorry)
un centre-ville	a town centre
un homme-grenouille	a frogman
une pause-café	a coffee break
une porte-fenêtre	a French window (a door combined with a window)
une voiture-restaurant	a dining-car

3 Noun + prepositional phrase compounds usually take the gender of the first noun.

un arc-en-ciel	a rainbow
un chef-d'œuvre	a masterpiece
une langue-de-chat	a finger biscuit
la main-d'œuvre	the workforce

Exceptions: *un tête-à-queue* (a spin in a car from head to tail), *un tête-à-tête* (a tête-à-tête conversation)

4 Adverb, preposition or prefix + noun compounds usually take the gender of the noun.

l'arrière-plan (m.)	background
un demi-tarif	half-fare
une arrière-pensée	an ulterior motive
une ex-femme	an ex-wife
la sous-location	subletting

Exceptions: *l'après-guerre* (m.) (the post-war period), *un en-tête* (a letterhead), *le sans-gêne* (cheekiness). Note also *une sans-abri* (a homeless woman), as opposed to *un sans-abri* (a homeless man).

5 Verb + noun compounds are usually masculine.

un gratte-ciel	a skyscraper
un tire-bouchon	a corkscrew
un essuie-mains	a hand towel
un pare-brise	a windscreen
un pare-chocs	a bumper
un porte-monnaie	purse
un soutien-gorge	a bra

The compound noun is masculine even if the noun that forms one element of it is feminine, e.g. *un porte-monnaie* (a purse) even though *la monnaie* (change) is feminine.

This explains why the following nouns, which were originally compounds, are masculine. Learners of French often wrongly assume that they are feminine, because *la chute*, *la pluie* and *la feuille* are all feminine.

un parachute	a parachute
un parapluie	an umbrella
un portefeuille	a wallet

Exceptions: *un / une garde-malade* (a home nurse), according to the sex of the person concerned, and *une garde-robe* (a wardrobe)

6 Verbal phrase compounds are masculine.

le on-dit	gossip
le ouï-dire	hearsay
un m'as-tu-vu	a show-off
un faire-part	an announcement of a birth, marriage or death
le savoir-faire	know-how

Exercises

EXERCISE 1. Complete the sentences by choosing between the alternatives given. The correct choice depends on the gender of the noun in each case.

1 Sa voiture a fait (un / une) tête-à-queue sur le verglas et s'est heurtée contre un arbre. (Quel / Quelle) manque de chance!
2 Les vieillards sont souvent les (premiers / premières) victimes (du / de la) froid.
3 L'inauguration (officiel / officielle) (du / de la) musée de Picardie eut lieu en 1867.
4 (Ce / Cette) bâtiment date (du / de la) fin (du / de la) dix-neuvième siècle.

5 Les œuvres d'art (conservés / conservées) au Louvre font partie (du / de la) patrimoine (du / de la) nation.
6 (Le / La) circulation dans (le / la) centre-ville est à l'arrêt.
7 J'ai eu (un / une) peur (bleu / bleue) quand j'ai découvert que (mon / ma) portefeuille avait disparu.
8 La Grande-Bretagne a connu deux après-guerres depuis 1900, (l'un / l'une) après l'armistice de 1918, l'autre après (le / la) capitulation (allemand / allemande) de 1945.
9 (Le / La) question (du / de la) féminisme reste (pertinent / pertinente).
10 Il a poursuivi (le / la) thème (du / de la) symbolisme devant (un / une) auditoire (attentif / attentive).
11 (Le / La) comité d'entreprise se réunira demain pour discuter (du / de la) stratégie à adopter.
12 Si tu fais (le / la) comparaison entre ces deux enregistrements (du /de la) concerto pour violon de Beethoven, tu verras bien (le / la) différence. (Le premier / La première) est nettement (supérieur / supérieure).
13 C'est (un / une) génie sans (aucun / aucune) doute.
14 (Le / La) squelette (humain / humaine) se compose de 206 os.
15 (Un / une) groupe (animé / animée) d'étudiants attendaient devant (le / la) cafétéria.
16 Dans (ce /cette) cimetière de voitures, nous avons trouvé (un vieux / une vieille) Jaguar.
17 Ce musicien qui a fait (le / la) couverture (du / de la) magazine est (un / une) connaissance de mon mari.
18 Mon fils joue (du / de la) violoncelle tandis que ma fille joue (du /de la clarinette).
19 Nous avons planté des peupliers (blancs / blanches) à des intervalles (réguliers / régulières).
20 (Le / La) Maine était (un / une) bastion des révolutionnaires.

EXERCISE 2. Identify the noun whose gender is different from the rest of the group and write it with either an indefinite or definite article, as specified.

1 image / stage / village / voyage (indefinite)
2 Belgique / Chine / Mexique / Norvège (definite)
3 espèce / groupe / légume / manque (indefinite)
4 betterave / carotte / concombre / courge (indefinite)
5 différence / patience / silence / violence (definite)
6 Dordogne / Loire / Rhône / Seine (definite)
7 bâtiment / enseignement / jugement / jument (indefinite)
8 numéro / photo / piano / studio (indefinite)
9 aubaine / domaine / douzaine / semaine (indefinite)

10 choix / croix / foi / noix (definite)
11 confiture / figure / injure / murmure (indefinite)
12 agenda / cinéma / opéra / pizza (indefinite)
13 bonheur / couleur / déshonneur / moteur (definite)
14 caractère / hémisphère / ministère / misère (definite)
15 bastion / exception / question / situation (indefinite)
16 couteau / peau / seau / veau (definite)
17 ambassade / façade / salade / stade (indefinite)
18 emploi / loi / roi / tournoi (indefinite)
19 café / clé / marché / thé (indefinite)
20 idée / journée / musée / traversée (indefinite)

Nouns that change meaning according to their gender

Mnemonic device

The two sentences below should help you to remember that some nouns in French have two genders and two different meanings.

> Le Tour de France est une course cycliste.
> (The Tour de France is a cycle race.)
>
> La Tour Eiffel est un icône de Paris.
> (The Eiffel Tower is an icon of Paris.)

The following list does not seek to be exhaustive. It focuses instead on the pairs of nouns that you are most likely to meet and gives examples of their use.

un aide	a male assistant
l'aide (f.)	help; female assistant

C'est un aide-cuisinier qui promet.
(He is a promising assistant cook.)

Il a apporté une aide considérable à sa famille.
(He has been a great help to his family.)

un chèvre	a goat's cheese
la chèvre	goat

Un chèvre est un produit laitier. Une chèvre est un animal.
(A goat's cheese is a dairy product. A goat is an animal.)

un crème	a white coffee
la crème	cream

Un crème, ou un café-crème, est un café additionné d'un peu de crème ou de lait.
(A white coffee is an espresso coffee with a little cream or milk added.)

La crème est la matière grasse du lait avec laquelle on fait le beurre.
(Cream is the fat part of milk with which butter is made.)

le crêpe	crepe (fabric); black veil or armband
la crêpe	pancake

Le crêpe de Chine est un tissu léger de soie ou de laine.
(Crepe de Chine is a fine silk or woollen fabric.)

Une crêpe est une galette légère cuite à la poêle.
(A pancake is a thin flat cake cooked in a frying pan.)

le critique	critic
la critique	criticism, review; critical opinion generally

Le critique musical du *Figaro* a fait la critique du concert.
(The music critic of *Le Figaro* reviewed the concert.)

un espace	a space (most senses)
une espace	a space (in printing)

Cette forêt couvre un espace important.
(This forest covers a sizeable area.)

J'ai noté qu'il avait omis de laisser une espace entre ces deux mots.
(I noted that he had omitted to leave a space between these two words.)

le livre	book
la livre	pound (money); half a kilo

Ce livre d'art coûte trente livres irlandaises.
(This art book costs thirty Irish pounds.)

J'ai acheté une livre de beurre.
(I bought half a kilo of butter.)

le manche	handle
la manche	sleeve; part of a game or match
la Manche	the English Channel

Le manche de la casserole s'est brisé.
(The saucepan handle has broken.)

Je cherche un chemisier à manches courtes pour l'été.
(I'm looking for a short-sleeved blouse for summer.)

Ce jeu se joue en deux manches.
(This is a game of two halves.)

Elle veut traverser la Manche à la nage.
(She wants to swim the Channel.)

Note also the familiar expression: **faire la manche** (to pass the hat round; to beg)

le manœuvre	unskilled worker
la manœuvre	manoeuvre

Un manœuvre est un ouvrier qui exécute des travaux manuels.
(An unskilled worker is a worker who carries out manual work.)

J'ai dû faire plusieurs manœuvres (f.) pour me garer.
(I had to make several manoeuvres in order to park.)

le mémoire	memo; dissertation
la mémoire	memory

Il a écrit son mémoire sur les romans de Mauriac si j'ai bonne mémoire.
(He wrote his dissertation about the novels of Mauriac if I remember rightly.)

un merci	a thank you
la merci	mercy

J'ai dit un grand merci à ma collègue. Sans elle j'aurais été à la merci de mon patron.
(I've said a big thank you to my colleague. But for her, I would have been at the mercy of my boss.)

le mode	way, mode
la mode	fashion

Elle ne comprend pas ce mode de vie. Pour elle, ce qui compte surtout c'est la mode.
(She doesn't understand this way of life. For her, fashion is what counts above all.)

un mort	a dead man; a fatality
la mort	death

L'attentat n'a fait qu'un mort, mais deux des blessés sont à deux doigts de la mort.
(The attack left only one dead, but two of the wounded are at death's door.)

le moule	mould; tin (for cake etc.)
la moule	mussel

Je cherche un moule à fond amovible pour faire ce gâteau.
(I'm looking for a loose-bottomed tin to make this cake.)

Une moule est un coquillage comestible.
(A mussel is an edible shellfish.)

le page	page (boy)
la page	page (of book)

Jadis un page était un jeune noble au service d'un noble de rang supérieur.
(In the past, a page was a young noble in the service of a noble of higher rank.)

Il manque une page dans ce livre.
(A page is missing from this book.)

le physique	physical appearance; physique
la physique	physics

Elle a un physique agréable.
(She is good-looking.)

Elle étudie la physique.
(She is studying physics.)

le poêle	stove; pall
la poêle	frying pan

Ils ont installé un poêle à bois.
(They have put in a wood-burning stove.)

Un poêle est le drap mortuaire dont on couvre un cercueil.
(A pall is the cloth covering a coffin.)

Je vais passer ce filet de saumon à la poêle.
(I'm going to fry this salmon fillet.)

le poste	position, job; (radio, TV) set; (telephone) extension
la poste	post office; postal service

Elle a décroché un poste d'enseignement au lycée.
(She has landed / got a teaching post in the high school.)

Elle a un poste de télévision dans sa chambre.
(She has a television set in her bedroom.)

Pourrais-je avoir le poste 569?
(Could I have extension 569?)

On parle de privatiser la Poste.
(They are talking about privatising the postal service.)

le rose	pink (colour)
la rose	rose (flower)

Le rose lui va très bien.
(Pink really suits her/him.)

La rose est un symbole de l'amour.
(The rose is a symbol of love.)

le solde	balance (of account); (plural) sale
la solde	(soldier's) pay

Il y a un solde de 500 euros en notre faveur.
(There is a balance of 500 euros in our favour.)

Il y aura des soldes tentants à la fin d'août.
(There will be some tempting sales at the end of August.)

Le soldat touche sa solde demain.
(The soldier gets his pay tomorrow.)

le somme	sleep, nap
la somme	sum, amount

Il fait un petit somme.
(He's having a little nap.)

Ils ont perdu une grosse somme d'argent.
(They have lost a large amount of money.)

le tour	turn; movement around; look; trick
la tour	tower

À qui le tour?
(Whose turn is it?)

Il a fait le tour de l'Écosse en stop.
(He has hitchhiked around Scotland.)

On va faire le tour du problème avant d'aller plus loin.
(We're going to have a look at the problem before we go any further.)

Il leur a joué un sale tour.
(He played a nasty trick on them.)

J'ai visité la Tour de Londres plusieurs fois.
(I have visited the Tower of London several times.)

le vase	vase
la vase	mud, silt

J'ai mis les fleurs dans un vase en cristal.
(I put the flowers in a crystal vase.)

Cette barque échouée s'est enfoncée dans la vase.
(This beached boat has sunk into the mud.)

le voile	veil; headscarf, hijab
la voile	sail; sailing

La mariée porte un voile.
(The bride is wearing a veil.)

Ils font de la voile depuis trois ans.
(They've been going sailing for three years.)

Finally, the following words, though not identical in form to one another, sometimes cause difficulty.

le droit	right, entitlement; law (referring to a body of laws or to law as a discipline)
la droite	right (as opposed to left)

Nous avons le droit de savoir.
(We have the right to know.)

Le droit fiscal est très compliqué.
(Tax law is very complicated.)

Elle ne connaît pas sa droite de sa gauche.
(She can't tell right from left.)

Exercises

EXERCISE 3. Choose the words that best complete the sentence, paying attention to gender, meaning and context.

1. Je n'ai jamais réussi à faire (un crêpe / une crêpe). Peut-être que je ne chauffe pas assez (le poêle / la poêle) avant d'ajouter la pâte.
2. Ces deux frères ont été coulés dans (le même moule / la même moule); ils partagent les mêmes valeurs.
3. Pour terminer mon repas, j'adore prendre du fromage, surtout (du chèvre / de la chèvre). Si je prends un café c'est toujours (un crème /une crème).
4. On m'a demandé de faire (le critique / la critique) de ce nouveau film.
5. (Le manœuvre / La manœuvre) a manqué (le manœuvre / la manœuvre) de la grue et a heurté un arbre situé à (son droit / sa droite).
6. À l'école la récréation offre (un espace / une espace) de liberté aux enfants.
7. (Le mode / La mode) de paiement par virement bancaire est très commode.
8. Il n'est pas là, mais vous pouvez le joindre (au poste / à la poste) 259.
9. Cet ordinateur a (un mémoire / une mémoire) de 750 Go.
10. Elle joue de (son physique / sa physique) pour réussir dans la vie.
11. Ce jeune homme a trouvé (le mort / la mort) dans un accident de moto. Il laisse une veuve et deux enfants.
12. C'est la goutte d'eau qui fait déborder (le vase / la vase).
13. Cette jeune femme fournit (un somme / une somme) énorme de travail. C'est une étudiante en (droit / droite).
14. (Un voile / une voile) de brume s'étendait sur le paysage.
15. Le gagnant de la course cycliste a fait (un tour / une tour) d'honneur du stade.
16. Le tunnel sous (le Manche / la Manche) relie l'Angleterre à la France.
17. (Le rose / La rose) est une des couleurs qui la flattent.
18. À l'heure actuelle (le livre /la livre) sterling est une monnaie forte.
19. Il faut tourner (le page / la page) pour lire la suite du message.
20. Le prisonnier est (au merci / à la merci) de ceux qui l'ont capturé. Ils sont (au solde / à la solde) de l'ennemi.

Nouns whose gender varies according to use

The first three nouns are the most common and the most important to learn.

1 **Chose** (thing) is feminine, but compound expressions including **chose**, such as *autre chose* (something else), *quelque chose* (something), *peu de chose* (nothing much), are all masculine. **Quelque chose** is followed by **de** and a masculine adjective. Compare and contrast these two examples.

C'est une bonne chose en soi.
(It's a good thing in itself.)

Je cherche quelque chose de nouveau.
(I'm looking for something new)

2 **Gens** (people) is normally masculine plural. However, if an adjective that immediately precedes the noun has a distinct feminine form, e.g. *bonne* (good), *mauvaise* (bad), *vieille* (old), the feminine plural form is used, e.g. *les vieilles gens* (old people). If such a phrase is preceded by *tout* (all) or *quel* (what! which?), these adjectives are also feminine, e.g. *toutes les vieilles gens* (all old people), *quelles mauvaises gens*! (what bad people!). However, this does not apply if the immediately preceding adjective, e.g. *braves* (fine, good), does not have a distinct feminine form. The masculine form, *tout / tous* or *quel(s)*, is used in such cases, e.g. *tous les braves gens* (all good people). In the phrase, *tous les gens* (everyone), the preceding adjective, *tous*, is separated from the noun by the definite article, so the feminine form, *toutes*, is not used.

Adjectives that follow the noun **gens** are always masculine, even when the noun is immediately preceded by an adjective with a distinct feminine form. This can produce an odd mixture of masculine and feminine, as in the following example.

Les vieilles gens de la campagne sont souvent très prudents.
(Old country people are often very cautious.)

3 **Une personne** (a person) is feminine, but the negative pronoun **personne** (no one) is masculine.

Une personne inconnue est arrivée. Personne n'est arrivé.
(An unknown person has arrived. No one has arrived.)

4 Some other less common nouns

Délice (delight) is masculine in the singular and feminine in the plural.

Cette pêche est un vrai délice.
(This peach is quite delicious.)

Il s'est laissé tenter par toutes les délices d'une vie de luxe.
(He gave in to all the delights of a life of luxury.)

Noël (Christmas) is normally masculine. However, when it refers to the holiday period, *la fête de Noël*, it is preceded by a feminine article.

Nous restons toujours chez nous à Noël.
(We always stay at home at Christmas.)

Joyeux Noël!
(Happy Christmas!)

Pour la Noël elle va chez ses parents en Suisse.
(She is going to her parents' home in Switzerland for Christmas.)

Œuvre (work) is normally feminine in the singular and always feminine in the plural.

Mon mémoire est une œuvre de longue haleine. J'étudie les premières œuvres de Chopin.
(My dissertation is a long-term piece of work. I'm studying the early works of Chopin.)

However, the masculine singular may be used to refer to the complete work of an artist.

Il a passé de longues années à étudier l'œuvre peint de Michel-Ange.
(He has spent long years studying the paintings of Michelangelo.)

The masculine singular is also used in the set phrase **le gros œuvre** (the main building work).

Ils ont fini le gros œuvre.
(They've finished the main building work.)

Orgue (organ) is masculine, but the feminine plural is used in the set expression, **les grandes orgues** (the great organ), to refer to a singular instrument, usually a church organ.

Il cherche un orgue électrique.
(He is looking for an electric organ.)

Avez-vous entendu les grandes orgues de la cathédrale?
(Have you heard the great organ in the cathedral?)

Pâques (Easter) is feminine plural in set expressions, such as greetings, but it is masculine singular when viewed as an event or a point in time.

Je te souhaite de joyeuses Pâques / de bonnes Pâques.
(I wish you a Happy Easter.)

On se reverra à Pâques prochain.
(We'll meet again next Easter.)

Exercises

EXERCISE 4. Choose the appropriate words to complete the sentence, depending on the gender of the noun in the context given.

1 Je cherche quelque chose de (bon / bonne) à manger.
2 Les gens d'affaires doivent être très (motivés / motivées) pour réussir.

3 (Seuls certains gens / Seules certaines gens) savent ce qui se passe.
4 (Tous / Toutes) les gens qui habitent le coin sont au courant de l'affaire.
5 50% des personnes (interrogés / interrogées) ont répondu qu'ils voulaient que l'Écosse devienne indépendante.
6 (Quel / Quelle) délice de passer les vacances en Italie!
7 Cette photographie est (un vrai œuvre / une vraie œuvre) d'art.
8 Cette exposition fait un tour d'horizon de (l'œuvre sculpté / l'œuvre sculptée) de Rodin.
9 Cette année-là, Pâques est (tombé / tombée) en mars.
10 On dit (Joyeux / Joyeuse) Noël, mais (Joyeux / Joyeuses) Pâques!

Number

The plural of nouns

In spoken French, there is often no audible distinction between the singular and plural forms of a noun. It is usually only the determiner (the article or the demonstrative or possessive adjective, etc.) that serves as a plural marker in the spoken language.

However, in written French, many nouns do carry a plural marker, and you must take care to remember this.

1 Regular plurals

The plural of most nouns is formed by adding **-s** to the singular form. This applies to both masculine and feminine nouns, for example:

un enfant	des enfants	(child / children)
un regard	des regards	(look / looks)
une loi	des lois	(law / laws)
une maison	des maisons	(house / houses)

2 Nouns ending in **-s**, **-x**, **-z**

There is no change in the plural, for example:

un cas	des cas	(case / cases)
une voix	des voix	(voice / voices)
un nez	des nez	(nose / noses)

3 Nouns ending in **-au, -eau, -eu, -œu**

The plural is formed by adding **-x**, for example:

un tuyau	des tuyaux	(pipe / pipes)
un bateau	des bateaux	(boat / boats)

un cheveu	des cheveux	(hair / hairs)
un vœu	des vœux	(wish / wishes)

Exceptions in -s:

un bleu	des bleus	(bruise / bruises)
un pneu	des pneus	(tyre / tyres)

4 Nouns ending in **-ou**

In most cases, the plural is formed by adding -s, for example:

un trou	des trous	(hole / holes)
un voyou	des voyous	(yob / yobs)

However, there are **seven exceptions** that form the plural with **-x**. These are:

un bijou	des bijoux	(jewel / jewels)
un caillou	des cailloux	(pebble / pebbles)
un chou	des choux	(cabbage / cabbages)
un genou	des genoux	(knee / knees)
un hibou	des hiboux	(owl / owls)
un joujou	des joujoux	(toy / toys)
un pou	des poux	(louse / lice)

5 Nouns ending in **-al**

Most nouns ending in **-al** change to **-aux** in the plural, for example:

un cheval	des chevaux	(horse / horses)
un idéal	des idéaux	(ideal / ideals)
le mal	les maux	(evil / evils; ache / aches)

Exceptions in -s:

un bal	des bals	(dance / dances)
un carnaval	des carnavals	(carnival / carnivals)
un festival	des festivals	(festival / festivals)
un récital	des récitals	(recital / recitals)
un régal	des régals	(culinary or other delight / delights)

6 Nouns ending in **-ail**

Most nouns form the plural in the regular way by adding -s, for example:

un détail	des détails	(detail / details)

Exceptions in -aux:

un bail	des baux	(lease / leases)
un corail	des coraux	(coral / corals)
un émail	des émaux	(enamel / enamels)
un travail	des travaux	(work / works)
un vitrail	des vitraux	(stained glass window / windows)

7 Nouns with irregular plurals

The most common are:

un ciel	des cieux	(sky / skies, heavens)
un œil	des yeux	(eye / eyes)
Monsieur	Messieurs	
Madame	Mesdames	
Mademoiselle	Mesdemoiselles	

The regular form, *les ciels*, is used for 'skies' in climates and in paintings, e.g. *les ciels d'Afrique*, *les ciels de Constable*.

Note also the following irregularities in the spoken language.

The final consonant of *un os* (a bone), *un bœuf* (a bullock), *un œuf* (an egg) is pronounced in the singular, but the ending of the plural forms, *des os*, *des bœufs*, *des œufs*, is completely silent.

8 Nouns that have only a plural form in French include the following:

les abats (m.)	offal; giblets
les affres (f.)	agonies; pangs (of hunger)
les alentours (m.)	surrounding area
les annales (f.)	annals
les archives (f.)	archives
les arrhes (f.)	deposit (e.g. on a flat)
les bestiaux (m.)	livestock
les ciseaux (m.)	scissors
les condoléances (f.)	condolences
les entrailles (f.)	entrails
les environs (m.)	surroundings
les félicitations (f.)	congratulations
les fiançailles (f.)	engagement
les frais (m.)	expenses
les fringues (f.) (colloquial)	clothes
les funérailles (f.)	funeral

les gens (m. normally)	people
les graffiti (m. invariable)	graffiti
les honoraires (m.)	fees
les intempéries (f.)	bad weather
les mœurs (f.)	customs
les pourparlers (m.)	talks
les obsèques (f.)	funeral
les spaghetti (m. invariable)	spaghetti
les ténèbres (f.)	darkness
les vêpres (f.)	vespers
les victuailles (f.)	victuals
les vivres (m.)	food, supplies

The corresponding noun in English is sometimes singular, e.g. *verser des arrhes* (to put down a deposit).

The plural of compound nouns

The rules for the formation of the plural are quite complex, but it helps to divide the nouns into categories as follows.

1 In adjective + noun (or noun + adjective) compounds, both elements become plural.

une belle-fille	des belles-filles
un cerf-volant	des cerfs-volants

2 In noun + noun compounds, the usual pattern is for both nouns to become plural.

un camion-citerne	des camions-citernes
une pause-café	des pauses-cafés

Exceptions with only one noun becoming plural

une auto-école	des auto-écoles	(a driving school / driving schools)
un hôtel-Dieu	des hôtels-Dieu	(a main hospital / main hospitals)
un timbre-poste	des timbres-poste	(a postage stamp / postage stamps)

3 In noun + prepositional phrase compounds, only the first noun becomes plural.

un arc-en-ciel	des arcs-en-ciel
un chef-d'œuvre	des chefs-d'œuvre

Exceptions with no change in the plural

un tête-à-queue	des tête-à-queue
un tête-à-tête	des tête-à-tête

4 In adverb, preposition or prefix + noun compounds, the noun alone becomes plural.

un demi-tarif	des demi-tarifs
une ex-femme	des ex-femmes

Exception with no change in the plural

un / une sans-travail	des sans-travail

5 In verb + noun compounds, **the golden rule is not to add a plural -s on the verb**. For the noun, there are two general patterns, though in practice there is so much fluctuation that the only safe way of proceeding is to consult a good dictionary.

a. The compound remains invariable whether the singular form contains a noun in the singular or the plural.

un gratte-ciel	des gratte-ciel
un essuie-mains	des essuie-mains
un pare-brise	des pare-brise

b. The noun becomes plural.

un tire-bouchon	des tire-bouchons
un couvre-lit	des couvre-lits

There are a few cases where, despite the golden rule given above, there is an **-s** on the verbal element of the compound and not on the noun. However, in these cases the verbal element is no longer related to any existing verbal form, as the following examples show. The third-person singular present tense indicative form of the verbs in question would be *appuie* and *soutient*.

un appui-tête	des appuis-tête	(headrests)
un soutien-gorge	des soutiens-gorge	(bras)

6 Verbal phrase compounds are usually invariable in the plural.

un on-dit	des on-dit
un faire-part	des faire-part

Exercises

EXERCISE 5. Write the plural of the following nouns.

1 le chapeau ____________
2 le mois ____________
3 le travail ____________
4 le pneu ____________
5 un chou ____________
6 un mal de tête ____________
7 un œil ____________
8 Monsieur ____________
9 un bal ____________
10 un bail ____________
11 un vœu ____________
12 un trou ____________
13 un ciel de Turner ____________
14 un cheval ____________
15 un cheveu ____________

EXERCISE 6. Indicate the gender of the following compound nouns (*un* / *une*) and then write their plural forms.

1 ___ timbre-poste des ________________
2 ___ pause-café des ________________
3 ___ chef-d'œuvre des ________________
4 ___ tête-à-tête des ________________
5 ___ demi-heure des ________________
6 ___ pare-brise des ________________
7 ___ soutien-gorge des ________________
8 ___ tire-bouchon des ________________
9 ___ faire-part des ________________
10 ___ grand-parent des ________________

Differences between French and English in the treatment of the plural

1 Some nouns that are singular in English are plural in French and vice versa. The following examples are a common source of difficulty for English speakers.

English singular	French plural
applause	les applaudissements (m.)
holiday, vacation	les vacances (f.)
hair	les cheveux (m.)
information	les informations (f.), les renseignements (m.)
knowledge	les connaissances (f.)
news (on radio, TV)	les informations (f.)
to make progress	faire des progrès (m.)
to do research / my research	faire des recherches (f.) / mes recherches

Note that *un cheveu* is a single strand of hair and *un renseignement* or *une information* is a single item of information or news.

English plural	French singular
economics	l'économie (f.)
grapes	du raisin
linguistics	la linguistique
physics	la physique
pyjamas	un pyjama
shorts	un short
stairs	un escalier
tights	un collant
trousers	un pantalon
underpants	un slip

Note that a single grape in French is *un grain de raisin*.

Remember that the singular form is used in French for a single pair of pyjamas, shorts, tights or trousers. If you used the plural, it would mean several pairs, e.g.

Je dois m'acheter des pantalons d'été.
(I must buy some pairs of summer trousers.)

2 When referring to a family, the plural article is used, but the name itself does not change. Avoid the common mistake of adding a plural **-s** as we would do in English.

Nous avons invité les Dupont à dîner samedi.
(We have invited the Duponts to dinner on Saturday.)

3 Collective nouns referring to groups of people or things are singular in form. Common examples include the following:

l'assistance (f.)	audience
le comité	committee
le conseil	council
l'équipe (f.)	team
la foule	crowd
le gouvernement (m.)	government
le peuple (m.)	people
la police	police

Such nouns take a singular verb in French. Note the contrast to English where the verb can be singular or plural.

Le gouvernement ne sait pas quelle politique adopter.
(The government does not / do not know what policy to adopt.)

Le comité va se réunir demain.
(The committee is / are going to meet tomorrow.)

4 If the collective noun is followed by *de* + a plural noun, the verb can be either singular or plural, but is more usually plural.

Un groupe d'étudiants faisait / faisaient la queue devant le bâtiment d'administration.
(A group of students was / were queuing outside the administration building.)

5 The collective phrase, *tout le monde* (everyone / everybody), must always be followed by a singular verb in French, as in English.

Tout le monde le sait.
(Everyone knows.)

Exercises

EXERCISE 7. Choose between the singular and plural alternatives given in brackets to complete the following sentences.

1. Il a fait (du progrès / des progrès) en (linguistique / linguistiques) cette année.
2. Elle fait (de la recherche / des recherches) sur le cancer.
3. Prenez (du raisin / des raisins) pour manger avec le fromage.
4. Nous allons partir en (vacance / vacances) demain.
5. L'enfant a déchiré (son pantalon / ses pantalons) en tombant dans (l'escalier / les escaliers).
6. Elle possède (une connaissance approfondie / des connaissances approfondies) en (physique / physiques).
7. Il a quitté la salle sous un tonnerre d'(applaudissement / applaudissements).
8. Les (Pléchot / Pléchots) habitent la maison d'en face.
9. La police (arrive / arrivent). Tout le monde (est / sont) au courant.
10. Nous regardons (l'information / les informations) de 20 heures à la télévision.

The agreement of adjectives: common problems

Adjectives must agree in gender (masculine or feminine) and number (singular or plural) with the noun or pronoun that they qualify. Many of these agreements, particularly the plural forms, are inaudible in the spoken language, but you must take care to make them when writing French.

1 The first step is to check the gender of the noun, hence the importance of the first part of this chapter! The next step, if you are unsure, is to revise the formation of the feminine and the plural of adjectives in one of the reference grammars listed in the Bibliography. There is space to mention only one important irregularity here.

The masculine plural of **tout** is **tous**. The feminine plural, **toutes**, is regular.

2 Watch out for examples where the adjective does not stand immediately next to the noun, but is separated from it by a verb, such as *être* or *devenir*, and remember to make the necessary agreement, for example:

Tous les musées sont fermés.
(All the museums are closed.)

La concurrence est devenue acharnée.
(The competition has become cut-throat.)

3 When an adjective qualifies two or more nouns of different genders, the adjective is masculine plural, e.g.

> un père et une mère indulgents (an indulgent father and mother)

4 With expressions of the type, *l'un des jardins les plus célèbres du monde* (one of the most famous gardens in the world), the adjective describes all the gardens, not just the particular one in question, and so it is plural.

5 When a noun is accompanied by a phrase, *de* + noun, and further qualified by an adjective, the adjective agrees with the noun that it actually qualifies, which is not necessarily the noun immediately next to it. In the following example, it agrees with the masculine noun, *point*.

> Du point (m.) de vue (f.) médical, il n'y a pas de problème
> (From a medical point of view, there is no problem.)

6 If an adjective appears at the beginning of the clause, remember to think ahead and make it agree with the noun that it qualifies, for example:

> Haute de 112 mètres, la flèche de la cathédrale d'Amiens domine la ligne des toits.
> (At 112 metres high, the spire of Amiens cathedral dominates the skyline.)

7 Take particular care with the word, **même**. If it is used as an adjective, meaning 'same' or 'very', it agrees with the noun, but if it is used as an adverb, meaning 'even', it is invariable.

> Cette étudiante a fait les mêmes erreurs que son frère.
> (This student made the same mistakes as her brother.)

> Ce sont les termes mêmes que j'ai employés.
> (Those are the very / exact words that I used.)

> Même les Français font parfois des erreurs d'accord.
> (Even the French sometimes make agreement mistakes.)

8 Finally, remember that all adverbs are invariable, so never put a plural **-s** on *beaucoup* or *ensemble*.

> Ils sont partis tous ensemble.
> (They all left together.)

Exercises

EXERCISE 8. Make the words shown in brackets agree as and when necessary.

1 Les vacances (scolaire) me semblent trop (long).
2 (Tout) les places de stationnement sont déjà (occupé).
3 Ce sont les lieux (même) de l'accident.
4 (Même) si elle a des goûts (douteux), elle sait ce qu'elle veut.
5 Les renseignements (fourni) dans la brochure sont (inexact).
6 (Tout) les gens (interviewé) sont du (même) avis.
7 Ce musée est sans (aucun) doute l'un des plus (important) du monde.
8 (Seul), elle ne viendra jamais à bout de cette tâche.
9 Cet enfant souffre de maux de tête (continuel). Son frère et sa sœur (aîné), par contre, sont en (plein) forme.
10 Les garçons et les filles jouent (ensemble) dans la cour.

EXERCISE 9. Fill in the blanks, paying particular attention to the gender and number of nouns, to the agreement of verbs with their subject (singular / plural), and to any necessary adjective agreements.

Sandrine vient d'être nommée (1) ________ (language teaching assistant) à l'université d'Aberdeen. En ce moment elle fait (2) ______________ (some research) sur Internet pour trouver (3) ______________ (information) sur la ville et sur (4) ____________ (the region). Elle sait déjà que (5) _______________ (the surrounding area) de la ville (6) _________ (is) très (7) ________________ (picturesque) et que la ville elle-même est (8) _________ (a centre) de (9) ___________________ (the oil industry). Ce qu'elle ne savait pas, cependant, c'est que (10) ____________ (accommodation) coûte très cher. Il est évident qu'(11) ___________ (a studio flat) près (12) ______________ (to the town centre) sera au-dessus de ses moyens. Il lui faudra donc partager (13) __________________ (a flat) avec d'autres étudiants et (14) _____________ (the choice) est déjà très (15) __________ (limited), à (16) ____________ (this stage). Pour résoudre (17) ___________ (the problem), elle décide de partir tout de suite en Écosse. On lui a déjà payé (18) ____________ (an advance) sur (19) ____________ (her salary), pour qu'elle puisse (20) _______________ (put down a deposit) sur une chambre.

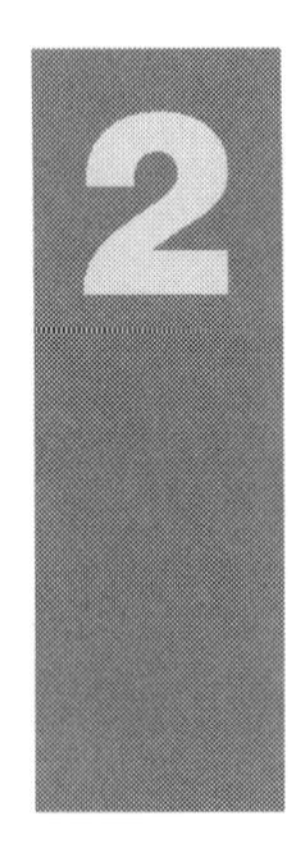

Mastering false friends: verbs

Although the following verbs look like English verbs, they often mean something very different. The first list consists of false friends that have a completely different meaning from their English lookalikes. The second list features verbs where there is some overlap of meaning with English, but an overlap that is only partial. Study the examples in the contexts given to help you remember the meanings of these verbs.

False friends

1 Achever

Achever means 'to complete', 'to put down (an animal)' or 'to finish off (a person)'.

Je me demande s'il va jamais **achever** sa thèse.
(I wonder if he is ever going to *complete* his thesis.)

Le vétérinaire a décidé d'**achever** le vieux chat malade.
(The vet decided to *put down* the sick old cat.)

Cette corvée administrative m'**a achevée**.
(That administrative task *finished* me *off*.)

* Learn also the pronominal intransitive verb, **s'achever** (to end / draw to a close). Le jour **s'achève.** (The day is ending / drawing to a close.)

► However, if you want to say 'to achieve', use **atteindre**, **arriver à** or **obtenir**.

Nous **avons atteint** tous ces objectifs.
(We have *achieved* all these goals.)

Ils **sont arrivés à** un large consensus.
(They have *achieved* a broad consensus.)

Elles **ont obtenu** des résultats époustouflants.
(They have *achieved* some amazing results.)

Note the difference between the following:

Son raisonnement **a achevé** de me convaincre.
(His argument *finally* convinced me.)

Son raisonnement **a réussi** à me convaincre.
(His argument *managed* to convince me.)

2 Agoniser

Agoniser is used in literary and / or figurative contexts to mean 'to be dying' or 'to be in the throes of death'.

Deux soldats blessés **agonisaient** dans le char abandonné.
(Two wounded soldiers *were dying* in the abandoned tank.)

Cette entreprise n'est plus ce qu'elle était; à vrai dire elle **agonise**.
(This company is no longer what it was; in fact it *is in its death throes*.)

► However, if you want to say 'to agonise', use **être au supplice** or **se tourmenter** (**à propos de quelque chose**).

Si je dois parler en public je **suis au supplice**.
(If I have to speak in public, *it is agony* for me.)

Il ne faut pas **vous tourmenter** à propos de cette décision.
(You mustn't *agonise* over this decision.)

3 Agréer

Agréer is used in formal style with a direct object to mean 'to accept', 'to approve' or followed by *à* + person to mean 'to suit'.

Le comité **a agréé** leur demande.
(The committee *accepted / approved* their request.)

Ce projet **agréait** parfaitement à leur collègue.
(This project *suited* their colleague perfectly.)

► However, if you want to say 'to agree to do something', use **s'accorder à** or **convenir de**. For 'to agree' about something, use **être d'accord**.

Nous nous accordons à accepter votre proposition.
(We *agree* to accept your proposal.)

Ils **ont convenu** à l'unanimité **d'**accepter sa démission.
(They *agreed* unanimously to accept his resignation.)

Nous **sommes d'accord avec** vous là-dessus.
(We *agree* with you on that.)

* Note the use of **agréer** in formal letter-closing formulae, such as:

Veuillez **agréer**, Monsieur / Madame, mes sentiments distingués.
(Please *accept* my distinguished regards, i.e. Yours faithfully.)

4 Altérer

Altérer means 'to change something for the worse', in other words 'to spoil' or 'to impair'. It can also mean 'to falsify'.

Le soleil **a altéré** les couleurs des étoffes.
(The sun has *faded* the colours of the fabrics.)

Le neveu cupide **a altéré** le testament de sa tante.
(The grasping nephew *falsified* his aunt's will.)

* Note also the pronominal intransitive verb **s'altérer (**to change for the worse, to become impaired). Sa santé commence à **s'altérer**. (His / her health is beginning *to decline*.)

► However, if you want to say 'to alter' (not for the worse), use **changer**, **modifier** or **transformer**.

Ils ont **changé** / **modifié** / **transformé** l'aspect extérieur de la maison.
(They have *altered* the outside appearance of the house.)

* Note that in formal usage, **altérer** can mean 'to make thirsty'. You are unlikely to meet this very frequently, but you will come across its semantic opposite, **désaltérer** (to quench thirst). Le thé **désaltère** mieux que le café. (Tea is more *thirst-quenching* than coffee.) You will also find the pronominal verb **se désaltérer** (to quench one's thirst). J'ai bu de l'eau fraîche pour **me désaltérer**. (I drank some cold water *to quench my thirst*.)

5 Balancer

Balancer means 'to rock', 'to sway', 'to hesitate / be torn between' or, colloquially, 'to chuck (out)'.

L'enfant **balançait** la tête de droite à gauche.
(The child *was rocking* his head from right to left.)

Les branches **balançaient** au vent.
(The branches *were swaying* in the wind.)

Je **balance** entre les deux candidats.
(I *am hesitating* / *am torn* between the two candidates.)

Tu devrais **balancer** ces saletés.
(You should *chuck out* this rubbish.)

► However, if you want to say 'to balance', use **équilibrer** (with a direct object) or **se tenir en équilibre** (intransitive).

Il faut **équilibrer** son emploi du temps.
(You need to *balance* your schedule.)

Il tient à **équilibrer** les comptes.
(He is anxious to *balance* the books.)

Elle **se tient en équilibre** sur la pointe des pieds.
(She *is balancing* on tiptoe.)

* Learn the colloquial expression: **je m'en balance** (I don't give a damn)

6 Blinder

Blinder means ‘to reinforce’, ‘to armour’ or, in familiar language, ‘to harden’.

Ils ont **blindé** la porte de l’abri.
(They *reinforced* the door of the shelter.)

Son expérience dans l’armée l’**a blindé** contre les horreurs de la guerre.
(His experience in the army has *hardened* him to the horrors of war.)

► However, if you want to say ‘to be blinded’ or ‘to blind’, use **perdre la vue**, **aveugler or éblouir**.

Elle **a perdu la vue** dans un incendie.
(She *was blinded* in a fire.)

Il est **aveuglé** par l’amour.
(He is *blinded* by love.)

Le soleil m’**éblouit**.
(The sun *is blinding* me.)

* Learn the expressions: **une porte blindée** (a security door); **une voiture blindée** (an armoured car)

7 Conforter

Conforter means ‘to consolidate’ or ‘to confirm’.

Ces événements l’**ont conforté** dans son opinion.
(These events *confirmed* him in his opinion.)

► However, if you want to say ‘to comfort’, use **consoler** or, more strongly, **réconforter**.

Tu as failli réussir, si ça peut te **consoler**.
(You almost passed, if that is any *comfort* to you.)

Cette bonne nouvelle l’**a réconfortée**.
(This good news *comforted* her / cheered her up.)

8 Crier

Crier means ‘to shout’, ‘to cry out’ or ‘to protest’.

Ne **criez** pas, nous vous entendons!
(There’s no need to *shout*, we can hear you!)

Le malade **a crié** de douleur.
(The patient *cried out* in pain.)

Dreyfus **a crié** son innocence.
(Dreyfus *protested* his innocence.)

► However, if you want to say 'to cry' or 'to weep', use **pleurer**.

Elle **a pleuré** de joie.
(She *cried / wept* for joy.)

* Learn the expression: **pleurer à chaudes larmes** (to cry one's eyes / heart out)

9 Demander

Demander means 'to ask for' or 'to expect'.

Il **a demandé** un conseil à son frère.
(He *asked* his brother *for* a piece of advice.)

Elle **demande** beaucoup de son assistant.
(She *expects* a lot of her assistant.)

► However, if you want to say 'to demand (forcefully)' or 'to require as essential', use **exiger**.

Elle a **exigé** qu'ils partent tout de suite.
(She *demanded* that they should leave immediately.)

Les prématurés **exigent** des soins constants.
(Premature babies *require* constant care.)

* Learn the expressions: **comme l'exige la loi** (as required by law); **permis de conduire exigé** (driving licence essential)

10 Disposer

Disposer de means 'to have at one's disposal' or 'to use'.

Je ne **dispose** que **d'**une demi-heure pour terminer ce travail.
(I *have* only half an hour to complete this work.)

Il nous a invité à **disposer de** son appartement à Cannes cet été.
(He has invited us *to use* his flat in Cannes this summer.)

► However, if you want to say 'to dispose of', use **se débarrasser de**, **vendre** or **expédier**.

Nous voulons **nous débarrasser de** ces vieux livres.
(We want *to dispose of* these old books.)

Il voulait **vendre** la maison de ses parents le plus tôt possible.
(He wanted *to dispose of* his parents' house as soon as possible.)

Elle **a expédié** ce problème en un clin d'œil.
(She *disposed of / dealt with* this problem in a flash.)

* Learn the expressions: **Disposez de moi comme vous voudrez** (You can employ me as you like); **le droit des peuples à disposer d'eux-mêmes** (the right of peoples to self-determination); **merci, vous pouvez disposer** (thank you, you may go)

11 Exténuer

Exténuer means 'to exhaust'.

Ce long voyage les **avait exténués**.
(This long journey *had exhausted* them.)

► However, if you want to say 'to extenuate', use **atténuer**, found most commonly in the expression: **circonstances atténuantes** (extenuating or mitigating circumstances).

12 Hurler

Hurler means 'to yell' or 'to howl'.

Il a **hurlé** des injures à son adversaire.
(He *yelled* insults at his opponent.)

L'animal **hurlait** de frayeur.
(The animal *was howling* with fear.)

► However, if you want to say 'to hurl', use **lancer**.

Il a **lancé** la balle par-dessus la barrière.
(He *hurled* the ball over the fence.)

For 'to hurl oneself', use **se lancer** or **se jeter**.

Il **s'est lancé / jeté** dans le vide.
(He *hurled himself* into space.)

13 Intoxiquer

Intoxiquer means 'to poison' or, figuratively, 'to brainwash'.

La femme avait essayé d'**intoxiquer** son mari.
(The woman had tried *to poison* her husband.)

Cet homme politique cherche à **intoxiquer** le public.
(This politician seeks *to brainwash* the public.)

See Chapter 3 for the expression **intoxication alimentaire** (food poisoning).

► However, if you want to say 'to intoxicate', use **enivrer**, **soûler** or **griser**.

Ses camarades de classe essayaient de l'**enivrer** / de le **soûler** à la bière.
(His classmates were trying *to intoxicate* him / *get him drunk* on beer.)

Le dictateur s'est laissé **griser** par le pouvoir.
(The dictator let power *intoxicate* him / *go to his head*.)

14 Molester

Molester means 'to manhandle' or, more familiarly, 'to rough someone up'.

Les responsables de la sécurité **ont molesté** les intrus.
(The security officers *manhandled* the intruders.)

► However, if you want to say 'to molest', use **agresser sexuellement** for sexual abuse, or **importuner** for 'bothering' someone in an importunate and unacceptable way.

Le professeur a été reconnu coupable d'**avoir agressé sexuellement** deux enfants.
(The teacher has been found guilty of *having molested* two children.)

Il n'est pas acceptable d'**importuner** les gens à cette heure de la nuit.
(It is not acceptable to *bother* / *disturb* people at this time of night.)

15 Passer (un examen / un test)

Passer un examen ou un test means 'to sit' or 'to take an examination / a test'. There is no presumption of success.

Demain elle doit **passer son examen** final.
(Tomorrow she has to *take her* final *examination*.)

► However, if you want to say 'to pass an examination', use **réussir à** or **être reçu à un examen**.

Elle **a réussi à** son examen de rattrapage.
(She *passed* her re-sit examination.)

Il a été **reçu à** son examen d'entrée.
(He *passed* his entrance examination.)

* Learn the expressions: **passer son permis de conduire** (to take one's driving test); **faire passer un test / des tests à quelqu'un** (to give someone a test / tests in a learning context); **passer des tests** (to have tests done in a medical context); **faire passer des tests à quelqu'un** (to carry out tests on someone in a medical context)

16 Pondre

Pondre means 'to lay' (an egg). Colloquially, it means 'to produce' or 'to churn out'.

Les poulent **pondent** bien en ce moment.
(The hens *are laying* well just now.)

J'**ai pondu** ma disserte en deux heures.
(I *produced / churned* out my essay in two hours.)

► However, if you want to say 'to ponder', use **considérer**, **réfléchir à** or **méditer sur**.

Nous **avons considéré** toutes les options avant de décider.
(We *pondered* all the options before deciding.)

Il faut **réfléchir à** ses motifs avant de le juger.
(You must *ponder* on his motives before judging him.)

Il **a médité** longtemps sur ce problème.
(He *pondered* for a long time over this problem.)

17 Prétendre

Prétendre means 'to claim' or 'to aspire to'.

Il n'est pas aussi intelligent qu'on le **prétend**.
(He is not as bright as they *claim*.)

Elle **prétend** à un poste supérieur.
(She *aspires* to a higher post.)

It is only possible to use **prétendre à** to translate 'pretend' in the sense of 'lay claim to'.

Je crains que le prince ne **prétende** au trône.
(I fear that the prince may *pretend / lay claim to* the throne.)

► However, if you want to say 'to pretend', meaning 'to make believe', use **faire semblant de + infinitive**.

L'enfant **fait semblant d'**être malade.
(The child *is pretending* to be ill.)

18 Remarquer

Remarquer means 'to notice' or 'to observe'.

J'**ai remarqué** qu'elle avait beaucoup maigri.
(I *noticed* that she had lost a lot of weight.)

Vous **remarquerez** que ses papiers sont dans le plus grand désordre.
(You will *observe* that his papers are in a complete mess.)

► However, if you want to say 'to remark', use **faire remarquer à quelqu'un**.

Elle a **fait remarquer à l'étudiant** qu'il avait mal orienté ses efforts.
(She *remarked* to the student that he had misdirected his efforts.)

Mnemonic device
Remember that by remarking (saying) something, you are drawing something to someone's attention, pointing it out to them and *making* them *notice* it.

* Learn the expression: **se faire remarquer** (to get oneself noticed, to draw attention to oneself)

19 Replacer

Replacer means 'to put back (again)' or, figuratively, 'to set (back) in context'.

On m'a demandé de **replacer** ces livres dans les rayons.
(I was asked to *put* the books *back* on the shelves.)

Le professeur **a replacé** ces événements dans leur contexte international.
(The teacher *set* these events *back* in their international context.)

► However, if you want to say 'to replace', meaning 'to take over from' or 'to replace with', use **remplacer**.

M. Dupont **remplace** M. Dumas à la direction.
(M. Dupont *is replacing / taking over from* M. Dumas as director.)

Ils ont **remplacé** leur piano par un clavier.
(They have *replaced* their piano *with* a keyboard.)

20 Reporter

Reporter means 'to postpone', 'to copy out', 'to take back' or 'to take back in time'.

Nous avons **reporté** notre départ d'une semaine.
(We have *postponed* our departure by a week.)

J'ai **reporté** les noms des candidats sur une nouvelle liste.
(I *copied out* the names of the candidates in a new list.)

Il faut **reporter** ces livres à la bibliothèque avant la fin du trimestre.
(You must *take* these books *back* to the library before the end of term.)

Parler de ces choses-là me **reporte** longtemps en arrière.
(Speaking about those things *takes* me *back* a long time.)

▶ However, if you want to say 'to report', use **rapporter** or **signaler**.

Il m'a demandé de **rapporter** leurs propos.
(He asked me *to report* what they said.)

Il n'y a rien à **signaler**.
(There is nothing *to report*.)

21 Ressentir

Ressentir means 'to feel' (an emotion).

Je **ressens** de la sympathie pour elle.
(I *feel* sympathy for her.)

▶ However, if you want to say 'to resent', use **en vouloir à quelqu'un** or **ne pas supporter quelque chose**.

Il lui **en veut** pour son succès.
(He *resents* her success.)

Elle **ne supporte pas** qu'ils soient mieux payés qu'elle.
(She *resents* their being better paid than her.)

However, the noun **ressentiment** does have the meaning of 'resentment'.

J'éprouve un vif **ressentiment** à leur égard.
(I feel deeply *resentful* towards them.)

22 Rester

Rester means 'to stay' or 'to remain'.

Je **suis restée** un an à Paris.
(I *stayed* in Paris for a year.)

Il **est resté** six mois au chômage.
(He *remained* unemployed for six months.)

▶ However, if you want to say 'to rest', use **se reposer**.

Va **te reposer**.
(Go and *rest*.)

* Learn the expressions: **rester assis** / **debout** (to remain sitting / standing); **reste tranquille**! (keep still)

23 Résumer

Résumer means 'to summarise' or 'sum up'.

Il nous fallait **résumer** le texte en 300 mots.
(We had to *summarise* the text in 300 words.)

► However, if you want to say 'to resume', use **reprendre** or **se remettre à**.

Il **a repris** son travail après le déjeuner.
(He *resumed* work after lunch.)

Elle **s'est remise** aux études à l'âge de trente ans.
(She *resumed* her studies at the age of thirty.)

24 User

User means 'to wear out'.

Il **a usé** l'embrayage en conduisant mal.
(He has *worn out* the clutch by driving badly.)

► However, if you want to say 'to use' or 'to make use of', use **employer**, **se servir de** or **utiliser**.

Il nous faudra **employer** une nouvelle méthode pour résoudre ce problème.
(We will have *to use* a different method to resolve the problem.)

Il **s'est servi d'**une pince-monseigneur pour ouvrir la fenêtre.
(He *used* a crowbar to open the window.)

Il ne faut pas **utiliser** ce produit pour nettoyer le PVC.
(You must not *use* this product to clean PVC.)

However, note that in a formal register, **user** followed by **de** does mean 'to use' or 'to exercise'.

Il faut **user de** diplomatie dans une telle situation.
(You must *use / exercise* diplomacy in such a situation.)

* Learn the expressions: **user ses vêtements jusqu'à la corde** (to wear one's clothes out); **une guerre d'usure** (war of attrition); **avoir quelqu'un à l'usure** (to wear someone down); **des semelles inusables** (hardwearing soles).

Mnemonic device
The adjective **inusable**, meaning 'hardwearing' or 'impossible to wear out', will help you to remember the meaning of the verb **user** (to wear out). It does not mean 'unusable'! To say 'unusable', you need **inutilisable**. See Chapter 4.

Partial overlap in meaning

1 Abuser

Abuser de can mean 'to abuse' in the sense of 'to take advantage of'.

Il **a abusé de** son autorité.
(He *abused* his authority.)

It can also be used for sexual abuse and even as a euphemism for 'to rape'.

Il **a abusé de** la femme.
(He *sexually abused / raped* the woman.)

It also means 'to abuse' in the sense of 'to use to excess'.

Elle **abuse des** sucreries.
(She *overindulges in* sweet things.)

► However, when followed directly by a noun, **abuser** means 'to fool'.

Ses excuses n'**abusent** plus personne.
(His / her excuses no longer *fool* anyone.)

* Learn the expressions: **se laisser abuser** (to be fooled / taken in); **si je ne m'abuse** (if I am not mistaken)

2 Assister

Assister can mean 'to assist' or 'to help'.

Je les **assiste** dans leur travail.

(I am *helping* them with their work.)

► However, **assister à** means 'to attend' or 'to be present at'.

Hier nous **avons assisté à** une réunion du syndicat.

(Yesterday we *attended* a union meeting.)

3 Commander

Commander can mean 'to command', in the sense of 'being in command of' or 'to demand'.

Le général **commande** cette division de l'armée.
(The general *is in command of* this division of the army.)

Ses exploits **commandent** le respect.
(His exploits *command / demand* respect.)

► However, it also means 'to order' or 'to place an order for', particularly in a restaurant.

Êtes-vous prêts à **commander**?
(Are you ready *to order*?)

4 Confronter

Confronter can mean 'to confront' in a legal sense.

L'enquêteur **a confronté** les témoins pour contrôler l'exactitude de leurs déclarations.
(The investigator *confronted / brought together* the witnesses to check the accuracy of their statements.)

Etre confronté avec quelqu'un / **à** quelque chose means 'to be confronted with'.

Nous **sommes confrontés à** un problème inattendu.
(We *are confronted by* an unexpected problem.)

► However, **confronter** can also mean 'to compare'.

Nous avons dû **confronter** trois manuscrits pour établir une édition du texte.
(We had *to compare* three manuscripts to establish an edition of the text.)

5 Contrôler

Contrôler can mean 'to control'.

Les troupes américaines **contrôlent** cette zone.
(The American troops *control* this zone.)

► However, it often means 'to check' or 'to inspect'.

L'inspecteur doit **contrôler** la qualité de la marchandise.
(The inspector has *to check* the quality of the goods.)

Le douanier **a contrôlé** leurs bagages.
(The customs officer *inspected* their luggage.)

6 Évoluer

Évoluer can mean 'to evolve' in the sense of 'to change' or 'to develop'.

Depuis qu'il est allé à l'université il **a** beaucoup **évolué**.
(Since he went to university, he *has changed* a great deal.)

► However, it can also mean 'to move around' or 'to glide about'.

Les danseurs **évoluaient** avec grâce sur la scène.
(The dancers *were gliding* gracefully *about* the stage.)

7 Excéder

Excéder can mean 'to exceed' in a formal register of language.

Le coût de ce voyage **excède** mes moyens.

(The cost of this journey *exceeds* my means.)

► However, it often means 'to tire / wear out' or 'to infuriate'.

Cet enfant m'**excède** avec ses caprices.
(That child *is wearing* me *out* / *infuriating* me with his / her tantrums.)

8 Ignorer

Ignorer can mean 'to ignore'.

Quand elle me voit, elle m'**ignore**.
(When she sees me she *ignores* me.)

► However, it more often means 'not to know' or 'to be unaware of'.

Je sais qu'il y a eu un accident, mais j'**ignore** les détails.
(I know that there has been an accident, but I *don't know* the details.)

J'**ignorais** l'existence de ce monument.
(I *was unaware of* the existence of this monument.)

Mnemonic device
Remember the meaning of **ignorer** by thinking of the English phrase 'to be ignorant of'.

9 Réaliser

Réaliser can mean 'to realise' in the sense of 'to become aware of something', though **se rendre compte** is more usually used for this.

Ils n'**avaient** pas **réalisé** / Ils ne **s'étaient** pas **rendu compte** à quel point sa santé s'était altérée.

(They hadn't *realised* the extent to which his / her health had deteriorated.)

► However, **réaliser** more often means 'to realise' in the sense of 'to make real' something that was a dream or an ambition.

Il **a** enfin **réalisé** son rêve de faire le tour du monde.
(He finally *realised / achieved* his dream of going round the world.)

* Note that it also has a specialised meaning, 'to direct' a film or a television programme, and remember the noun **un réalisateur** (film director).

10 Succéder

Succéder à means 'to succeed' in the sense of 'to follow on from'.

Henri IV **a succédé à** Henri III.
(Henry IV *succeeded* Henry III.)

Le désespoir **succéda à** la défaite.
(Despair *followed* the defeat.)

► However, if you want to say 'to succeed', meaning 'to have success in', use **réussir à**.

Nous **avons réussi à** vendre notre appartement.
(We have *succeeded in* selling our flat.)

Exercises

EXERCISE 1. Choose the appropriate word or words to fill the blanks and make any necessary changes.

1 Elle est ________ par l'amour.
a) aveuglée b) blindée

2 J'entends les écoliers qui ______ à l'heure de la sortie.
a) crient b) pleurent

3 Elle _______ à propos de cette décision.
a) agonise b) se tourmente

4 Il a _______ tous ses objectifs.
a) achevé b) atteint

5 J'ai décidé d' / de ________ le dessin de mon jardin.
a) altérer b) transformer

6 J'ai du mal à ________ mon emploi du temps.
a) balancer b) équilibrer

7 Je voudrais __________de ce vieux fauteuil.
a) disposer b) me débarrasser

8 Les soldats cherchaient à _______ la nouvelle recrue à la bière.
a) enivrer b) intoxiquer

9 Il a _____ son rapport en une demi-heure.
a) considéré b) pondu

10 En le revoyant pour la première fois depuis son mariage, j'ai ______ qu'il avait grossi, mais je ne lui en ai rien dit.
a) remarqué b) fait remarquer

11 J'ai ________ mon portable par une tablette.
a) remplacé b) replacé

12 Les enfants jouent à _______.
a) faire semblant b) prétendre

13 Il est difficile de ________ son travail après de longues vacances.
a) reprendre b) résumer

14 Il ne _______ jamais tranquille.
a) se repose b) reste

15 J'ai été obligé de ________ mon départ de trois jours.
a) rapporter b) reporter

16 Il _________ qu'elle soit mieux payée que lui.
a) ressent b) ne supporte pas

17 Il a _____ son pantalon aux genoux.
a) usé b) utilisé

18 Les plantes de serre _______ des soins constants.
a) demandent b) exigent

19 Il y aura sans doute des circonstances __________ pour expliquer ce retard.
a) atténuantes b) exténuantes

20 Il va _______ son permis de conduire demain.
a) passer b) réussir à

21 Nous avons ______ d'accepter ces conditions.
a) agréé b) convenu

22 En divulguant son adresse email on risque de se faire ______ à toute heure.
a) importuner b) molester

EXERCISE 2. Match each underlined verb or phrase in the sentences below with the closest synonym from the box and rewrite the whole sentence, making any necessary changes.

abuser de (see example below); altérer; assister à; commander; conforter; confronter; considérer; contrôler; crier; disposer de; évoluer; excéder; exténuer; ignorer; intoxiquer; prétendre; réaliser; replacer; ressentir; réussir à; user

Example: Elle mange trop de sucreries. Elle abuse des sucreries.

1 Ils ont rapproché trois textes différents pour les comparer.
2 Les soucis l'ont épuisé.
3 J'ai été témoin d'un incident regrettable.
4 Des avions allaient et venaient dans le ciel pendant le meeting aérien.
5 Il ne pourra jamais mettre à exécution tous ses projets.
6 Cet enfant m'exaspère avec ses petites manies.
7 Je ne sais pas où ils habitent.
8 Le directeur doit vérifier la fiabilité du texte.
9 Nous avons demandé la fourniture d'une caisse de vin.
10 Cet attentat l'a confirmé dans l'idée d'être journaliste.
11 L'humidité a abîmé la décoration de la chambre.
12 L'accusé a protesté de son innocence.
13 Si vous avez l'usage d'une voiture, vous pourrez y aller.
14 Ces longues heures de travail l'avaient fatigué à l'extrême.
15 Elle avait été empoisonnée par des champignons vénéneux.
16 Il a été reçu à son examen de rattrapage.
17 Elle a moins d'expérience qu'on ne l'affirme.
18 On nous a demandé de remettre les chaises dans la salle de classe.
19 Il faut réfléchir aux conséquences avant d'agir.
20 Il éprouve de la colère contre elle.

EXERCISE 3. Use the verb from the box that best completes each sentence. Conjugate it as appropriate.

s'abuser; s'achever; agréer; balancer; blinder; contrôler; désaltérer; exiger; griser; prétendre; réaliser; remarquer; faire remarquer; remplacer; replacer; se reposer; se servir de; signaler; user; en vouloir (à quelqu'un)

1 Tu as l'air fatigué. Tu devrais aller _______.
2 Les malheurs de sa vie l'ont ________ contre la sentimentalité.
3 Ce poste ne lui est pas accessible, parce que l'on ________ un permis de conduire.
4 Je leur _________ de m'avoir caché la vérité.
5 Il ne faut pas vous laisser _____ par les flatteries.
6 Je dois faire un grand rangement et ______ toutes mes vieilles fringues.
7 Sa carrière sportive s'est _________ sur une victoire inespérée.

8 Je trouve qu'une glace me _______ aussi bien qu'une boisson fraîche.
9 Veuillez ______, Madame, mes salutations distinguées.
10 Il nous a __________ le changement d'horaire.
11 Il a _____ ses vêtements jusqu'à la corde.
12 C'est un escroc, si je ne _______.
13 Il a su _________ cette situation pour faire avancer sa carrière.
14 Savez-vous qui a _______ le film *Caché*?
15 N'avez-vous pas ______ combien il a changé depuis sa récente maladie?
16 Elle est chargée de _____ les billets à l'entrée de la salle.
17 Qui va _______ Madame Morel pendant son absence?
18 Il ________ à des indemnités après son accident.
19 Voulez-vous ________ ces papiers dans le classeur?
20 Il m'a ________ d'un ton dédaigneux que j'avais fait très peu de progrès.

EXERCISE 4. Fill in the blanks with the most appropriate verbs and verbal expressions that you have learnt in this chapter.

Chère Julie,

Demain je dois (1) ________ (sit / take) mon examen de français et j'ai bien peur. Si seulement je pouvais le (2) ___________ (postpone) à la semaine prochaine, mais tant pis. Je suis sûre que tu (3) ___________(realise) de mes problèmes, même si mon professeur croit parfois que j'essaie d'inventer des circonstances (4) __________ (mitigating). Il est évident qu'il ne veut pas (5) ________ (to be fooled). Je n'ai pas (6) ________ (succeeded) à le convaincre qu'il est difficile de (7) ___________ (to resume) aux études à l'âge de trente ans quand on a d'autres responsabilités. Hier soir, par exemple, ma petite fille (8) __________ (was crying her heart out) parce que je lui avais demandé de ne pas m' (9) __________ (to bother) pendant une heure. Elle (10) __________ (resents it / holds it against me) de consacrer autant de temps à mes études. Parfois elle m' (11) ___________ (wears out / infuriates). En tout cas, le trimestre (12) ___________ (is coming to an end) et je pourrai bientôt (13) ___________ (rest). Pour ce qui est des résultats, je voudrais pouvoir dire que (14) _____________ (don't give a damn). En fin de compte j'ai fait de mon mieux avec les moyens dont je (15) ________ (have) et il faudra accepter ce que je ne peux pas (16) ________ (alter) et cesser de (17) ______________ (agonising).

Je t'embrasse,
Aurélie

Mastering false friends: nouns

Although the following nouns look like English nouns, they often mean something very different. The first list consists of false friends that have a completely different meaning from their English lookalikes. The second list features nouns where there is some overlap of meaning with English, but an overlap that is only partial. Study the examples in the contexts given to help you avoid misunderstanding.

False friends (Part 1)

1 Achèvement

Achèvement (m.) means 'completion' or 'conclusion'.

L'**achèvement** des travaux d'aménagement demandera encore quelques mois.
(The *completion* of the improvement work will take another few months.)

Nous espérons voir l'**achèvement** des discussions dans les jours prochains.
(We are hoping to see the *conclusion* of the talks in the next few days.)

► However, if you want to say 'achievement', use **la réussite**, **le succès** or **la réalisation**.

On ne peut pas nier ses nombreuses **réussites** / **succès** dans ce domaine.
(Her many *achievements* in this field cannot be denied.)

Il tient absolument à la **réalisation** de cette ambition.
(He is absolutely set on the *achievement* of this ambition.)

* Note the expressions: **en cours d'achèvement** and **en voie d'achèvement** (nearing completion).

2 Affluence

Affluence (f.) means 'crowd(s)'.

Il est étonnant de voir l'**affluence** des grands magasins quand c'est la saison des soldes.
(It's amazing to see the *crowds* in the department stores during the sales.)

Je préfère éviter le supermarché aux heures d'**affluence.**
(I prefer to avoid the supermarket at *busy* / *crowded* times.)

► However, if you want to say 'affluence', use **la richesse**.

Il n'a aucun scrupule à étaler sa **richesse**.
(He has no scruples about flaunting his *affluence*.)

3 Agenda

Un agenda is 'a diary' for forthcoming appointments.

J'ai noté le rendez-vous dans mon **agenda**.
(I've noted the appointment in my *diary*.)

► However, if you want to say 'agenda', use **l'ordre du jour** for the literal sense and **le programme** for the figurative sense of 'list of priorities'.

Cette question sera à l'**ordre du jour** de notre prochaine réunion.
(This matter will be on the *agenda* of our next meeting.)

Je suis sûr qu'ils ont un **programme** secret.
(I am sure that they have a hidden *agenda*.)

* Note the expressions: **un agenda de bureau** (desk diary), **un agenda électronique** (electronic personal organiser) and **un agenda de poche** (pocket diary).

4 Agonie

Agonie (f.) means 'death throes', and can refer to the slow demise of governments, monarchies or regimes, as well as to the death of living beings.

Elle est à l'**agonie**.
(She is *dying / at death's door*.)

Son **agonie** a été longue et terrible.
(He / she died a terrible, slow *death*.)

La monarchie était à l'**agonie**.
(The monarchy was in its *death throes*.)

► However, if you want to say 'agony', use **la douleur** for physical agony and **l'angoisse** (f.) for mental agony or anxiety.

Elle se tordait de **douleur**.
(She was writhing in *agony*.)

Je ne veux pas prolonger l'**angoisse** des étudiants qui attendent les résultats.
(I don't want to prolong the *agony* of the students who are waiting for the results.)

* Note the expression: **c'était l'horreur!** (it was agony!)

5 Agrément

Agrément (m.) means 'approval' and can also mean 'pleasure' or 'charm'.

Il a sollicité l'**agrément** de son supérieur avant de poursuivre la question.
(He sought the *approval* of his superior before proceeding with the matter.)

Nous trouvons de l'**agrément** à cette ville de province.
(We find a certain *charm* in this provincial town.)

► However, if you want to say 'agreement', use **un accord**.

Les leaders des deux partis sont parvenus à un **accord**.
(The leaders of the two parties have come to an *agreement*.)

6 Allée

Une allée is 'a path' in a garden, park or wood. It can also be an aisle between rows of chairs or a row (A, B, C etc.) of cars in a car park.

Vous trouverez une petite **allée** dans les bois qui mène à la chaumière.
(You will find a small *path* in the woods, which leads to the cottage.)

Il s'est avancé par l'**allée** centrale pour trouver sa place.
(He moved along the central *aisle* to find his seat.)

► However, if you want to say 'alley', use **la ruelle.**

J'ai pris une **ruelle** pour éviter la foule qui se pressait autour de l'entrée de la gare.
(I turned down an *alley* to avoid the crowd swarming around the station entrance.)

7 Altération

Altération (f.) means 'impairment', 'spoiling' or 'deterioration'. It can also mean 'distortion' or 'falsification'. In musical terminology, it means an 'accidental'.

L'**altération** de sa santé a été brusque et alarmante.
(The *deterioration* in his / her health was sudden and alarming.)

Le texte de cet article a subi des **altérations** importantes.
(The text of this article has been subject to significant *distortions*.)

Le dièse et le bémol sont des **altérations**.
(Sharps and flats are *accidentals*.)

► However, if you want to say 'alteration' in a neutral sense, use **la transformation**, **la modification** or **le changement**.

On a effectué des **transformations** importantes dans ce quartier de la ville.
(Major *alterations* have been carried out in this district of the town.)

Ils ont accepté son texte sans **modifications**.
(They accepted his text without *alterations*.)

Un incident imprévu a entraîné un **changement** de programme.
(An unforeseen incident caused an *alteration* to the programme.)

* Learn the expression: **travaux d'aménagement** (alterations / improvements to a building).

8 Avertissement

Un avertissement is 'a warning'. In sport, it is 'a caution'.

> Cet accident m'a servi d'**avertissement**.
> (This accident served as a *warning* to me.)

> L'arbitre a donné un **avertissement** au joueur.
> (The referee gave the player a *caution*.)

However, if you want to say 'advertisement', use **une annonce** or **une publicité**.

> J'ai fait passer une **annonce** dans le journal pour vendre ma voiture.
> (I've placed an *advertisement* in the paper to sell my car.)

> On passe une **publicité** pour le concert à la radio.
> (They are running an *advertisement* for the concert on the radio.)

9 Balancement

Balancement (m.) means 'swaying' or 'swinging'.

> Elle regardait le **balancement** des branches du cerisier.
> (She watched the *swaying* of the cherry tree branches.)

► However, if you want to say 'balancing', use **équilibrage** (m.).

> Il faut veiller à l'**équilibrage** des roues.
> (You must see to the *balancing* of the wheels.)

* Learn the figurative expression: **tenter d'atteindre un compromis** (to do a balancing act).

10 Blouse

Une blouse is 'an overall' or 'smock'. It is usually knee-length and is worn over the clothes for protection.

> Il faut mettre une **blouse** pour éviter de se salir.
> (You need to put on an *overall* to avoid getting dirty.)

► However, if you want to say 'blouse', use un **chemisier**.

> Elle portait un **chemisier** en soie.
> (She was wearing a silk *blouse*.)

* Learn the expression: **une blouse blanche** (a white coat, as worn by a doctor).

11 Car

Un car (or **un autocar**) is 'a coach' or bus.

Nous prenons le **car** pour aller à Londres.
(We are taking the *coach* to London.)

► However, if you want to say 'car', use **la voiture**.

J'ai vendu ma **voiture** l'année dernière et maintenant je fais les longs trajets en **car**.
(I sold my *car* last year and now I make long journeys by *coach*.)

For the dining or sleeping 'car' on a train, use **le wagon**.

Ce train n'a pas de **wagon-restaurant.** Par contre il y a **un wagon-lit.**
(This train does not have a *dining car*. On the other hand, there is a *sleeping car*.)

* Learn the useful expressions: **un car de police** (a police van), **un car scolaire** (a school bus) and **le tramway** (streetcar / streetcar line in American usage; tram / tramway in British usage).

12 Cargo

Un cargo is a 'cargo ship'.

Un grand **cargo** vient d'entrer dans le dock.
(A large *cargo ship* has just come into dock.)

Just to confuse things, it can also mean a pair of 'cargo pants'! Like **un pantalon** (a pair of trousers), it is singular.

Elle porte un **cargo** qui ne lui va pas du tout.
(She is wearing *cargo pants* that don't suit her at all.)

► However, if you want to say 'cargo', use **une cargaison**.

Les soldats ont commencé à décharger **la cargaison** d'équipement.
(The soldiers began to unload the *cargo* of equipment.)

* Learn the useful expressions: **un avion cargo** (a cargo plane) and **un cargo mixte** (a passenger-cargo ship).

13 Casserole

Une casserole is 'a saucepan'.

Remplissez une **casserole** d'eau et portez-la à ébullition.
(Fill a *saucepan* with water and bring it to the boil.)

► However, if you want to say 'casserole', use **une daubière**, **une cocotte** or **une marmite** if you mean the container, and **un ragoût en cocotte** or **un ragoût cuit au four** if you mean the food cooked inside it.

Ce bœuf n'est bon que si vous le faites cuire à la **cocotte**.
(This beef is only any good if you cook it in a *casserole.*, i.e. if you casserole / stew it.)

J'ai préparé un **ragoût en cocotte** pour ce soir.
(I've prepared a *casserole* for this evening.)

* Note the idiomatic expressions: **passer à la casserole** (to get into trouble; to be coerced into sex) and **chanter / jouer comme une casserole** (to sing / play atrociously badly).

14 Caution

Une caution is 'a deposit'. It can also mean 'bail' or 'support / backing'.

Nous avons versé une **caution** de 200 euros pour l'appartement.
(We paid a *deposit* of 200 euros for the flat.)

Il a été libéré sous **caution**.
(He has been released on *bail.*)

Le chef de parti a apporté sa **caution** au nouveau candidat.
(The party leader gave the new candidate his *support / backing.*)

* Note the expression **sujet(tte) à caution**, meaning 'in need of support / backing', i.e. 'open to doubt'.

On ne peut pas se fier à des affirmations aussi **sujettes à caution**.
(You can't trust such *dubious* assertions.)

► However, if you want to say 'caution', use **prudence** (f.). In a sporting context, use un **avertissement**. (See item 8 on p. 57.)

Il faut conduire avec **prudence** quand il y a du verglas.
(You need to drive with *caution* when there is ice.)

15 Cave

Une cave is 'a cellar', very often 'a wine cellar'.

Il a une bonne **cave**.
(He has a good *cellar.*)

► However, if you want to say 'cave', use **une caverne** or **une grotte**.

C'est une véritable **caverne** d'Ali Baba.
(It's a real Aladdin's *cave.*)

Il aime explorer les **grottes** sous-marines.
(He likes exploring underwater *caves*.)

16 Change

Change (m.) means 'foreign exchange' of money or 'exchange rate'.

Il y a un bureau de **change** à l'aéroport.
(There is a *foreign exchange* office at the airport.)

Les vacances en Europe sont plus abordables quand le **change** est avantageux.
(Holidays in Europe are more affordable when the *exchange rate* is favourable.)

► However, if you want to say a 'change', use **un changement.** For 'change' in the sense of coins, see **la monnaie** below.

Le **changement** d'horaire m'a prise au dépourvu.
(The *change* of schedule caught me by surprise.)

BE AWARE! Of all the false friends listed in this chapter, this is perhaps the most common source of mistakes.

Mnemonic device
The expression **bureau de change** should help you to remember that **change** in French means 'exchange'.

17 Chips

Chips (m. pl.) are 'potato crisps' (British usage).

J'ai acheté des **chips** goût bacon fumé parce que les enfants en raffolent.
(I bought smoky bacon *crisps* because the children are crazy about them.)

► However, if you want to say 'chips', meaning 'fried potatoes', use **les frites** (f. pl.).

Ce restaurant met un point d'honneur à ne pas servir de **frites**.
(This restaurant prides itself on not serving *chips*.)

* Note the expression: **une puce** (computer chip). It also means a flea!

18 Comédien

Un comédien / **une comédienne** is 'an actor / actress'.

Un **comédien** interprète des rôles dramatiques ou comiques.
(An *actor* plays dramatic or comic parts.)

► However, if you want to say 'comedian', use un(e) comique.

Ce **comique** écrit des sketches qui nous font tordre de rire.
(This *comedian* writes sketches that have us doubled up with laughter.)

19 Complainte

Une complainte is 'a lament', i.e. a sad song.

Elle ne chante que des **complaintes**. Je préfère écouter des chansons plus gaies.
(She only sings *sad songs / laments*. I prefer listening to more light-hearted songs.)

► However, if you want to say 'complaint', use **une plainte** or **une réclamation.**

Il a porté **plainte** contre son voisin.
(He lodged a *complaint* against his neighbour.)

Les ouvriers ont déposé une **réclamation** auprès de la direction.
(The workers lodged a *complaint* with the management.)

20 Complexion

Complexion (f.) means 'constitution'.

Cet enfant a une **complexion** délicate.
(This child has a delicate *constitution*.)

► However, if you want to say 'complexion', use **le teint**.

Elle a un joli **teint**. Sa peau est toute lisse.
(She has a lovely *complexion*. Her skin is very smooth.)

21 Conducteur

Un conducteur is 'a driver'.

Je ne crois pas qu'il soit bon **conducteur**. Il prend trop de risques.
(I don't think he is a good *driver*. He takes too many risks.)

► However, if you want to say 'conductor', use **le receveur** for a bus or tram, **le chef de train** for a train or **le chef d'orchestre** for an orchestra.

Il travaillait comme **receveur** de bus, mais ce travail se fait maintenant par le **conducteur**.
(He used to work as a bus *conductor*, but the job is done by the *driver* now.)

Les musiciens n'apprécient pas ce **chef d'orchestre.**
(The musicians don't like this *conductor*.)

22 Conférence

Une conférence is 'a public lecture'.

Il donne une **conférence** sur les plans de réaménagement.
(He is giving a *public lecture* about the redevelopment plans.)

Note that the usual word for a university lecture is **un cours**. If it is a lecture to a large audience, it is a **cours magistral**.

Le semestre prochain elle donnera des **cours** sur Proust.
(Next semester she will be giving *lectures* on Proust.)

► However, if you want to say 'conference', use **le congrès**.

Le **congrès** se déroulera à Rome du 5 au 7 avril.
(The *conference* will take place in Rome from 5 to 7 April.)

23 Convenance

In the singular, **convenance** (f.) means something that is 'to someone's liking' or that 'suits them'.

Cet appartement est à ma **convenance**.
(This flat is *to* my *liking* / *suits* me.)

It is only in fixed phrases, like **un mariage de convenance** (a marriage of convenience), that **convenance** means 'convenience'.

Convenances (f. pl.) means 'convention' or 'propriety'.

Elle n'a aucun scrupule à braver les **convenances**.
(She has no scruples about defying *convention*.)

► However, if you want to say 'convenience', use **les avantages** (m. pl.) or **la commodité**.

Les **avantages** d'habiter près de son lieu de travail sont évidents.
(The *convenience* of living near to one's workplace is obvious.)

J'ai acheté une quiche préparée pour raisons de **commodité**.
(I bought a ready-made quiche for the sake of *convenience*.)

* Note the expression: **pour convenances personnelles** (for personal reasons).

24 Course

Une course is 'a race' or the activity of running. In the plural, it means 'shopping'.

Nous suivons avec intérêt la **course** à la Maison Blanche.
(We are following with interest the *race* for the White House.)

Le frigo est vide; je dois aller faire des **courses**.
(The fridge is empty; I must go and do some *shopping*.)

► However, if you want to say 'course', use **un cours**.

Nous suivons un **cours** de littérature ce trimestre.
(We're taking a literature *course* this term.)

* Note the expressions: **au cours de l'année** (in the course of the year), **en cours de construction** (in the process of being built / under construction) and **en cours de route** (along the way).

25 Courtier

Un courtier is 'a broker' in the world of commerce or finance.

Je cherche un **courtier** en assurances.
(I'm looking for an insurance *broker*.)

► However, if you want to say 'courtier', use **un courtisan** or **une dame de cour**.

Le roi a assemblé tous ses **courtisans** dans la salle de bal.
(The king gathered all his *courtiers* together in the ballroom.)

* Note that **une courtisane** means 'a courtesan' and so should be used with care!

26 Déception

Une déception is 'a disappointment'.

Ce résultat est une vraie **déception** pour moi. J'espérais faire mieux.
(This result is a real *disappointment for me.* I was hoping to do better.)

► However, if you want to say 'deception', use **des tromperies** (f. pl.) or **une fraude.**

Les **tromperies** du gouvernement nous laissent interdits.
(We are dumbfounded by government *deception*.)

Il a obtenu le poste par **fraude**.
(He obtained the job by *deception*.)

27 Délai

Un délai is the 'period of time' allowed for doing something. It can also mean a 'deadline' or an 'extension' of the original time limit.

Nous avons un **délai** de quinze jours pour payer la facture.
(We have *a period* of a fortnight to pay the bill.)

Il faut que tous les étudiants respectent le **délai** pour les inscriptions.
(All students must meet the *deadline* for registration.)

On m'a accordé un **délai** de huit jours pour rendre mon mémoire.
(I have been given an *extension* of a week to hand in my dissertation.)

► However, if you want to say 'delay', use **le retard**.

Nous vous prions de nous excuser pour ce **retard**.
(We apologise for the *delay*.)

* Learn the useful expression **dans les plus brefs délais** (as soon as possible) and note the expression **sans délai** (without delay) where, exceptionally, **délai** does translate as 'delay'.

28 Destitution

Destitution (f.) means 'dismissal' or 'discharge'.

La **destitution** du directeur a fait du bruit.
(The *dismissal* of the manager caused a stir.)

► However, if you want to say 'destitution', use **le dénuement**, **l'indigence** (f.) or **la misère**.

Il se trouvait dans le plus grand **dénuement**.
(He was in a state of utter *destitution*.)

Elle vit dans l'**indigence** / dans la **misère**.
(She is living in *destitution*.)

29 Disgrâce

Disgrâce (f.) means 'misfortune'.

Ils ont connu des **disgrâces** humiliantes.
(They have come up against some humiliating *misfortunes*.)

► However, if you want to say 'disgrace', meaning something shameful, use **la honte** or **le déshonneur**.

C'est une **honte**.
(It's a *disgrace*.)

Il est le **déshonneur** de la famille.
(He is the *disgrace* / black sheep of the family.)

* Note, as exceptions, the expressions: **connaître la disgrâce / être en disgrâce** (to be in disgrace) and **tomber en disgrâce** (to fall into disgrace).

30 Dissertation

Une dissertation (une disserte in informal usage) is 'an essay' written by a student.

Je dois faire une **dissertation** sur le roman que nous venons d'étudier.
(I have to write an *essay* about the novel we have just studied.)

► However, if you want to say 'dissertation', use **un mémoire**.

Pour obtenir mon diplôme, je dois écrire un **mémoire** de 15 000 mots.
(To get my degree, I have to write a *dissertation* of 15,000 words.)

* Note the difference in gender and in meaning between **le mémoire** (dissertation) and **la mémoire** (memory). See also Chapter 1.

31 Donjon

Un donjon is 'a castle keep'.

Ce château fort se fait remarquer par son beau **donjon** en pierre de taille.
(This castle is remarkable for its fine *keep* in dressed stone.)

► However, if you want to say 'dungeon', use **un cachot**.

Le prisonnier a été relégué au **cachot**.
(The prisoner was banished to the *dungeon*.)

32 Engin

Un engin is a device for a particular purpose. In the plural, it means 'equipment'. In a military context, it is the generic term for weapons of war.

Les alpinistes se sont munis de tous leurs **engins**.
(The climbers brought all their *equipment* with them.)

L'armée a montré ses **engins** les plus sophistiqués lors du défilé du 14 juillet.
(The army displayed its most sophisticated *weapons of war* in the parade on 14 July.)

Also note the colloquial expression:

Qu'est-ce que c'est que cet **engin**?
(What's that *contraption*?)

▶ However, if you want to say 'engine', use **un moteur**.

J'ai laissé la voiture avec le **moteur** en marche.
(I've left the car with the *engine* running.)

33 Étable

Une étable is 'a cowshed'.

En hiver on rentre les vaches dans l'**étable**.
(In winter, the cows are brought into *the cowshed*.)

▶ However, if you want to say 'stable', use **une écurie**.

Il a mené le cheval à l'**écurie**.
(He led the horse to *the stable*.)

34 Évidence

Une évidence means 'obviousness', either an obvious fact or position. You can remember this by associating it with the adjective **évident** (obvious).

C'est l'**évidence** même.
(It's glaringly *obvious*.)

J'ai laissé les clés en **évidence**.
(I left the keys in an *obvious place*.)

▶ However, if you want to say 'evidence', use une **preuve** or **un témoignage**.

Les **preuves** sont insuffisantes pour qu'on l'interpelle.
(There is insufficient *evidence* for him to be brought in for questioning.)

Il a été condamné sur le **témoignage** de son voisin.
(He was convicted on the *evidence* of his neighbour.)

* Learn the expressions: **de toute évidence** (obviously) and **mettre en évidence** (to highlight).

35 Grief

Un grief is 'a grievance'.

Elle a un **grief** contre eux à cause de leur chien qui aboie tout le temps.
(She has a *grievance* against them because of their dog that barks all the time.)

The expression, **faire grief à quelqu'un de quelque chose** means 'to hold something against someone'.

Il nous **fait grief** de ne pas lui avoir rendu visite à l'hôpital.
(He *holds it against* us that we didn't visit him in hospital.)

► However, if you want to say 'grief', use **le chagrin** or **la douleur**.

La mort de sa mère lui a causé un profond **chagrin**.
(The death of his mother caused him great *grief*.)

Elle est accablée de **douleur**.
(She is *grief*-stricken.)

36 Habileté

L'habileté (f.) means 'skill'.

Elle a exécuté le morceau avec **habileté**.
(She performed the piece *skilfully*.)

► However, if you want to say 'ability / abilities', use **la capacité** or **les compétences** (f. pl.).

Je doute de ma **capacité** à faire ce travail.
(I doubt my *ability* to do this work.)

Ses **compétences** intellectuelles sont évidentes.
(His / her intellectual *ability* is obvious.)

37 Halle

Une halle is 'a market hall'. It is more usually found in the plural, meaning 'covered market'.

Les Halles de Paris abritent un bistro de renom.
(The *covered market* in Paris houses a famous bistro.)

► However, if you want to say 'hall', use **l'entrée** (f.) in a house, **le hall** in a hotel, airport or station, and **une salle** where 'hall' means a large public room.

J'ai laissé mon parapluie dans **l'entrée**.
(I've left my umbrella in the *hallway*.)

Nous nous sommes donné rendez-vous dans le **hall** de départ de l'aéroport.
(We arranged to meet in the departures *hall* of the airport.)

La réunion aura lieu dans la **salle** polyvalente de la commune.
(The meeting will take place in the local village *hall*.)

* Note that both **la halle** and **le hall** begin with an aspirate 'h' and see Chapter 1.

38 Incidence

Incidence (f.) means 'effect' or 'impact'.

La hausse des prix a eu une **incidence** sur leur niveau de vie.
(The increase in prices has had an *effect / impact* on their standard of living.)

▶ However, if you want to say 'incidence', use **la fréquence** or **le taux**.

La **fréquence** de vols dans le quartier nous laisse inquiets.
(The *incidence* of thefts in the neighbourhood worries us.)

Il y a un **taux** élevé de mortalité infantile dans le tiers-monde.
(There is a high *incidence* of infant mortality in the Third World.)

39 Inconvenance

Inconvenance (f.) means 'impropriety'.

L'**inconvenance** de leur conduite me laisse interdite.
(*The impropriety* of their behaviour dumbfounds me.)

▶ However, if you want to say 'inconvenience', use **le dérangement** in the sense of 'trouble, bother' and **l'inconvénient** (m.) in the sense of 'disadvantage'.

Ils m'ont causé beaucoup de **dérangement**.
(They put me to great *inconvenience*.)

Le fait de ne pas avoir de voiture nous cause souvent des **inconvénients**.
(Not having a car often causes us *inconvenience*.)

40 Ingénuité

Ingénuité (f.) means 'ingenuousness'.

Cette question naïve démontre l'**ingénuité** totale de l'enfant.
(This naïve question shows the complete *ingenuousness* of the child.)

▶ However, if you want to say 'ingenuity', use **l'ingéniosité** (f.).

En trouvant la solution au mystère elle a fait preuve d'une **ingéniosité** remarquable.
(In solving the mystery, she showed remarkable *ingenuity*.)

41 Injure

Une injure is 'an insult'.

Il a considéré notre absence comme une **injure** personnelle.
(He considered our absence to be a personal *insult*.)

► However, if you want to say 'injury', use **une blessure**.

Le soldat a subi une grave **blessure** à la tête.
(The soldier sustained a serious head *injury*.)

42 Intoxication

Intoxication (f.) means 'poisoning' or 'brainwashing'.

Il y a eu 5 cas d'**intoxication** alimentaire.
(There have been 5 cases of food *poisoning*.)

Il s'agit d'une véritable **intoxication** des esprits par la propagande.
(It's a case of real *brainwashing* by propaganda.)

► However, if you want to say 'intoxication', use **l'ivresse** (f.) or **l'ébriété** (f.).

On l'a trouvé en état d'**ivresse** / d'**ébriété**.
(He was found in a state of *intoxication*.)

43 Issue

Une issue means 'an exit', 'a solution' or 'way out' of a situation, or 'an outcome'.

L'**issue** principale était bloquée.
(The main *exit* was blocked.)

Cette situation est sans **issue**.
(There is no *way out* of this *situation*.)

On craint une **issue** tragique.
(A tragic *outcome* is feared.)

► However, if you want to say 'issue', meaning 'topic for discussion', use **le problème** or **la question**.

Ce n'est pas **le problème** / **la question**.
(That's not the *issue*.)

Ce qui est en **cause** est la validité du projet.
(The point at *issue* is the viability of the project.)

C'est leur avenir qui est en **question**.
(Their future is at *issue*.)

Mnemonic device
The expression: **issue de secours** (emergency exit) should help you to remember that **une issue** does not translate the English word 'issue'.

Exercises

EXERCISE 1. Choose the most appropriate noun to fill the blanks and make any other necessary choices depending on the gender of the noun chosen.

1 L'enquête a servi à mettre en _________ le lien entre ces événements.
a) évidence b) preuve c) témoignage
2 Elle doit ses ________ à sa persévérance.
a) achèvements b) réalisations c) succès
3 Tout ce qu'ils racontent n'est que mensonges et _________.
a) déceptions b) fraudes c) tromperies
4 Ils vivent dans l' / la _________.
a) agonie b) destitution c) misère
5 Avez-vous noté l' / le ________ d'adresse?
a) altération b) change c) changement
6 Le directeur a adressé un(e) _________ à ses employés.
a) annonce b) avertissement c) caution
7 On nous a accordé un(e) _________ de huit jours pour payer la facture.
a) délai b) retard c) issue
8 Le ministre est tombé en _______.
a) déshonneur b) disgrâce c) honte
9 Il a été reconnu coupable de conduite en état d'________.
a) inconvenance b) intoxication c) ivresse
10 Il a couvert son adversaire de / d' ____________.
a) avertissements b) blessures c) injures
11 Les __________ de cette commune datent du quinzième siècle.
a) halles b) halls c) salles
12 Ses croyances religieuses ne sont pas en ________.
a) issue b) problème c) question
13 Les travaux nous ont causé de nombreux / -euses _________.
a) dérangements b) désavantages c) inconvenances
14 Son fils lui a fait du / de la _______.
a) chagrin b) douleur c) grief
15 Je ne doute pas de vos _________ d'imagination.
a) capacités b) compétences c) habiletés
16 Je prépare un(e) __________ de 20 000 mots sur la Révolution française.
a) course b) dissertation c) mémoire
17 Nous suivons un(e) ____________ de mathématiques ce trimestre.
a) conférence b) cours c) course
18 Le ministre a démissionné pour __________ personnel(le)s.
a) avantages b) commodités c) convenances

19 C'est une question qu'il faut inscrire à l' / au _________ pour la prochaine réunion.
a) agenda b) ordre du jour c) programme
20 Elle a porté _______ contre la direction.
a) complainte b) plainte c) réclamation

EXERCISE 2. Connect each noun on the left with its most logical companion or associate from the list on the right.

Example: une allée + un jardin

1	un agenda	a	une vache
2	une blouse	b	des esprits
3	le balancement	c	personnelle
4	un car	d	un sketch
5	une issue	e	blanche
6	une altération	f	une pièce de théâtre
7	une caution	g	en cocotte
8	une caverne	h	des hanches
9	un comédien	i	scolaire
10	un ragoût	j	de train
11	un teint	k	en assurances
12	le chef	l	mixte
13	un courtier	m	de secours
14	le donjon	n	de poche
15	un comique	o	un château fort
16	une étable	p	d'Ali Baba
17	le taux	q	de 100 euros
18	l'intoxication	r	le bémol
19	une injure	s	de chômage
20	un cargo	t	de pêche

EXERCISE 3. Insert the noun from the box that best completes each sentence.

affluence; l'agonie; l'altération; une annonce; une casserole; caution; la cave; commodité; convenance; cours; courses; délai; une inconvenance; ingénuité; retard; les témoignages

1 Elle trouve difficile d'accepter _________ de sa santé.
2 Elle chante comme __________.
3 Son avocat a demandé la mise en liberté sous _______.
4 Il s'agit d'un mariage de _____________.
5 Mon train a une heure de ______.

6 La police s'appuie sur ___________ de la famille.
7 Ce serait ___________ de ne pas répondre à cette invitation.
8 Ce projet est en _________ d'achèvement.
9 Elle a posé la question en toute ________.
10 Nous sommes allés le voir à l'hôpital sans _____.
11 Aux heures d'________ il est difficile de se garer en centre-ville.
12 Ce régime est à _________.
13 Nous avons fait passer __________ dans le journal pour louer notre appartement.
14 J'ai cherché partout du grenier à ______ sans trouver mon agenda.
15 J'ai loué un appartement près de mon lieu de travail pour raisons de ________.

False friends (Part 2)

44 Lecture

La lecture means 'reading'.

La **lecture** à voix haute nous plaît beaucoup.
(We very much like *reading* aloud.)

► However, if you want to say 'lecture', use **une conférence** for a public lecture or **un cours** for a lecture given at university.

Hier soir nous avons assisté à une **conférence** sur la musique contemporaine.
(Last night, we attended a *lecture* about contemporary music.)

J'ai un **cours** d'informatique à dix heures.
(I have a computing *lecture* at 10 o'clock.)

45 Libraire

Un / une libraire is 'a bookseller'.

Ce **libraire** a le sens des affaires.
(This *bookseller* is a good businessman.)

► However, if you want to say 'librarian', use **un / une bibliothécaire**.

Elle travaille comme **bibliothécaire** à l'université.
(She works as a *librarian* at the university.)

46 Librairie

Une librairie is 'a bookshop'.

Il aime flâner dans des **librairies** de livres anciens, mais il n'y achète jamais rien.
(He likes browsing in antiquarian *bookshops*, but he never buys anything there.)

► However, if you want to say 'library', use **une bibliothèque**.

Il y a moins de **bibliothèques** publiques en France qu'en Grande-Bretagne.
(There are fewer public *libraries* in France than in Great Britain.)

47 Licence

Une licence is a French university degree awarded after a year's study following the DEUG (diplôme d'études générales universitaires) or DEUST (diplôme d'études universitaires scientifiques et techniques).

Elle prépare une **licence** en espagnol.
(She is doing a *degree* in Spanish.)

► However, if you want to say 'licence', meaning permit, use **le permis**.

Il s'est fait retirer son **permis** de conduire.
(He has had his driving *licence* taken away from him.)

48 Location

La location means 'renting', 'rented accommodation', 'hire' or 'booking'.

Nous cherchons une **location** à Nice pour les vacances.
(We're looking for *rented accommodation* in Nice for the holidays.)

La location des places pour le festival d'Aix est déjà ouverte.
(*Booking* for the Aix festival is already open.)

► However, if you want to say 'location', use **un emplacement**.

Ce n'est pas l'**emplacement** idéal pour la tente, mais tant pis.
(It's not the ideal *location* for the tent, but never mind.)

49 Logeur

Un logeur / **une logeuse** is 'a landlord / landlady'.

Un **logeur** ou une **logeuse** est une personne qui loue des chambres meublées.
(A *landlord* or *landlady* is someone who rents out furnished rooms.)

► However, if you want to say 'lodger', meaning 'tenant', use **un / une locataire** for someone who simply rents a room, but use **un / une pensionnaire** for someone who also pays for meals.

Elle a une chambre à louer et cherche un **locataire**.
(She has a room to rent and is looking for a *lodger*.)

50 Luxure

Luxure (f.) means 'lust'.

La luxure est l'un des péchés mortels.
(*Lust* is one of the mortal sins.)

► However, if you want to say 'luxury', use **le luxe**.

Ils vivent dans le **luxe**.
(They live in *luxury*.)

Mnemonic device
The adjectival phrase **de luxe** (luxury), as in **une boutique de luxe** (a luxury boutique), will help you to remember that the word for luxury is **le luxe**.

51 Misère

La misère is 'extreme poverty' or 'destitution'.

Son mari prodigue l'a réduite à la **misère**.
(Her spendthrift husband has reduced her to *poverty*.)

► However, if you want to say 'misery', use **la souffrance**.

Elle a une vie de **souffrance**.
(She leads a life of *misery*.)

* Learn the expression: **acheter quelque chose pour une misère** (to buy something for a pittance / for a song).

52 Monnaie

La monnaie means 'currency' or 'change'.

Le franc suisse est une **monnaie** forte.
(The Swiss franc is a strong *currency*.)

Est-ce que vous pouvez me faire la **monnaie** de 20 euros.
(Can you give me *change* for 20 euros?)

► However, if you want to say 'money', use **l'argent** (m.).

Il en veut pour son **argent**.
(He wants his *money*'s worth.)

53 Motoriste

Un / une motoriste is 'a car mechanic'.

Il travaille comme **motoriste**.
(He works as a *car mechanic*.)

► However, if you want to say 'motorist', use **un / une automobiliste**.

À la suite de l'accident, l'**automobiliste** a subi un alcootest.
(Following the accident, the *motorist* was breathalysed.)

54 Patron

Un patron is 'a manager' or 'a boss'.

Il aime être son propre **patron**.
(He likes to be his own *boss*.)

► However, if you want to say 'patron', use **un mécène** for someone who supports the arts and **un client** for a customer.

Ce jeune artiste bénéficie du soutien d'un **mécène** anonyme.
(This young artist benefits from the support of an anonymous *patron*.)

Cette boutique de luxe attire des **clients** cossus.
(This luxury boutique attracts well-off *patrons / customers*.)

55 Pétrole

Le pétrole is 'crude oil'.

On vient de fermer cette raffinerie de **pétrole**.
(This *oil* refinery has just been closed.)

► However, if you want to say 'petrol', use **l'essence** (f.).

Le prix de l'**essence** a encore augmenté.
(The price of *petrol* has gone up again.)

56 Pétulance

Pétulance (f.) means 'exuberance'.

La **pétulance** de son petit-fils le fait sourire.
(The *exuberance* of his grandson makes him smile.)

▶ However, if you want to say 'petulance', use **l'irascibilité** (f.) or **l'irritabilité** (f.).

Son **irascibilité** / **irritabilité** la rend difficile à vivre.
(Her *petulance* makes her difficult to live with.)

57 Physicien

Un physicien means 'a physicist'.

C'est un **physicien** nucléaire.
(He is a nuclear *physicist*.)

▶ However, if you want to say 'physician', use **un médecin**.

Les **médecins** ont découvert qu'il était diabétique.
(The *physicians* diagnosed him as a diabetic.)

58 Politicien

Un politicien is a pejorative word for 'a politician'.

Ce **politicien** a la réputation d'être fourbe.
(This *politician* has a reputation for cunning.)

▶ However, if you want a neutral word for 'politician', use **un homme** / **une femme politique.**

En tant qu'**homme politique** il a passé 30 ans de sa vie au service de la communauté.
(As a *politician*, he has spent 30 years of his life in service to the community.)

59 Préjudice

Préjudice (m.) means 'harm' or 'detriment' caused to someone's rights or interests.

Les actions de son frère lui ont porté **préjudice**.
(The actions of his brother caused him *harm*.)

J'ai accepté ce compromis au **préjudice** de ma famille.
(I agreed to this compromise to the *detriment* of my family.)

▶ However, if you want to say 'prejudice', use **le préjugé**.

Il a des **préjugés** contre les travailleurs immigrés.
(He is *prejudiced* against immigrant workers.)

* Note that **un préjugé** is a noun, not an adjective. If you want to say 'prejudiced' in French, use **avoir des préjugés contre** (against) or **en faveur de** (in favour of).

60 Préservatif

Un préservatif means 'a condom'.

L'usage d'un **préservatif** protège contre les MST.
(Use of a *condom* protects against STDs.)

► However, if you want to say 'preservative', use **un agent de conservation**.

Il faut se méfier des **agents de conservation** dont les plats cuisinés sont remplis.
(You have to watch out for the *preservatives* that ready meals are full of.)

61 Procès

Un procès means 'a trial' or 'a lawsuit'.

Il a dû subir un **procès** médiatique.
(He had to undergo a *trial* by media.)

Par suite d'une dispute familiale, ils sont en **procès** avec leurs cousins.
(Due to a family disagreement, they are involved in a *lawsuit* with their cousins.)

► However, if you want to say 'process', use **le processus** in general, or **le procédé** for a particular technique.

Le **processus** biologique de la digestion est intéressant à étudier.
(The biological *process* of digestion is interesting to study.)

On a mis au point un **procédé** chirurgical révolutionnaire.
(A revolutionary surgical *process / technique* has been developed.)

* Note the very common expression: **être en train de faire quelque chose** (to be in the process of doing something).

62 Rente

Rente (f.) is income earned from private means such as investment, rather than from employment.

Il ne travaille plus; il vit de ses **rentes.**
(He doesn't work any more; he lives on his *private income.*)

► However, if you want to say 'rent' on property, use **le loyer**.

J'ai dû payer deux mois de **loyer** à l'avance.
(I had to pay two months' *rent* in advance.)

63 Rétribution

Une rétribution means 'a remuneration' or 'reward'.

Ils ont demandé une **rétribution** en reconnaissance de leurs efforts.
(They asked for *remuneration / reward* in recognition of their efforts.)

► However, if you want to say 'retribution' or 'punishment,' use **le châtiment** for the former and **la punition** for the latter.

C'est le juste **châtiment** pour ce crime.
(It is the just *retribution* for this crime.)

Comme **punition** tu seras privé de dessert ce soir.
(As a *punishment*, you will go without pudding tonight.)

64 Rudesse

La rudesse means 'harshness' or 'severity'.

La **rudesse** de l'hiver à la campagne les a pris au dépourvu.
(The *harshness / severity* of winter in the countryside took them by surprise.)

► However, if you want to say 'rudeness', use **impolitesse** (f.).

Rien n'excuse leur **impolitesse**.
(There's no excuse for their *rudeness*.)

65 Scientiste

Un / une scientiste means 'a follower of scientism'.

► However, if you want to say 'scientist', use **un / une scientifique.**

Il n'y a pas assez de dialogue entre les **scientifiques** et les littéraires.
(There isn't enough dialogue between *scientists* and arts specialists.)

* Note that **scientifique** is also an adjective, meaning 'scientific'.

66 Square

Un square is 'a small public garden', often found in the middle of a square and surrounded by railings.

Les enfants jouaient dans le **square**.
(The children were playing in the *small public garden*.)

► However, if you want to say 'square', use **la place**.

La foire se tiendra sur la **place** du marché.
(The fair will be held in the market *square*.)

67 Stage

Un stage means 'a period of training' or 'work experience'.

Elle fait un **stage** non rémunéré en entreprise.
(She is doing some unpaid *work experience* in a company.)

► However, if you want to say 'stage', use **un stade** or **une phase** for a stage in a process and **une étape** for a stage on a journey. For the theatrical stage, use **la scène.**

La première **phase** / Le premier **stade** d'un processus est souvent difficile.
(The first *stage* of a process is often difficult.)

Elle a été en **scène** pendant deux heures.
(She was on *stage* for two hours.)

* If you follow the Tour de France, you will become familiar with the word, **une étape,** for a stage of the race.

68 Studio

Un studio usually means 'a small flat'. It can also be 'a broadcasting studio for television or radio'.

Elle a loué un **studio** à Paris pour un mois plutôt que de payer une chambre d'hôtel.
(She has rented a *small flat* in Paris for a month rather than paying for a hotel room.)

La chanson a été enregistrée en **studio**.
(The song was recorded in the *studio*.)

► However, if you mean 'the studio of a painter', use **un atelier.**

Il lui faut un vaste **atelier** pour ses toiles.
(He needs a very big *studio* for his canvases.)

69 Trouble

Trouble (m.) means 'unrest' or 'confusion'. It can also mean 'emotion' or a 'medical disorder'.

Son discours a produit un certain **trouble** dans l'assemblée.
(His speech caused some *unrest* among those present.)

Il faut dominer son **trouble** et essayer de s'exprimer clairement.
(You have to overcome your *confusion* and try to express yourself clearly.)

Elle ne veut pas trahir le **trouble** qu'elle ressent en sa présence.
(She doesn't want to give away the *emotion* she feels in his presence.)

Les **troubles** du sommeil sont difficiles à traiter.
(Sleep *disorders* are difficult to treat.)

► However, if you want to say 'trouble', meaning 'inconvenience' or 'difficulty', use **la peine** or **la difficulté**.

Cela n'en vaut pas la **peine**.
(It's not worth the *trouble*.)

Cette entreprise a des **difficultés** financières.
(This firm is in financial *trouble*.)

70 Venue

Une venue is 'a visit' or 'an arrival'. **La venue au monde** means 'birth'.

Nous attendons la **venue** de nos invités.
(We are awaiting the *arrival* / *visit* of our guests.)

La **venue au monde** de leur petit-fils les a remplis de joie.
(The *birth* of their grandson gave them great joy.)

► However, if you want to say 'venue', use **le lieu**.

On a annoncé un changement de **lieu** pour la réunion.
(A change of *venue* for the meeting has been announced.)

71 Vers

Un vers means 'a single line of verse'.

Un alexandrin est un **vers** de douze syllabes.
(An alexandrine is a *line* of twelve syllables.)

► However, if you want to say 'verse', meaning 'poetry', use **la poésie**. For a verse, meaning 'a stanza', use **une strophe**.

Elle aime faire de la **poésie**.
(She likes writing *verse*.)

La première **strophe** de ce poème se compose de 6 **vers**.
(The first *verse* / *stanza* of this poem is made up of 6 *lines*.)

72 Veste

Une veste means 'a jacket'.

Cette **veste** jure avec mon pantalon.
(This *jacket* clashes with my trousers.)

► However, if you want to say 'vest', use **un maillot de corps**.

Un **maillot de corps** est un sous-vêtement indispensable en hiver.
(A *vest* is a vital undergarment in winter.)

Partial overlap in meaning

1 Assistance

Assistance (f.) can mean 'assistance' or 'aid'.

Il ne serait pas parvenu à monter l'escalier sans l'**assistance** d'une infirmière.
(He would not have managed to climb the stairs without the *assistance* of a nurse.)

► However, it can also mean 'audience' or 'attendance'.

Il y avait une **assistance** nombreuse et enthousiaste.
(There was a large and enthusiastic *audience*.)

Leur **assistance** à mon cours est très irrégulière.
(Their *attendance* at my class is very irregular.)

* Remember that the verb **assister** + *à* means 'to attend'. See Chapter 2.

2 Audience

Une audience can mean a 'TV or radio audience' or 'an audience granted by a head of state', for example:

Les indicateurs d'**audience** pour le nouveau feuilleton sont encourageants.
(The *audience* ratings for the new serial are encouraging.)

Le chef d'État a accordé une **audience** à l'ambassadeur.
(The Head of State granted an *audience* to the ambassador.)

► However, it can also mean a 'judicial hearing'.

L'**audience** a été suspendue.
(The *hearing* has been adjourned.)

* Note that the usual word in French for the 'audience' in a theatre, cinema etc. is **le public**. See also **assistance** above.

3 Collège

Un collège can mean 'a college', but only in very particular contexts.

Le **collège** des cardinaux se réunit en conclave pour élire le Pape.
(The *college* of cardinals meets in conclave to elect the Pope.)

► However, it more usually means a 'secondary school' for pupils aged 11–15.

Il est actuellement au **collège,** mais l'année prochaine il ira au lycée.
(He is currently at *secondary school,* but next year he will go on to the high school.)

* If you want to say higher education 'college' in French, use **un établissement d'enseignement supérieur.**

4 Complaisance

Complaisance (f.) can mean 'complacency'.

Il considérait ses réussites avec **complaisance.**
(He regarded his achievements with *complacency.*)

▶ However, it more usually means 'kindness' or 'willingness to oblige'.

Il les a accompagnés en voiture à l'aéroport par **complaisance.**
(He drove them to the airport out of *kindness.*)

Hence, the phrase **sans complaisance** means 'candid' or 'objective'.

On voit bien que c'est un portrait **sans complaisance.**
(It is clearly a *candid* portrait.)

5 Conscience

La conscience can mean moral 'conscience'.

Je leur ai écrit pour me donner bonne **conscience.**
(I wrote to them to ease my *conscience.*)

▶ However, it can also mean 'awareness' or 'consciousness'.

La **conscience** de mes responsabilités pèse lourd sur moi.
(*Awareness* of my responsibilities weighs heavily on me.)

Il a repris **conscience.**
(He has regained *consciousness.*)

6 Contrôle

Le contrôle can mean 'control'.

Il a perdu le **contrôle** de son véhicule.
(He lost *control* of his vehicle.)

▶ However, it can also mean a 'check' of various sorts, including a school or university 'test'.

Avant d'accéder au stade il faut passer par un **contrôle** de sécurité.
(Before you get into the stadium, you have to go through a security *check.*)

Je dois réviser pour mon **contrôle** de géographie demain.
(I must revise for my geography *test* tomorrow.)

* Remember that the verb **contrôler** can mean 'to check' as well as 'to control'. See Chapter 2.

7 Étiquette

Étiquette (f.) can sometimes mean 'etiquette'.

Cet homme politique trouve difficile de se plier aux exigences de l'**étiquette**.
(This politician finds it difficult to submit to the demands of *etiquette*.)

► However, it more usually means a 'label'.

J'ai mis mon nom et mon adresse sur l'**étiquette** à bagages.
(I've put my name and address on the luggage *label*.)

8 Évolution

Une évolution does usually mean 'change' or 'development'.

Nous suivons de près l'**évolution** de la situation.
(We are following closely the *development* of the situation.)

► However, in the plural it can mean 'graceful gliding movements'.

Ils suivaient les **évolutions** des patineurs sur le lac.
(They were watching the skaters' *gliding movements* on the lake.)

* Remember that the verb **évoluer** can also mean 'to move around' or 'to glide about'. See Chapter 2.

9 Expérience

Expérience (f.) often does mean 'experience'.

Il manque d'**expérience**, mais il apprend vite.
(He lacks *experience*, but he is a quick learner.)

► However, it can also mean an 'experiment'.

Ils s'opposent aux **expériences** sur les animaux.
(They are against *experiments* on animals.)

10 Figure

Une figure can mean a 'figure', either a personality or a geometric figure.

Les grandes **figures** du passé passent souvent dans la légende.
(The great *figures* of the past often become legends.)

J'ai du mal à dessiner cette **figure** géométrique.
(I find it difficult to draw this geometric *figure*.)

► However, it often means 'face'.

Je me suis lavé la **figure**.
(I washed my *face*.)

11 Formation

Une formation can mean 'formation'.

Avez-vous remarqué cette **formation** nuageuse?
(Did you notice that cloud *formation*?)

► However, it often means 'education' and / or 'training'.

Quelle est votre **formation**?
(What education and *training* have you had?)

12 Hôte

Un hôte can mean 'a host'.

J'ai remercié nos **hôtes** de leur hospitalité.
(I thanked our *hosts* for their hospitality.)

► However, it can also mean 'guest'.

Il passe quinze jours chez nous en tant qu'**hôte** payant.
(He is spending a fortnight with us as a paying *guest*.)

13 Occasion

Une occasion can mean 'an occasion'.

Il faut fêter les grandes **occasions**!
(Special *occasions* must be celebrated!)

► However, it usually means an 'opportunity'.

Il ne faut pas laisser passer l'**occasion** de visiter les États-Unis.
(You mustn't miss the *opportunity* of visiting the USA.)

It can also mean 'something bought second-hand'.

Cette télévision n'est qu'une **occasion**, mais elle nous convient.
(This television is only *second-hand*, but it suits us.)

J'ai acheté ma voiture d'**occasion**.
(I bought my car *second-hand*.)

14 Office

Office (m.) can mean 'office' or 'agency' in certain compound expressions.

L'**Office de Tourisme** se trouve en face de la cathédrale.
(The *Tourist Information Office* is opposite the cathedral.)

► However, it usually means 'duty' or 'purpose'.

Elle fait **office** d'interprète.
(She is serving as, i.e. serving the *purpose* of, an interpreter.)

It can also mean a 'religious service'.

Il va à l'**office** du matin tous les dimanches.
(He attends the morning *service* every Sunday.)

* Note that the usual word in French for an 'office', meaning a place of work is **le bureau**.

15 Parent

Un parent can mean 'a parent'.

Ce sont ses **parents** adoptifs. Il ne connaît pas ses **parents** biologiques.
(They are his adoptive *parents*. He does not know his biological *parents*.)

► However, it can also mean 'relative'.

Il est orphelin. Son **parent** le plus proche est sa tante maternelle.
(He is an orphan. His closest *relative*, i.e. next of kin, is his maternal aunt.)

16 Pièce

Une pièce does sometimes mean 'piece'.

Le vase s'est brisé en mille **pièces**.
(The vase broke into a thousand *pieces*.)

► However, its more usual meanings are: 'room', 'coin', 'play' or 'part' of an engine / car / machine.

Ces deux **pièces** donnent au sud.
(These two *rooms* face south.)

Avez-vous une **pièce** d'un euro?
(Do you have a one euro *coin*?)

Les étudiants montent une **pièce** de Molière.
(The students are putting on a *play* by Molière.)

SEAT offre une garantie de 2 ans **pièces** et main d'œuvre.
(SEAT offers a 2-year guarantee for *parts* and labour.)

* Note the useful expressions: **une pièce d'identité** (identification / identity papers) and **pièce(s) jointe(s)** (enclosures in a letter; attachments to an email).

17 Voix

Une voix does usually mean 'voice'.

Elle parle d'une **voix** douce.
(She speaks in a gentle *voice*.)

► However, in a political context, it means 'vote'.

Ils ont gagné par 300 **voix** contre 154.
(They won by 300 *votes* to 154.)

Exercises

EXERCISE 4. Choose the most appropriate noun to fill the blanks and make any other necessary choices depending on the gender of the noun chosen.

1 Je n'ai pas de petit(e) ________.
a) argent b) monnaie c) pièce

2 Pour ton / ta ___________ tu rangeras ta chambre.
a) châtiment b) punition c) rétribution

3 Le premier jour il a accompli un(e) ___________ de 100 kilomètres.
a) étape b) stage c) stade

4 Il s'est donné le / la __________ de venir nous chercher à la gare.
a) difficulté b) peine c) trouble

5 Je cherche une co-____________ pour partager mon appartement.
a) locataire b) logeuse c) pensionnaire

6 Il a acheté la maison pour une _________.
a) misère b) occasion c) pièce

7 Il prépare un(e) ___________ en histoire.
a) course b) licence c) stage

8 Les _________ à Paris sont élevé(e)s.
a) logeurs b) loyers c) rentes

9 Il a perdu son _______ pour corruption.
a) procédé b) procès c) processus

10 Il est arrivé en retard, parce qu'il n'avait pas noté le changement de _______.
a) lieu b) place c) venue

11 Cette scène a été tournée en _______.
a) atelier b) stage c) studio

12 Un décasyllabe est un(e) _________ de dix syllabes.
a) poème b) strophe c) vers

13 Tout le monde s'est levé quand le juge est entré dans la salle d'_______ .
a) assistance b) audience

14 Les ___________ sont des mécaniciens.
a) automobilistes b) conducteurs c) motoristes

15 Cette logeuse a des _________ contre les étudiants.
a) préjudices b) préjugés c) licences

16 Ils étaient en ______ de manger quand je suis passé les voir.
a) procès b) processus c) train

17 C'est un _________nucléaire.
a) médecin b) physicien c) scientiste

18 Cette pièce est un chef-d'œuvre du / de la _______ française.
a) scène b) stade c) stage

19 Ces ___________ de la mémoire le gênent de plus en plus dans son travail.
a) difficultés b) peines c) troubles

20 Ils n'ont pas encore les moyens d'acheter un appartement; ils sont en __________.
a) location b) occasion c) pièces

EXERCISE 5. Connect each noun on the left with its most logical companion or associate from the list on the right.

Example: une allée + un jardin

1	un permis	a	des avions
2	une veste	b	la contraception
3	un préservatif	c	au monde
4	un stage	d	de séjour
5	une rétribution	e	en tweed
6	la venue	f	de chimie

7	les évolutions	g	le dynamisme
8	un collège	h	en faveur de
9	une licence	i	de la personnalité
10	une étiquette	j	le Tour de France
11	une expérience	k	d'enseignement secondaire
12	un hôte	l	non rémunéré
13	un procès	m	scientifique
14	la pétulance	n	à bagages
15	un agent de conservation	o	pour meurtre
16	une étape	p	du climat
17	la rudesse	q	un peintre
18	des préjugés	r	la nourriture
19	un atelier	s	de 1 000 euros
20	des troubles	t	payant

EXERCISE 6. Insert the noun from the box that best completes each sentence, using a plural form where necessary.

> bibliothèque; essence; figure; formation; librairie; occasion; office; parent; patron; pétrole; pièce; préjugé; préjudice; scientifique; trouble

1 Son nouveau roman sera en vente dans toutes les __________ dès lundi.
2 Cette pièce me fait _______ de cabinet de travail.
3 Quand il a entendu cette nouvelle, sa _________ s'est allongée.
4 Cette statue est faite d'une seule ________.
5 Un autre étudiant a demandé ce livre et je dois le rendre à la _________.
6 J'ai acheté cette veste d'_______.
7 Il a reçu une ________ d'architecte.
8 La voiture est tombée en panne d'_______.
9 Il n'a pas de __________ contre les étrangers.
10 Je l'ai encouragé à parler de ses vacances pour essayer de dissiper son _______.
11 Il ne croit pas au scientisme; c'est tout simplement un ________.
12 Son ________ le plus proche est sa nièce.
13 J'essaie de trouver le bon moment pour demander un congé au _______.
14 À la suite du krach, ils ont subi un grave __________ financier.
15 Ce Texan est un magnat du __________.

EXERCISE 7. Fill in the blanks with the most appropriate nouns that you have studied in this chapter.

Chère Julie,

Je t'écris pour te demander des conseils. Notre fils aîné, Pierre, prépare une (1)____________ (degree) de littérature comparée et cet été il voudrait faire un (2) __________ (period of work experience) en France. Il voudrait travailler soit dans une (3) _____________ (bookshop), soit dans une (4) _______________ (library). Il ne cherche pas de (5) _____________ (remuneration); ce qui compte pour lui c'est acquérir de l' (6) _______________ (experience) et avoir l'(7) _________ (opportunity) d'améliorer son français. Est-ce que tu pourrais lui proposer des idées? À part sa (8) ___________ (training) littéraire, il a un (9) _________ (licence) de conduire et c'est un bon (10) _______________ (driver). En ce moment il est en (11) ____________ (the process) d'achever son / sa (12) ___________ (dissertation) de fin d'année et il n'a pas le temps de t'écrire lui-même. Il faut quand même penser à lui trouver un logement. Il n'aura pas assez d' (13) _________ (money) pour louer un (14) ____________ (small flat). Est-ce que tu connais peut-être quelqu'un qui prenne des (15) ____________ (lodgers with meals provided) ou bien des étudiants qui cherchent un co-(16) _________ (flatmate / co-tenant)? Toutes les idées seront les bienvenues, mais ne te dérange pas trop. Cela n'en vaut pas la (17) _____ (trouble)! Ce sera à Pierre de trouver une (18) __________ (solution / way out) quand il aura terminé ses études.

Nous espérons te revoir bientôt à l'(19) __________ (occasion) de ton prochain (20) ______________ (conference) à Londres.

Avec nos amitiés,

Anne et Michael

Mastering false friends: adjectives and adverbs

Students of French tend to find the following adjectives and adverbs difficult to remember. Although a French word may look very similar to an English word, it frequently means something quite different. Even where there is some overlap in meaning, the match is often only partial. Try to learn the different meanings of each French adjective and adverb below by studying the contexts given.

False friends

1 Abusif

Abusif means 'excessive', 'unfair' or 'improper'.

Il a fait un usage **abusif** de citations.
(He has made *excessive* use of quotations.)

Ils se sont arrogé des privilèges **abusifs**.
(They have claimed *unfair* privileges.)

Voilà un emploi **abusif** du terme.
(That is an *improper* / *incorrect* use of the term.)

► However, if you want to say 'abusive', meaning 'rude' or 'insulting', note the following:

Il a réagi d'une façon **grossière**.
(He reacted in an *abusive* / *rude* way.)

Ce sont des remarques très **injurieuses**.
(These are very *abusive* / *insulting* remarks.)

* Learn the expression: **une mère abusive** (an over-protective mother)

2 Académique

This adjective usually has a pejorative sense, referring to 'an artist or writer who conforms narrowly to the tradition in which they were trained'.

C'est un peintre **académique**.
(He is an *academic* painter.)

More neutrally, it can refer to something associated with the Académie Française, or to something associated with a particular local education authority, or *académie*, as it is known in France.

Elle travaille à l'inspection **académique** d'Amiens.
(She works in the *local schools* inspectorate of Amiens.)

► However, if you want to say 'academic' in the English sense, there are various possibilities.

Elle a accepté un poste **universitaire**.
(She has taken up an *academic* post.)

Il n'est pas très **doué pour les études**.
(He is not very *academic*.)

Ce débat est d'un intérêt **théorique**.
(This debate is a matter of *academic* interest.)

3 Actuel / Actuellement

The adjective **actuel** and the corresponding adverb **actuellement** do not mean 'actual' or 'actually'. They both express a connection with the present time.

La forme **actuelle** de sa thèse n'est qu'une ébauche.
(The *present* / *current* shape of his thesis is only a draft.)

Nous ne disposons **actuellement** que de deux ordinateurs.
(*At present* we have only two computers.)

► However, if you want to say:

actual → **exact, réel, même** (following the noun)
actually → **en fait, vraiment, exactement**

Je ne me rappelle pas le coût **exact.**
(I don't remember the *actual* cost.)

Je ne peux pas imaginer son motif **réel.**
(I can't imagine his / her *actual* reason.)

Voici la maison **même** où Shakespeare est né.
(This is the *actual* house where Shakespeare was born.)

En fait elle cuisine très bien.
(She's *actually* a very good cook.)

Ils n'ont pas **vraiment** refusé de l'aider.
(They didn't *actually* refuse to help him.)

À quelle heure sont-ils arrivés **exactement**?
(What time did they *actually* arrive?)

4 Compréhensif

Compréhensif means 'understanding'.

C'est un professeur **compréhensif,** toujours prêt à écouter les étudiants.
(He is an *understanding* teacher, always ready to listen to students.)

► However, if you want to say 'comprehensive', meaning all-embracing, use **complet** or **détaillé.**

Il a rédigé un rapport **complet** / **détaillé** sur le problème.

(He wrote a *comprehensive* report about the problem.)

* Learn the expression: **assurances tous risques** (comprehensive insurance policy).

5 Conséquent

Conséquent means 'substantial' or 'consistent / coherent'.

Les réfugiés ont reçu une aide **conséquente**.
(The refugees have received *substantial* aid.)

Il faut être **conséquent** avec soi-même.
(It is essential to be *consistent*.)

► However, if you want to say 'consequent', a verbal expression is better.

Le référendum et les discussions **qu'il a entraînées**
(The referendum and the *consequent* discussions.)

* Learn the expression: **par conséquent** (therefore, as a result).

6 Content

Content means 'pleased'.

Je suis **contente** qu'elle soit là.
(I am *pleased* that she is here.)

► However, if you want to say 'content', use **satisfait.** Compare and contrast the following:

Ce n'est pas un élève doué, mais je suis **satisfaite** de son travail.
(He's not a gifted pupil, but I am *content / satisfied* with his work.)

Il a fait des progrès remarquables et je suis très **contente** de son travail.
(He has made remarkable progress and I am very *pleased* with his work.)

7 Disgracieux

Disgracieux means 'ugly', 'unsightly', 'awkward' or 'unbecoming'.

Les boutons d'acné sont **disgracieux**.
(Acne spots are *unsightly*.)

Elle portait une robe très **disgracieuse**.
(She was wearing a very *unbecoming* dress.)

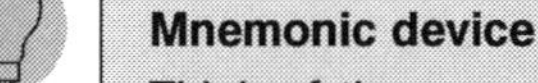

Mnemonic device
Think of the associated noun **grâce** (grace). **Disgracieux** means 'lacking grace / attraction'.

▶ However, if you want to say 'disgraceful', meaning 'shameful', use **honteux** or **scandaleux.**

C'est une attitude **honteuse**.
(That's a *disgraceful* attitude.)

Ce sont des propos **scandaleux**.
(Those are *disgraceful* remarks.)

* Learn the expressions: **C'est une honte** or **C'est un scandale** (It's disgraceful).

8 Effectif / Effectivement

Effectif means 'real' or 'actual'. **Effectivement** means 'indeed' or 'actually'.

Il a de bonnes intentions, mais son travail **effectif** ne vaut pas grand-chose.
(He has good intentions, but his *actual* work does not amount to much.)

La situation est **effectivement** délicate.
(It is *indeed* a delicate situation.)

▶ However, if you want to say 'effective' or 'effectively', use **efficace** or **efficacement**.

C'est un remède très **efficace**.
(It's a very *effective* treatment.)

Elle est intervenue **efficacement** dans les pourparlers.
(She intervened *effectively* in the talks.)

* Learn the expressions: **devenir effectif** (to come into effect) and **oui / non, effectivement** (yes / no, that's right – in answer to a previous question).

9 Engagé

Engagé means 'politically committed'.

Camus est un écrivain **engagé**.
(Camus is a *politically committed* writer.)

▶ However, if you want to say 'engaged', use **fiancé** for 'engaged to be married' and **occupé** for 'occupied' or 'busy'.

Elle est **fiancée** à mon neveu.
(She is *engaged* to my nephew.)

La toilette est **occupée**. La ligne est **occupée**.
(The toilet is *engaged*. The line is *engaged*.)

10 Éventuel / Éventuellement

Éventuel means 'possible'. **Éventuellement** means 'possibly'.

> Il faut penser aux conséquences **éventuelles** d'une telle démarche.
> (You need to think about the *possible* consequences of such a step.)

> Vous aurez **éventuellement** des difficultés à comprendre le dialecte sicilien.
> (You will *possibly* have difficulty understanding the Sicilian dialect.)

► However, if you want to say 'eventual' or 'eventually', use **à la longue, à long terme**, **finalement** or **finir par**.

> Ce qu'elle a l'intention de faire **à long terme** c'est de devenir médecin.
> (Her *eventual* goal is to become a doctor.)

> Il a **fini par** comprendre.
> (*Eventually* he understood.)

11 Fastidieux

Fastidieux means 'tedious' or 'tiresome'.

> La correction des devoirs est un travail **fastidieux**.
> (Marking homework is a *tedious* task.)

► However, if you want to say 'fastidious' use **méticuleux** in a positive sense, or **délicat** in a negative sense.

> Elle est **méticuleuse** dans son travail.
> (She is *fastidious* in her work.)

> Elle est **délicate** sur la nourriture.
> (She is *fastidious* / *fussy* about food.)

12 **Génial** means 'brilliant', 'fantastic', 'great'.

> C'est une idée **géniale**.
> (That's a *brilliant* / *great* idea.)

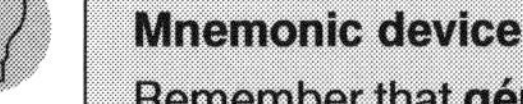

Mnemonic device
Remember that **génial** is related to the noun **génie** (genius) and so it means, literally, 'full of genius'.

► However, if you want to say 'genial', use **cordial** (*genial* / *warm-hearted*) or **bienveillant** / **doux** (*genial* / *gentle* / *mild*).

C'est une personne très **cordiale**.
(He / she is a very *genial* / *warm-hearted* person.)

Elle a un regard **bienveillant** / **doux**.
(She has a *genial* / *gentle* expression / look.)

13 Hardi

Hardi means 'bold' or 'impudent'.

C'est un explorateur **hardi**.
(He is a *bold* explorer.)

L'élève a été bien **hardi** de parler au professeur sur ce ton.
(The pupil was very *impudent* to speak to the teacher in that way.)

► However, if you want to say 'hardy', use **robuste.**

C'est un arbre **robuste** qui résistera à ce climat.
(It's a *hardy* tree that will withstand this climate.)

14 Incessamment

Incessamment means 'very shortly'.

Nous attendons des nouvelles **incessamment**.
(We are expecting news *very shortly*.)

► However, if you want to say 'unceasingly' or 'constantly', use **sans cesse**.

Il a travaillé **sans cesse**.
(He has worked unceasingly / constantly.)

* Learn the humorous expression **incessamment ou sous peu** (in next to no time). This is effectively saying the same thing twice; **sous peu** (very shortly) means much the same as **incessamment.** It's a good way of remembering the meaning of **incessamment**.

15 Inusable

Inusable means 'hardwearing'.

J'achète toujours des pneus **inusables**.
(I always buy *hardwearing* tyres.)

► However, if you want to say 'unusable', use **inutilisable**.

Ce produit est contaminé et tout à fait **inutilisable**.
(This product is contaminated and completely *unusable*.)

16 Large / Largement

Large means 'broad' or 'wide'.

Cette avenue est très **large**.
(This avenue is very *wide*.)

► However, if you want to say 'large', use **grand, gros or important**.

Ce magasin se spécialise dans les **grandes** tailles.
(This shop specialises in *large* sizes.)

Ils ont perdu de **grosses** / d'**importantes** sommes d'argent.
(They have lost / wasted *large* amounts of money.)

* Learn the expressions: **dans une large mesure** (to a large extent), **avoir les idées larges** (to be broad-minded / liberal) and **avoir l'esprit large** (to be broad-minded).

Largement most commonly means 'widely'.

C'est une attitude **largement** répandue.
(It's a *widely* held attitude.)

However, it can sometimes mean 'largely / to a large extent'.

Elle est **largement** responsable de l'organisation des cours de langue.
(She is *largely* responsible for organising the language classes.)

It also has other idiomatic uses, including:

Tu as **largement** le temps.
(You have *plenty of* time.)

C'est **largement** suffisant.
(That's *more than* enough.)

17 Luxurieux

Luxurieux means 'lustful' and is characteristic of literary usage. The associated noun is **la luxure** (lust).

Une attitude **luxurieuse** se trahit dans son comportement envers ces jeunes femmes.
(A *lustful* attitude is apparent in his behaviour towards these young women.)

► However, if you want to say 'luxurious', use **luxueux.** The associated noun is **le luxe** (luxury).

Ils mènent un train de vie **luxueux**.
(They have a *luxurious* lifestyle.)

Mnemonic device
The expression **hôtel de luxe** (luxury or deluxe hotel) should help you to remember that the French noun for 'luxury' is **luxe**, not **luxure**, and therefore that the French adjective for 'luxurious' is **luxueux,** not **luxurieux**.

18 Pathétique

Pathétique means 'full of pathos' or 'moving'.

J'ai trouvé cette scène vraiment **pathétique**.
(I found that scene really *moving*.)

► However, if you want to say 'pathetic', meaning 'inadequate' or 'contemptible', use **misérable**, or, more colloquially, **lamentable.**

Il gagne un salaire **misérable**.
(He earns a *pathetic* wage.)

Cette dissert est **lamentable**.
(This essay is *pathetic*.)

19 Pétulant

Pétulant means 'exuberant'.

Je n'ai jamais connu un enfant si débordant d'énergie, si **pétulant**.
(I have never known a child so brimming with energy, so *exuberant*.)

► However, if you want to say 'petulant', use **irascible or irritable**.

Cet adolescent est très **irascible** / **irritable**. Il se met en colère pour un rien.
(This teenager is very *petulant*. He flies into a rage at the slightest thing.)

20 Présentement

Présentement means 'at present' or 'at the moment'. It is a synonym for the more commonly used **actuellement**. See above.

Le directeur est **présentement** en voyage d'affaires.
(The director is on a business trip *at the moment*.)

► However, if you want to say 'presently', meaning 'in a moment from now', use **tout à l'heure**.

Le médecin vous verra **tout à l'heure**.
(The doctor will see you *presently*.)

Remember the expression: **À tout à l'heure** (See you later).

Note that **tout à l'heure** can refer to time past as well as to future time, e.g.

Il est passé **tout à l'heure**.
(He called by *just now / a little while ago*.)

21 Roman

Roman means 'Romanesque' (or Norman in Great Britain), as applied to the style of architecture used in western and southern Europe from the ninth to the twelfth century, characterised by rounded arches and massive masonry wall construction. It also means 'Romance', as applied to languages.

La cathédrale de Durham est un bel exemple du style **roman**.
(Durham cathedral is a fine example of *Romanesque / Norman* style.)

Les langues **romanes**, telles que le français et l'italien, sont dérivées du latin.
(*Romance* languages, such as French and Italian, are derived from Latin.)

► However, if you want to say 'Roman', use **romain**.

On trouve d'importants vestiges **romains** dans le Midi.
(There are significant *Roman* remains in the South of France.)

22 Rude

Rude means 'hard', 'harsh' or 'severe'.

Le métier des armes est **rude.**
(An army career is *hard*.)

Nous avons vécu des hivers **rudes.**
(We have lived through some *harsh / severe* winters.)

► However, if you want to say 'rude', use **impoli**.

C'était très **impoli** de sa part de partir sans rien dire.
(It was very *rude* of him / her to leave without saying anything.)

* Learn the expression: **avoir une santé de fer** (to be in rude health).

23 Sensible means 'sensitive' or 'perceptible'.

Elle a la peau **sensible**.
(She has *sensitive* skin.)

La différence est à peine **sensible**.
(The difference is hardly *perceptible*.)

► However, if you want to say 'sensible', meaning 'reasonable', use **sensé** or **raisonnable**.

C'est une personne très **sensée / raisonnable**.
(He / she is a very *sensible* person.)

24 Sympathique

Sympathique means 'nice', 'friendly' or 'pleasant'.

Ce sont des gens **sympathiques**. Ils créent une ambiance **sympathique**.
(They are *nice* people. They create a *friendly* atmosphere.)

► However, if you want to say 'sympathetic', meaning 'understanding', use **compatissant**.

Elle se montrait **compatissante** envers les élèves moins doués.
(She was *sympathetic* to the weaker pupils.)

25 Valable

Valable means 'valid'.

Mon passeport est **valable** jusqu'à la fin de juillet.
(My passport is *valid* until the end of July.)

► However, if you want to say 'valuable', use **de valeur** or **précieux**.

Il est évident que ce sont des objets **de valeur**.
(They are clearly *valuable* objects.)

La bibliothèque abrite des manuscrits **précieux**.
(The library houses some *valuable* manuscripts.)

Partial overlap in meaning

1 Actif

The adjective **actif** can sometimes mean 'active'.

Elle a joué un rôle **actif** dans la campagne.
(She has played an *active* role in the campaign.)

► However, it frequently translates the idea of 'working'.

Il s'est vite habitué à la vie **active**.
(He quickly became used to *working* life.)

Le nombre des femmes **actives** est en progression constante.
(The number of *working* women is steadily increasing.)

2 Amusant

Amusant does sometimes mean 'amusing' or 'funny'.

Il nous a raconté une histoire très **amusante**.
(He told us a very *funny* story.)

► However, it often means 'entertaining'. In this sense, it is the opposite of **ennuyeux** (boring).

J'avais peur que les enfants ne s'ennuient au théâtre, mais en fait ils ont trouvé le spectacle très **amusant**.

(I was the afraid the children would be bored at the theatre, but actually they found the show very *entertaining*.)

3 Ancien

Ancien is one of a small group of adjectives in French that change their meaning according to their position.

When placed after the noun, **ancien** does literally mean 'ancient'.

Elle étudie le grec **ancien**.
(She is studying *ancient* Greek.)

► However, when placed before the noun, **ancien** means 'old' in the sense of 'former'.

Ce sont nos **anciens** voisins.
(They are our *old / former* neighbours.)

* Learn the following set expressions with **ancien** before the noun: **un ancien combattant** (a veteran), **un(e) ancien(ne) étudiant(e)** (former student / alumnus / a), **l'Ancien Monde** (the Old World), **l'Ancien Régime** (the pre-Revolutionary regime in France) and **l'Ancien Testament** (the Old Testament).

4 Attractif

The adjective **attractif** is used to describe 'a physical force of attraction'.

L'aimant a une force **attractive**.
(The magnet has an *attractive* force.)

► However, if you want to express the idea of 'attractive' in a more general sense:

an *attractive* person → une personne **séduisante / charmante**
an *attractive* offer → une offre **attrayante**
an *attractive* price → un prix **intéressant**

5 Aussi

The most common meaning of the adverb **aussi** is indeed 'also'.

Mon père était professeur, lui **aussi**.
(My father was *also* a teacher).

▶ However, when placed before an adjective or adverb, it means 'so'.

Je ne savais pas qu'elle était **aussi** grande.
(I didn't know she was *so* tall.)

In the construction, **aussi . . . que,** it means 'as . . . as'.

Il n'est pas **aussi** plein d'entrain que son frère.
(He is not *as* lively *as* his brother.)

When placed at the beginning of a clause or sentence, **aussi** expresses a consequence, 'so' or 'therefore'. In careful French, the subject and verb are inverted, as in the following example:

Le président du comité est malade. **Aussi** la réunion est-elle reportée.
(The chair of the committee is ill. *So* the meeting is postponed.)

6 Brave

When placed after the noun, **brave** does literally mean 'brave' or 'courageous'.

It is a synonym for the more commonly used **courageux**.

Malgré sa jeunesse, il s'est montré un combattant **brave**.
(Despite his youth, he proved to be a *brave* fighter.)

▶ However, when placed before the noun, **brave** means 'nice' or 'decent'.

C'est un **brave** type. Ce sont de **braves** gens.
(He's a *nice* guy. They are *nice* people.)

* Learn the following expressions: **Courage**! (Be brave!); **il a été très courageux** (he has been very brave); **dans le meilleur des mondes** (in a brave new world).

7 Civil

Civil means 'civilian' or 'civil', as opposed to 'religious'.

Le soldat s'est acheté des vêtements **civils**.
(The soldier bought himself some *civilian* clothes.)

Le mariage **civil** a été célébré mercredi à la mairie.
(The *civil* marriage ceremony took place on Wednesday at the Town Hall.)

► However, if you want to say

civil service → la fonction **publique**
civil servant → un **fonctionnaire**

To say 'civil' in the sense of 'polite', use **courtois.**

* Learn the expressions: **ingénieur des travaux publics** (civil engineer) and **résistance passive** (civil disobedience).

8 Différent

Différent means 'different' in nature when it is placed after the noun.

L'année dernière il a étudié le français et l'espagnol, mais cette année il a choisi des matières **différentes.** Il ne veut plus étudier les langues.

(Last year he studied French and Spanish, but this year he has chosen *different* subjects. He doesn't want to study languages any more.)

► However, when placed before the noun, **différent** means 'various' or 'a number of'.

En première année les étudiants ne peuvent pas se spécialiser dans une seule discipline. Ils doivent suivre un programme composé de **différentes** matières.
(In the first year, students cannot specialise in a single discipline. They must take a programme made up of *various / a number of* subjects.)

9 Important

Important often does mean 'important'.

Il occupe un poste **important**.
(He holds an *important* post.)

► However, when placed before or after the noun, it can also mean 'considerable', either in size or seriousness. See also **large** above.

Elle a reçu un **important** héritage.
(She received a *sizeable* inheritance.)

Nous n'avions pas prévu des conséquences aussi **importantes**.
(We hadn't foreseen such *serious* consequences.)

10 Inférieur

Inférieur does sometimes mean 'inferior' in quality.

Son travail est **inférieur** au vôtre.
(His work is *inferior* to yours.)

► However, it often means simply 'lower' or 'smaller'.

Les étages **inférieurs** sont à préférer.
(The *lower* floors are to be preferred.)

Compare **supérieur**.
(See below.)

11 Intéressant

Intéressant does often mean 'interesting'.

► However, it sometimes means 'attractive' (see also **attractif** above), especially from a financial point of view.

Ils pratiquent des tarifs très **intéressants**.
(They are offering very *attractive* rates.)

* Learn the informal idiomatic expression: **être dans une situation intéressante** (to be pregnant).

12 Populaire

Populaire can sometimes mean 'popular' in the sense of 'well-liked', but more commonly it means something associated with the working classes.

Cet acteur est d'origine **populaire**.
(This actor comes from a *working-class* background.)

► If you want to say something is 'popular,' use **prisé** or **en vogue**.

C'est un produit très **prisé** / très **en vogue** chez les bourgeois.
(It's a very *popular* product with the middle classes.)

* Learn the expressions: **avoir du succès auprès du public (**to have popular appeal) and **l'opinion générale au sujet de quelque chose** (the popular view of something).

13 Simple

Simple does usually mean 'simple'.

Il écrit des phrases **simples** mais correctes.
(He writes *simple* but correct sentences.)

► However, it can also mean 'single'.

Je prends une glace **simple**, s'il vous plaît.
(I'll have a *single* scoop of ice cream, please.)

Mnemonic device
Remember that the difference between the **passé simple** (or past historic) and the **passé composé** is that the former consists of a single verb form, whereas the latter is composed of two – an auxiliary verb + a past participle. Most students would agree that the **passé simple** is not a simple tense to learn!

14 Supérieur

Supérieur does sometimes mean 'superior' in quality.

Cet hôtel est **supérieur** à l'autre.
(This hotel is *superior* to the other one.)

► However, it often means simply 'higher' or 'greater'.

Nous avons subi des pertes **supérieures** à la moyenne.
(We have incurred *higher* than average losses.)

Compare **inférieur** above and remember the expression: **l'enseignement supérieur** (higher education).

15 Terrible

Terrible usually means 'terrible'.

Il y a eu une catastrophe **terrible**.
(There has been a *terrible* catastrophe.)

► However, in informal language, it means 'fantastic' or 'wonderful'.

C'est un film **terrible**.
(It's a *fantastic* film.)

Exercises

EXERCISE 1. Choose the appropriate word or expression to fill the blanks.

1 _________, les étudiants se sont très bien débrouillés.
a) Actuellement b) En fait

2 L'université tient à maintenir de bonnes relations avec ses ______ étudiants.
a) anciens b) vieux

3 L'agence de voyages propose des excursions à des prix ________.
a) attractifs b) intéressants

4 C'était très _______ de sa part de penser à nous.
a) civil b) courtois

5 La vie _______ ne lui plaît pas du tout. Il préférerait poursuivre ses études.
a) active b) travailleuse

6 Le journaliste a donné une interprétation ________ de leur conduite.
a) abusive b) grossière

7 L'offre des postes _______ en Grande-Bretagne ne correspond pas à la demande.
a) académiques b) universitaires

8 Elle dorlote ses enfants. C'est une mère vraiment _____.
a) abusive b) injurieuse

9 A l'heure _____, nous ne savons pas les résultats des examens.
a) actuelle b) même

10 La première guerre mondiale et les bouleversements sociaux ________ ont transformé toute l'Europe.
a) conséquents b) qu'elle a entraînés

11 Il est ______ que tu aies reçu une si mauvaise note.
a) disgracieux b) honteux

12 Bien que ce ne soit pas le résultat que j'espérais obtenir, j'en suis largement _______.
a) contente b) satisfaite

13 Cet étudiant a peu de chances de réussir aux examens ; il est ___________ absent.
a) incessamment b) sans cesse

14 Son comportement grossier a ______________ entraîné des poursuites disciplinaires.
a) éventuellement b) finalement

15 Elle a vendu des bijoux ______.
a) précieux b) valables

16 Je passerai te voir ___________.
a) présentement b) tout à l'heure

17 Elle a des idées très peu _______.
a) raisonnables b) sensibles

18 Avant d'être interrompue de façon si ______, j'allais vous expliquer mon retard.
a) impolie b) rude

19 Elle a un physique ______.
a) attractif b) séduisant

20 Ils ont investi de / d' _______ sommes d'argent.
a) grandes b) importantes

21 Nous cherchons des plantes _____ qui résisteront à l'hiver.
a) hardies b) robustes

22 Elle a assumé ses responsabilités très _________.
a) effectivement b) efficacement

23 La salle de bains est d'une propreté _________.
a) fastidieuse b) méticuleuse

24 Il nous a donné une explication __________ du retard.
a) compréhensive b) détaillée

25 Patientez un moment s'il vous plaît. La ligne est ________.
a) engagée b) occupée

26 Ses notes au dernier contrôle ont été _________.
a) lamentables b) pathétiques

27 On a passé une soirée très _________.
a) compatissante b) sympathique

28 Ce papier est humide. Il est complètement _________.
a) inusable b) inutilisable

EXERCISE 2. Match each underlined word or phrase on the left with the closest synonym on the right and rewrite the whole sentence, making any necessary changes and agreements.

Example: un spectacle amusant = divertissant
Rewrite as: un spectacle divertissant

1	Ce sont des pouvoirs excessifs.	a	efficace
2	Elle est actuellement en vacances.	b	en fait
3	Ainsi a-t-il résolu de ne jamais revenir.	c	présentement
4	Elle portait une robe qui ne lui allait pas.	d	génial
5	Vous pourrez vous en servir le cas échéant.	e	aussi
6	Quelle idée fantastique!	f	conséquent
7	Les portes s'ouvriront sous peu.	g	prisé
8	Elle a perdu une grosse somme d'argent.	h	académique
9	Ce sont des objets de valeur.	i	large
10	Cette marque est très en vogue.	j	important
11	C'est un artiste sans aucune originalité.	k	différent

12	Ce remède a de l'effet.	l	pétulant
13	À vrai dire, elle écrit très mal.	m	incessamment
14	Il y a diverses explications.	n	scandaleux
15	Elle a épousé un garçon gentil.	o	précieux
16	Cela représente une réduction importante.	p	éventuellement
17	Elle a des connaissances étendues.	q	disgracieux
18	Il est très exubérant.	r	brave
19	Son salaire est moins élevé que le tien.	s	abusif
20	Il mène une vie déplorable.	t	inférieur

EXERCISE 3a. Insert the adjective from the box that best completes each sentence. Make each adjective agree as appropriate.

amusant; ancien; doué; effectif; grand; général; intéressant; large; public; sensible

1 Le / L'_____ Testament précède le Nouveau Testament.
2 Elle attend un enfant; elle est dans une situation ______.
3 Ils sont riches et ils mènent une vie _____.
4 Je suis ______ au froid.
5 Elle n'est pas aussi _____ pour les études que son frère.
6 Les jeux de questions-réponses m'ennuient, mais elle les trouve ______.
7 En général la fonction _______ paie moins bien que le secteur privé.
8 Le cessez-le-feu devient ______ à partir de minuit.
9 Ce modèle n'existe pas dans les ______ tailles.
10 L'opinion _______ sur le gouvernement est mitigée.

EXERCISE 3b. Insert the adverb from the box that best completes each sentence.

actuellement; aussi; effectivement; en fait; éventuellement; exactement; incessamment; largement; sensiblement; tout à l'heure

1 À quelle heure est-il arrivé _______ ?
2 Il sera là _______ ou sous peu.
3 Tu as oublié ton billet ? Oui, __________.
4 Elle pourrait _________ vous aider à trouver un logement.
5 L'année dernière il était à l'université en Angleterre, mais ______ il fait un stage en France.
6 Vous avez _______ le temps de passer les voir avant de partir.
7 Mes clefs étaient là _________, mais je ne les trouve plus.
8 La température a ___________ baissé cette semaine.
9 Elle a beaucoup travaillé, ______ a-t-elle réussi à ses examens.
10 Elle n'avait aucune expérience de l'enseigement, mais _____ elle s'est très bien débrouillée.

EXERCISE 4. Fill in the blanks with the most appropriate adjectives or adverbs that you have studied in this chapter. Remember to make the adjectives agree as necessary.

Chère Amélie,

Je me plais très bien à l'université en Écosse. Si je t'explique que mon programme se compose de (1) _________ (various) matières tu comprendras que j'avais peur au début d'être surchargée. Cependant j'ai eu l'idée (2) _________ (brilliant) de choisir le gaélique comme une de mes options. Pour une Bretonne comme moi, c'est (3) _________ (fantastic), bien plus facile que les langues (4) ________ (Romance). Je ne veux pas travailler (5) __________ (constantly), donc c'est un moyen (6) ________ (effective) de faciliter les choses. Tu sais bien que je ne suis pas (7) _______ (as) (8) ____________ (academic) que toi.

J'ai eu la chance de trouver un appartement en ville que je partage avec deux autres étudiantes. Ce n'est pas (9) __________ (luxurious), mais c'est sympa. Il est vrai que le coût de la vie à Aberdeen est (10) ________ (higher) à la moyenne, mais l'argent que je reçois de ma bourse est (11) _________ (more than) suffisant. J'aurai (12) __________ (possibly) l'occasion de visiter Édimbourg la semaine prochaine. Ma carte d'étudiant me permet d'acheter des billets de train à un tarif (13) _________ (attractive).

On m'avait dit que l'hiver en Écosse pourrait être (14) ________(harsh), mais jusqu'ici je trouve le climat assez (15) __________ (mild). Quant aux Écossais, ils sont vraiment (16) _________ (genial), bien que l'accent continue à me poser des problèmes. 17) _________ (Actually) il y a plusieurs accents (18) _________ (different) que je commence maintenant à distinguer. Je n'avais pas prévu d'avoir des difficultés de compréhension (19)___________ (as) (20) ___________ (serious) au début.

J'espère avoir bientôt de tes nouvelles.

Je t'embrasse,
Laurence

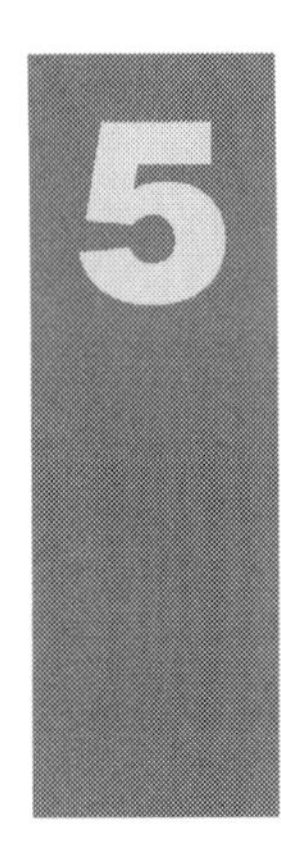

5 Common verb phrases and idiomatic expressions

TOMBER DES NUES = TO BE FLABBERGASTED

This chapter contains many common verb phrases and idiomatic phrases that are important to know. It would be impossible to include them all, so the focus is on the expressions that are likely to be most useful. If you are ever puzzled by the idiomatic use of a common verb that doesn't make sense literally, look it up in a good dictionary.

Expressions with *aller*, *avoir*, *donner* and *être*

1 **Aller** literally means 'to go', but it has different meanings in a number of common expressions.

aller + infinitive	referring to future events

Elle va bientôt partir.
(She will soon be leaving.)

Je vais lui dire au revoir.
(I'm going to say goodbye to her.)

aller à quelqu'un	to suit someone

Cette robe lui va très bien.
(That dress really suits her.)

aller de soi	to go without saying; to be obvious

Il va de soi que nous t'accompagnons à la gare.
(It goes without saying that we'll take you to the station.)

Le lien entre les deux choses allait de soi.
(The link between the two things was obvious.)

aller bien / mal	to be going well / badly; to be good / bad

Les affaires vont bien / mal.
(Business is good / bad.)

Comment allez-vous?	How are you?
Ça va?	How are things?
Ça va. . .	Is it OK / Does it suit . . .?

Ça te va si on se voit lundi?
(Is it OK with you if we meet on Monday?)

y aller	to get on with something

Vas-y. Dis-le-moi.
(Go on. Tell me.)

il y va de . . .	to be at stake

Il y va de ton bonheur.
(Your happiness is at stake.)

il en va de même . . . the same goes for . . .

Tout le monde devra s'y habituer et il en va de même pour vous.
(Everyone will have to get used to it and the same goes for you.)

il en va autrement . . . things happen differently

Il en va autrement en Afrique.
(Things happen differently / are different in Africa.)

s'en aller to go away; to leave; to go by

Va-t'en!
(Go away!)

Nous nous en allons bientôt.
(We're leaving soon.)

Les années s'en vont et tout change.
(The years go by and everything changes.)

2 **Avoir** literally means 'to have' or 'to get', but it is also used in many expressions that take the verb 'to be' in English.

a. Expressions where **avoir** means 'to have', 'to get', or a closely related idea.

avoir un bus, un train etc. to catch a bus, a train etc.

Je n'ai pas eu mon train hier soir.
(I didn't catch my train last night.)

avoir . . . pour un certain prix to get . . . for a certain price

J'ai eu ce portable pour 60 euros.
(I got this mobile for 60 euros.)

avoir quelqu'un to beat (at sport)

L'équipe de Bordeaux les a eus.
(The Bordeaux team beat them.)

avoir quelqu'un to have, to con someone

Ils nous ont bien eus avec leur fourberie.
(They've really conned us with their double-dealing.)

avoir quelqu'un (au téléphone) to get through to someone (by telephone); to put someone through to

Pouvez-vous m'avoir votre adjoint à Rouen?
(Can you get me / put me through to your assistant in Rouen?)

avoir un vêtement to wear, to have on

Elle avait une blouse pour se protéger.
(She was wearing an overall for protection.)

b. Common expressions

avoir l'air to look, to seem

Elle a l'air excédé(e)
(She looks harassed.)

The adjective may agree (m. sing.) with **air** or with the subject.

avoir beau to do something in vain

J'ai beau essayer, je n'arrive pas à comprendre ce texte.
(It's no good my trying, I can't understand this text.)

avoir besoin de to need

Elle a besoin d'un coup de main.
(She needs a helping hand.)

avoir confiance en quelqu'un to trust someone

Nous avons confiance en lui.
(We trust him.)

avoir envie de to feel like; to want to

Ils ont envie de changer d'air.
(They want a change of scene.)

avoir l'intention de to intend to

J'avais l'intention de préparer mon cours ce soir.
(I intended to prepare my class this evening.)

avoir lieu to take place

La réunion aura lieu mercredi après-midi.
(The meeting will take place on Wednesday afternoon.)

avoir mal to have an ache / pain

J'ai mal à la gorge. Il a mal à la tête.
(I have a sore throat. He has a headache.)

avoir du mal à to find it hard to

J'ai du mal à comprendre ce qu'ils disent.
(I find it hard to understand what they are saying.)

avoir de quoi to have enough / good reason

Si vous avez de quoi vivre, vous avez de quoi être satisfait.
(If you have enough to live on, you have good reason to be satisfied.)

avoir à + infinitive to have something to do

J'ai beaucoup à faire, moi. N'as-tu rien à faire?
(I have a lot to do. Don't you have anything to do?)

n'avoir qu'à + infinitive to have only to

Il n'avait qu'à le dire.
(He had only to say so.)

en avoir pour + time to take; to be . . .

J'en ai pour cinq minutes. Il n'en a pas pour longtemps.
(It will take me five minutes. It won't take him long / He won't be long.)

en avoir pour + money to cost

J'en aurai pour combien? J'en ai eu pour 100 euros.
(How much will it cost me? It cost me 100 euros.)

c. Common expressions where the verb 'to be' is used in English

avoir affaire à to be dealing with

Nous avons affaire à un fainéant.
(We're dealing with a time-waster.)

avoir . . . ans to be . . . years old.

Il a douze ans.
(He is twelve years old.)

avoir quelques minutes d'avance to be a few minutes early

Nous avons dix minutes d'avance.
(We are ten minutes early.)

avoir du chagrin to be sad

Elle a du chagrin.
(She is sad.)

avoir un gros chagrin to be very upset (of a child)

L'enfant a eu un gros chagrin à la mort de son chien.
(The child was very upset when his dog died.)

avoir de la chance to be lucky

Il a toujours de la chance.
(He is always lucky.)

avoir chaud / froid to be hot / cold

Nous avions froid, mais maintenant nous avons trop chaud.
(We were cold, but now we are too hot.)

avoir du courage to be brave

Il faut admettre qu'elle a du courage.
(You have to admit that she is brave.)

avoir faim / soif to be hungry / thirsty

Après ce long voyage il a faim, mais il a surtout soif.
(After this long journey he is hungry, but above all he is thirsty.)

avoir l'habitude de to be in the habit of

Ils ont l'habitude d'aller au cinéma le vendredi soir.
(They're in the habit of going to the cinema on Friday evenings.)

avoir honte de to be ashamed of

Il a honte de ses mauvaises notes.
(He is ashamed of his bad marks.)

avoir de la patience to be patient

Elle a beaucoup de patience avec les enfants.
(She is very patient with the children.)

avoir peur to be afraid of

Elle a peur du noir.
(She is afraid of the dark.)

avoir quelque chose something is wrong

Qu'est-ce que tu as? J'ai que mon fils est malade.
(What's wrong? My son is ill, that's what's wrong.)

avoir raison / tort to be right / wrong

Si tu as raison, il doit avoir tort.
(If you are right, he must be wrong.)

avoir du retard	to be late
avoir quelques minutes de retard	to be a few minutes late

Nous avons du retard. Notre train a vingt minutes de retard.
(We are late. Our train is twenty minutes late.)

avoir sommeil	to be sleepy

Si tu as sommeil, va te reposer.
(If you are sleepy, go and rest.)

en avoir marre de	to be fed up with
en avoir assez de	to have had enough of

J'en ai assez de ses caprices. J'en ai marre de le dire.
(I've had enough of his / her whims. I'm fed up of saying so.)

d. Expressions where **avoir** is used to give dimensions

avoir + noun + de + measurement	to be . . . high / wide etc.

Cette tour a une hauteur de trente mètres.
(This tower is thirty metres high.)

avoir + measurement + de + noun	to be . . . high / wide etc.

Cette tour a trente mètres de hauteur.
(This tower is thirty metres high.)

avoir + measurement + de + adjective	to be high / wide etc.

Cette tour a trente mètres de haut.
(This tower is thirty metres high.)

e. The impersonal expression, **il y a** (there is / there are)

This impersonal expression is always third-person singular. It can be followed by a singular or a plural noun and can be conjugated in all tenses of the indicative and subjunctive. The important thing to remember is that you are dealing with **avoir**, not **être**, even though it translates the English 'there is / there are'.

Hier il y a eu des protestations. Demain il y aura une grève.
(Yesterday there were protests. Tomorrow there will be a strike.)

It is also found in the infinitive, **y avoir**.

Il va y avoir de l'orage.
(There is going to be a storm = There's a storm brewing.)

Some common idiomatic uses are listed below.

il y a + expression of time — ago

J'ai visité Rome il y a dix ans.
(I visited Rome ten years ago.)

il y a + expression of time + que — for + time

The following verb is in the present tense if the action is still continuing, but in the past tense if the action was completed in the past.

Il y a trente ans que j'habite ici.
(I've lived here for thirty years.)

Il y a belle lurette qu'il a pris la retraite.
(It is ages since he retired.)

il y a + expression of distance — it is

Il y a 10 kilomètres d'ici à l'aéroport.
(It's 10 kilometres from here to the airport.)

il y a + à + infinitive — there is . . . to be + past participle

Il y a beaucoup à dire là-dessus.
(There is a lot to be said about that.)

Il y a beaucoup à faire, mais il n'y a pas à s'en plaindre.
(There's a lot to be done, but there's no need to complain.)

il y en a qui — there are those who

Il y en a qui arrivent toujours en retard.
(There are some people / those who always turn up late.)

il y en a pour + time — it takes

Il y en aura encore pour trois heures.
(It will take another three hours.)

il y en a pour + money — it costs

Il y en aura pour 500 euros.
(It will cost / come to 500 euros.)

il y a de quoi — there is good reason
il n'y a pas de quoi — don't mention it

On m'a conseillé de ne pas m'inquiéter, mais il y a de quoi.
(I was advised not to worry, but there is / I have good reason to do so.)

Merci beaucoup. Il n'y a pas de quoi.
(Thank you very much. Don't mention it.)

3 **Donner** literally means 'to give', but it is used with different meanings in some common expressions.

donner un âge à quelqu'un	to say someone is a certain age

Je lui donne 30 ans.
(I'd say he / she is 30.)

donner à boire à quelqu'un	to give someone something to drink
donner à manger à quelqu'un	to provide someone with food

Je leur ai donné à boire et à manger.
(I gave them something to eat and drink.)

You could also say:

Je leur ai donné quelque chose à boire et à manger.

donner faim / froid à quelqu'un	to make someone feel hungry / cold

Cette promenade m'a donné faim / froid.
(That walk has made me feel hungry / cold.)

donner un film / une pièce	to show a film; to put on a play

Qu'est-ce qu'on donne au théâtre en ce moment?
(What's on at the theatre just now?)

donner rendez-vous à quelqu'un	to arrange to meet someone

Je leur ai donné rendez-vous à midi.
(I arranged to meet them at midday.)

ne rien donner	not to have any effect

Leurs efforts pour le convaincre n'ont rien donné.
(Their efforts to convince him didn't have any effect.)

donner contre	to hit; to run into

Il a donné de la tête contre le mur.
(He hit his head against the wall.)

Note also the figurative usage:

Je ne sais plus où donner de la tête.
(I don't know which way to turn.)

donner sur; donner dans	to overlook; to lead into

Ma fenêtre donne sur le parc.
(My window looks out onto the park.)

L'entrée donne dans le salon.
(The hall leads into the living room.)

donner dans	to tend towards

Ce film donne dans l'expressionnisme.
(This film tends towards expressionism / has expressionistic tendencies.)

se donner à	to devote oneself to

Il se donne tout entier à cette cause.
(He is devoting himself wholeheartedly to this cause.)

se donner pour	to make oneself out to be

Elle se donne pour libérale, mais elle ne trompe personne.
(She makes herself out to be a liberal, but she doesn't fool anyone.)

se donner du mal pour quelqu'un	to go to a lot of trouble on someone's account
se donner du mal pour faire quelque chose	to go to a lot of trouble to do something

Ils se sont donné beaucoup de mal pour moi / pour m'aider.
(They went to a great deal of trouble on my account / to help me.)

4 **Être** literally means 'to be', but it is used in combination with the prepositions *à* and *de* and with the pronouns *en* and *y* with meanings that may not be immediately obvious. There are also some useful impersonal expressions to note.

a. In combination with *à*, *de*, *en* and *y*

être à	to belong to; to be with

Cette serviette est à moi. À qui est celle-là?
(This towel is mine. Whose is that one?)

Je suis à vous tout de suite.
(I'll be with you right away.)

être de + place	to come from

Nous sommes de Londres. D'où êtes-vous?
(We come from London. Where do you come from?)

être de + person / activity — to be one of / to take part in

Il est des nôtres. Êtes-vous du voyage aussi?
(He is one of us. Are you coming on the trip too?)

être d'un(e) + noun — to be so . . .

Elle est d'une ingénuité!
(She is so naïve!)

être en train de + infinitive — to be in the process of . . . -ing

Nous étions en train de déjeuner quand il est arrivé.
(We were in the middle of having lunch when he arrived.)

en être — to have reached a particular point

Où en es-tu?
(Where are you up to? / How far have you got?)

J'en suis au chapitre cinq.
(I'm up to / I've got as far as chapter five.)

y être — to be with it; to get it

D'abord je n'ai pas compris le calembour, mais maintenant j'y suis.
(At first I didn't understand the pun, but now I get it.)

b. Impersonal expressions

ceci / cela étant, . . . — this being so, . . .

il en est de même pour . . . — the same goes for . . .

Je préfère rester à Paris et il en est de même pour mon mari.
(I prefer to stay in Paris and the same goes for my husband.)

Il adore le sport, mais il n'en est pas de même pour son frère.
(He loves sport, but the same does not go / is not the case for his brother.)

Il en sera toujours ainsi. — It will always be so.

Il n'en est rien. — This isn't at all the case.

ne serait-ce que / ne fût-ce que . . . — if only . . .

Je voudrais passer la voir, ne serait-ce que pour dire bonjour.
(I'd like to call and see her, if only to say hello.)

C'est cela / ça. — That's right.

Ça y est! — That's it! / All done!

Ça m'est égal. — I don't mind either way.

Exercises

EXERCISE 1. In the sentences below, fill in the blanks with the correct form of **aller**, **avoir, donner** or **être** as appropriate to the context and make any other necessary choices.

1 Qu'est-ce que tu ____? Tu _____ l'air bouleversé.
2 Je ne comprends pas ce qui te retient. _____-y.
3 Quel âge lui ____-vous? Elle ______ d'une élégance!
4 Je voudrais visiter Paris, ne ______-ce que pour voir la Tour Eiffel.
5 Ne / n'_____ pas peur! Il ne va pas te manger.
6 Ils ______ beau essayer. Ils n'y arrivent pas.
7 Elle ne sait plus où ________ de la tête.
8 Ils ont _____ cette maison pour un million d'euros.
9 Il ___ de soi que nous avons confiance en vous.
10 Il paraît que la réunion a ____ lieu hier.
11 Qu'est-ce qu'on ______ au cinéma ce soir?
12 Je n'ai vraiment pas de préférence. Ça me / m'_____ égal.
13 Je vois que tu as commencé tes révisions. Où en ____-tu maintenant?
14 Tu devrais insister sur ce point. Il y ____ de ta sécurité.
15 Cette salle _____ dix mètres de long.
16 Nous organisons une soirée dimanche. J'espère que vous pouvez _____ des nôtres.
17 Cet escroc nous a bien _____.
18 _____-vous de quoi manger?
19 Il devrait ______ honte de sa conduite.
20 La chambre ________ dans la salle de bains.

EXERCISE 2. Fill in the blanks by choosing the most appropriate expression from the box below. Conjugate the verbs as necessary.

> à qui; s'en aller; avoir beau; ça y est; cela étant; c'est ça; donner dans; donner sur; ne . . . rien donner; se donner; se donner pour; en avoir pour longtemps; il y a de quoi; il n'y a pas de quoi; il y a belle lurette; il en va; il en va de même pour; il n'en est rien; il y en a; être en train de; y être

1 Elle a gagné à la loterie, mais ______________ qu'elle a tout dépensé.
2 ________ est cette veste? Elle traîne là depuis la semaine dernière.
3 A-t-il vraiment dit qu'il ne me connaît pas? Oui, _________.
4 Est-ce que vous ___________? Non, nous aurons bientôt terminé.
5 ______________! Tu m'embêtes.
6 Enfin, ______________! J'ai terminé ma dissertation.
7 Tu ne devrais pas t'étonner de l'absence de sa mère. __________ souvent ainsi.

8 Elle s'inquiète de son fils, et ___________.
9 La salle de bal ___________ le parc.
10 ___________ qui sont pour et d'autres qui sont contre ce programme.
11 La production de cet auteur _______________ le réalisme.
12 Merci beaucoup! _______________.
13 J'ai eu du mal à comprendre le mode d'emploi de cette imprimante, mais maintenant je / j'_______.
14 Ils ____________ essayer, ils n'arrivent pas à parler allemand.
15 Tous leurs efforts ______________. Ils n'ont pas eu de prix.
16 Je / J'______________ parler au téléphone quand on a sonné à la porte.
17 Je ne suis pas sportive et ______________ ma fille.
18 Il _____________ intellectuel, mais _____________.
19 Elle ne veut pas assister au mariage, et ___________, je ne peux pas y assister moi non plus.
20 C'est une étudiante assidue. Elle _________ tout entière à ses études.

Expressions with *faire, mettre, prendre, tenir, tomber* and *venir*

5 **Faire** literally means 'to do' or 'to make', but it is also used in many common expressions with a variety of meanings. You can also use it in impersonal expressions, particularly to describe the weather. In combination with a following infinitive, it forms a causative construction, meaning 'to make someone do something' or 'to get / have something done'.

a. Everyday expressions that should be part of your core vocabulary

faire du bien — to produce a good effect, to do good

Les vacances te feront du bien.
(The holidays will do you good.)

faire des courses — to go shopping

faire la cuisine — to cook

faire une promenade — to go for a walk

faire la queue — to queue

faire du sport, du tennis etc. — to play sports, tennis etc.

faire sa toilette — to get ready / dressed

faire un voyage — to go on a journey, trip

faire attention à to pay attention to; to be careful

faire confiance à to trust

faire la connaissance de qqn to meet someone

faire exprès to do something on purpose

Il faut le lui pardonner. Il ne l'a pas fait exprès.
(He has to be forgiven. He didn't do it on purpose.)

faire fortune to become rich

faire mal to hurt

Ça ne fait pas mal.
(It doesn't hurt.)

faire mal à quelqu'un to cause pain to / to hurt someone

Il lui a fait mal au bras.
(He hurt her arm.)

faire du mal à quelqu'un to harm, hurt someone

This is often found in the negative:

ne pas faire de mal à quelqu'un not to harm, hurt someone

Il ne voulait pas leur faire de mal.
(He didn't mean them any harm.)

Ça ne leur ferait pas de mal de s'excuser.
(It wouldn't hurt them to apologise.)

faire de son mieux to do one's best

faire part de quelque chose à quelqu'un to announce something to someone

Sophie et Marc Dumas sont heureux de vous faire part de la naissance de leur fils, Pierre.
(Sophie and Marc Bourget are pleased to announce the birth of their son, Pierre.)

Note that **un faire-part** is an official announcement of a birth / marriage / death.

faire de la peine à quelqu'un to hurt someone's feelings

Il leur a fait de la peine en disant cela.
(He hurt their feelings when he said that.)

faire peur à quelqu'un	to frighten, to scare someone
faire plaisir à quelqu'un	to please, to give pleasure to someone

Ça me ferait très plaisir de te revoir.
(I'd be delighted to see you again.)

faire son possible	to do one's best
faire semblant de + infinitive	to pretend

Elle fait semblant de travailler.
(She is pretending to be working.)

b. Some other very useful expressions

faire + adjective (invariable)	to look, to seem

Je trouve qu'elle fait très jeune et sa robe fait très élégant.
(I think she looks very young, and her dress looks very elegant.)

faire + illness	to have a medical problem

Il a fait une crise cardiaque.
(He has had a heart attack.)

faire le malade / le héros, etc.	to act, to pretend to be ill / the hero, etc.

Il n'a absolument rien, mais il fait le malade.
(There's absolutely nothing wrong with him, but he's pretending to be ill.)

faire de . . . autre chose	to make / turn . . . into something else

J'ai fait de cette chambre mon cabinet de travail.
(I've made this bedroom into my study.)

On a fait de lui un acteur.
(They turned him into an actor.)

ne faire que + infinitive	to only

Je ne faisais que plaisanter
(I was only joking.)

faire vite	to act quickly

Vas-y, mais fais vite!
(Go on, but be quick about it!)

faire in reported speech — to say

'Je vous remercie', fit-elle.
('Thank you', she said.)

c. Impersonal expressions with **il fait**

Il fait chaud / frais / froid — It is hot / cool / cold

Il fait beau / bon / mauvais — The weather is fine / nice / bad

Il fait du brouillard / du soleil / du vent — It is foggy / sunny / windy

Il fait jour / nuit — It is daylight / night

BE AWARE! You cannot use **faire** for all expressions concerning the weather. For example, if you want to say 'it is raining' or 'it is snowing', use the impersonal verbs **il pleut** or **il neige**.

d. Expressions with **cela / ça fait**

cela / ça fait + expression of time — duration of an action / state

Cela / Ça fait deux ans qu'elle est médecin.
(She has been a doctor for two years now.)

Ça ne fait rien. — That doesn't matter.

e. Causative expressions

faire + infinitive — to make someone do something

Il faut faire boire ta mère. Il faut la faire boire.
(You must make your mother drink. You must make her drink.)

In this example, the person being made to drink is treated as the direct object, but only because the following infinitive **boire** does not have a direct object of its own. If it did have one, then the person would become the indirect object, e.g.

Il faut faire boire la tisane à ta mère. Il faut lui faire boire la tisane.
(You must make your mother drink the herbal tea. You must make her drink the herbal tea.)

This can be tricky for an English speaker to understand. However, if you compare the French and English word order in the example above, you will see an explanation. In English, the two verbal elements are treated separately and each is followed by its own direct object: 'make your mother drink the tea'. By contrast, in French, **faire + infinitive** is treated as a single, uninterrupted unit that can have only one direct object, so the person, who may appear to an English speaker to be the direct object of **faire**, becomes the indirect object of **faire boire**. The direct object is *la tisane* (the herbal tea).

The translation of these verbal units depends on the verb following **faire**. Some common examples are as follows:

faire remarquer — to point out

faire savoir — to let know, to tell

Veuillez nous le faire savoir dans les plus brefs délais.
(Please let us know as soon as possible.)

faire venir — to call for, to send for

Nous avons dû faire venir le médecin.
(We had to call for the doctor.)

faire voir — to show

Il a fait voir la lettre à sa femme pour que'elle la lise elle-même.
(He showed the letter to his wife so that she could read it herself.)

faire + infinitive — to get / have something done

The thing to note here is that **faire** is always followed by an infinitive, whereas in English a past participle is used after 'to get' or 'to have'.

Il a fait construire une maison.
(He had a house built.)

f. The reflexive form, **se faire**

se faire + adjective — to become

Notre ancien collègue se fait vieux.
(Our former colleague is getting old.)

Il se fait tard et nous devons partir.
(It is getting late and we must leave.)

se faire mal — to hurt oneself

Il s'est fait mal en tombant.
(He hurt himself when he fell over.)

se faire plaisir + infinitive — to be delighted to do something

Elle se fera plaisir de vous aider.
(She will be delighted to help you.)

s'en faire — to worry

Ne t'en fais pas! Eux, ils ne s'en font pas du tout.
(Don't worry about it! They're not bothered at all.)

se faire à quelque chose — to get used to

J'ai du mal à me faire à cette situation.
(I'm finding it hard to get used to this situation.)

Cela / Ça se fait / ça ne se fait pas. It is / is not the done thing.

Ça ne se fait pas de se curer les dents en public.
(It's not the done thing / not polite to pick your teeth in front of other people.)

Il se fit que . . . (impersonal) — It (so) happened that . . .

Il se fit un grand silence.
(There was complete silence.)

Comment se fait-il que . . . ?
(How is it that . . . ?)

se faire + infinitive — to get / to make oneself + past participle

Attention! Ne te fais pas écraser.
(Be careful! Don't get run over.)

Il s'est fait comprendre tant bien que mal.
(He made himself understood with great difficulty.)

Note that in this causative construction, **se faire** is followed by an infinitive, whereas in English a past participle is used after 'to get' and 'to make onself'.

6 **Mettre** literally means 'to put' or 'to put on', but it is also used in some common and idiomatic expressions where it is often translated by a different verb.

mettre + article of clothing — to put on; to wear (habitually)

Elle a mis un chapeau.
(She put on a hat.)

Il ne met jamais de costume.
(He never wears a suit.)

mettre la table — to lay / set the table

mettre + time — to take

J'ai mis une heure pour préparer le repas.
(It took me an hour to prepare the meal.)

mettre à l'épreuve to test

Je doute que cette solution soit valable. Il faudra la mettre à l'épreuve.
(I doubt if this solution is viable. It will have to be tested.)

mettre à exécution to carry out; to implement

C'est un programme qu'on ne va jamais mettre à exécution.
(It's a plan that will never be implemented.)

mettre à jour to bring up to date; to update

Il faut mettre à jour cette banque de données.
(This data bank needs to be updated.)

mettre en exergue to highlight

Tout d'abord je voudrais mettre en exergue le problème essentiel.
(First of all, I would like to highlight the key issue.)

mettre en marche to start; to switch on

Il a mis l'ordinateur en marche.
(He switched on the computer.)

mettre en œuvre to implement

Le gouvernement veut mettre en œuvre la réforme aussitôt que possible.
(The government wants to implement the reform as soon as possible.)

mettre en scène to stage (a play); to direct (a film)

On met *Phèdre* en scène au festival cet été.
(*Phèdre* is being staged at the festival this summer.)

mettons let's say

On se donne rendez-vous à quelle heure? Mettons à dix heures.
(What time shall we arrange to meet? Let's say at 10 o'clock.)

mettons que + subjunctive supposing . . .

Mettons qu'il soit déjà parti, qu'est-ce que tu feras?
(Supposing he has already left, what will you do?)

se mettre to take up a position; to stand

Il s'est mis debout quand les autres sont arrivés.
(He stood up when the others arrived.)

se mettre à + noun / infinitive to take up; to begin; to turn

Cet été il va se mettre au tennis.
(This summer he is going to take up tennis.)

Mon ordinateur se met à avoir des problèmes.
(My computer is beginning to go wrong.)

Le temps s'est mis au mauvais.
(The weather has turned bad.)

7 **Prendre** literally means 'to take', but it is used with other meanings in some common and idiomatic expressions.

prendre + drink / food / meal to have

Qu'est-ce que vous prenez? Je prends un café.
(What are you having? I'm having a coffee.)

prendre un bain / une douche to have a bath / a shower

prendre conscience to become aware

J'ai pris conscience de leur hostilité.
(I became aware of their hostility.)

prendre contact avec to make contact with

Il a pris contact avec nous à l'aéroport.
(He made contact with us at the airport.)

prendre froid to catch a cold

prendre + weight to put on

On voit bien qu'il a pris du poids.
(You can see that he has put on weight.)

Elle a pris deux kilos en une semaine.
(She put on two kilos in a week.)

prendre + direction to take; to go

Il faut prendre la deuxième à gauche / à droite.
(You need to take the second on the left / right.)

Il a pris à gauche, mais moi j'ai pris au plus court.
(He went left, but I went the shortest way.)

à tout prendre all in all

C'est à prendre ou à laisser. Take it or leave it.

Qu'est-ce qui te prend? What's the matter with you?

se prendre pour to think of oneself

Elle se prend pour une beauté.
(She thinks she's a great beauty.)

Pour qui est-ce que tu te prends?
(Who do you think you are?)

s'en prendre à quelqu'un to set about someone

Le prisonnier mécontent s'en est pris à son compagnon de cellule.
(The discontented prisoner set about his cellmate)

s'y prendre to go about something

Comment vas-tu t'y prendre pour expliquer la situation à tes employés?
(How will you go about explaining the situation to your employees?)

s'y prendre avec to handle

Elle sait s'y prendre avec les élèves difficiles.
(She knows how to handle difficult pupils.)

8 **Tenir** literally means 'to hold', but it is used with other meanings in some common and idiomatic expressions.

tenir à + noun to like, to value

Cette vieille dame tient à son indépendance.
(This old lady values her independence.)

tenir à + infinitive to be keen / anxious to; to insist on

Il tient beaucoup à la revoir.
(He is really keen to see her again.)

Je tiens à rentrer avant que le temps ne se mette au mauvais.
(I'm anxious to get home before the weather turns bad.)

Elle tient à vous parler.
(She insists on speaking to you.)

tenir à + noun to be due to

Cet accident tient à leur négligence.
(This accident is due to their negligence.)

tenir de quelqu'un to take after someone

Je vois bien que tu tiens de ta mère.
(I can see that you take after your mother.)

tenir bon to last out

J'espère que mon ordinateur va tenir bon jusqu'aux examens.
(I hope my computer is going to last out until the exams.)

tenir le coup to hold out

Je ne sais pas si elle pourra tenir le coup jusqu'à la fin de l'année scolaire.
(I don't know if she'll be able to hold out until the end of the school year.)

se tenir to stay, to be, to stand

Il se tient caché derrière la porte.
(He is standing hidden behind the door.)

s'en tenir à to keep to

Il leur faut s'en tenir aux ordres.
(They have to stick to orders.)

Tiens! Oh!

Tiens, tu as raison!
(Oh yes, you're right!)

9 **Tomber** literally means 'to fall' but it is also used in some common and idiomatic expressions.

tomber sur to come across; to meet by chance

En feuilletant le journal je suis tombé sur votre petite annonce personnelle.
(When I was leafing through the paper I came across your personal ad.)

Elle est tombée sur une connaissance au cinéma.
(She ran into someone she knew at the cinema.)

tomber sur to fall upon, to attack

Les voleurs sont tombés sur le gardien.
(The thiefs attacked the security guard.)

tomber bien / mal to turn up at a good / bad time

Ça tombe bien. C'est exactement ce que je cherchais.
(That's lucky. It's exactly what I was looking for.)

Je suis désolé, mais tu tombes mal. Je pars à l'instant.
(I'm sorry, but you're unlucky / you've come at a bad time. I'm leaving right now.)

tomber bien / mal (of a garment) — to hang well / badly

Cette robe tombe bien et elle te va à merveille.
(That dress hangs well and it fits you like a dream.)

tomber dans — to get / lapse into

Son dernier roman ne me plaît pas; il tombe dans la sensiblerie.
(I don't like his / her latest novel; it lapses into sentimentality.)

laisser tomber — to drop; to give up / drop

Le gardien de but a laissé tomber le ballon.
(The goalkeeper dropped the ball.)

J'ai essayé le yoga, mais j'étais tellement nulle que je l'ai laissé tomber.
(I tried yoga, but I was so useless that I gave it up.)

Il a laissé tomber sa petite amie.
(He has dropped his girlfriend.)

Laisse tomber!
(Forget it!)

tomber amoureux — to fall in love

tomber malade — to fall ill

tomber des nues — to be flabbergasted

tomber en panne — to break down

Ma voiture est tombée en panne sur l'autoroute.
(My car broke down on the motorway.)

les bras m'en tombent — I am speechless

avoir les épaules qui tombent — to have sloping shoulders

Note also the informal expression:

tomber la veste — to take off one's jacket

10 **Venir** literally means 'to come', but it is used with other meanings in some common and idiomatic expressions.

venir de — to originate from; to be due to

Ces objets viennent du Moyen-Orient.
(These artefacts come from the Middle East.)

Sa réussite au concours vient d'un long travail de préparation.
(His / her success in the competitive exam is due to lengthy preparation.)

D'où vient qu'ils ne se parlent jamais?
(How come / Why is it that they never speak to one another?)

De là vient que tu es toujours fatigué.
(That's why / hence you are always tired.)

venir à quelqu'un to occur to someone

L'idée est venue à Marc qu'il pourrait aller vivre à l'étranger.
(It occurred to Marc that he could go and live abroad.)

Ça ne m'était jamais venu à l'esprit / l'idée.
(It had never occurred to me.)

venir de + infinitive to have just

Ce livre vient de paraître.
(This book has just come out / been published.)

Mon mari venait de partir quand nos invités sont arrivés.
(My husband had just left when our guests arrived.)

The present tense of **venir** is used for 'have just', the imperfect for 'had just'.

venir à + infinitive to chance to happen

Si elle venait à changer d'avis, il y aurait des problèmes.
(If she happened to / if she were to change her mind, there would be problems.)

en venir à to come to, to get to a particular point

Nous en venons au problème principal.
(We now come to the key problem.)

Il en est venu à abandonner ses études.
(He has got to the point of dropping out.)

Où veux-tu en venir au juste?
(What exactly are you getting at?)

en venir aux mains to come to blows

Ils en sont venus aux mains.
(They came to blows.)

à venir coming, future

Dans les années à venir, nous espérons voir de grands progrès.
(In future years, we hope to see great progress.)

qui vient coming, future

L'année qui vient vous apportera de meilleures choses, j'espère.

(The coming year will bring you better things, I hope.)

Exercises

EXERCISE 3. In the sentences below, fill in the blanks with the correct form of **faire**, **mettre**, **prendre**, **tenir**, **tomber** or **venir** as appropriate to the context.

1 D'où _____ que vous êtes si nerveuse? Tout se passera bien, j'en suis sûr.
2 Je suis très heureuse de _______ votre connaissance.
3 Il n'est jamais trop tard de se ________ à apprendre une deuxième langue.
4 Si jamais il ____________ à découvrir la vérité, il serait furibond.
5 Pourquoi la critiquer? Elle a _____ tout son possible pour vous aider.
6 Il est grand temps de __________ ce dossier à jour.
7 Tout à coup j'ai _________ conscience qu'on me suivait.
8 Quand on écrit une dissertation il est essentiel de s'en ________ au sujet.
9 Je suis désolé, mais vous ________ mal. Ils _________ de partir.
10 Qu'est-ce qui te _________? Tu as l'air excédé.
11 J'ai bien écouté le professeur, mais je ne comprends pas où il voulait en ______ .
12 Je m'excuse. C'était un accident. Je ne l'ai pas ________ exprès.
13 Je ne sais pas pour qui elle se ______, mais elle se donne de grands airs.
14 On ne saura s'il est capable de jouer ce rôle que si on le ________ à l'épreuve.
15 Nous avons ______ trois heures pour ________ le trajet de Paris à Calais.
16 Les bras m'en _________. Son insolence est absolument incroyable!
17 Ce sont des projets impracticables qu'on ne pourra pas _______ à exécution.
18 Les joueurs se sont disputés et ont fini par en ________ aux mains.
19 Elle est débrouillarde. J'admire la façon dont elle s'y ______ .
20 Tôt ou tard, il faudra en _______ à ce problème épineux.
21 Elle ________ à partir de bonne heure pour avoir son train.
22 En sortant du théâtre elle est __________ sur son anciennne co-locataire.

EXERCISE 4. Fill in the blanks by choosing the most appropriate expression from the box below. Conjugate the verbs as necessary.

cela fait; faire du bien; faire part; faire remarquer; faire venir; il se fit; laisser tomber; mettons; mettre en exergue; mettre en marche; prendre; tenir; tiens!; tomber; tomber sur; venir; se faire; se faire à; s'en faire; se mettre; se mettre debout; s'y prendre; se tenir

1 _______ que le théâtre soit complet ce soir, qu'est-ce que tu vas faire?
2 On m'a dit qu'un changement d'air me ___________ .
3 Si le bébé ne va pas mieux demain, il faudra __________ le médecin.
4 J'en ai marre de la pluie. Je me demande quand le temps va _________au beau.
5 Il a disparu. Je crois qu'il a dû _________ à droite au carrefour.
6 Il _________ tard et je vais me coucher.
7 Elle a perdu ses parents à un jeune âge. De là ______ qu'elle est toujours angoissée.
8 _____! Elle est toujours là. Elle a _______ le coup.
9 Il fera un bon instituteur. Il sait ___________ avec les enfants.
10 Je leur ai écrit pour leur ____________ de la naissance de la petite Agnès.
11 Le thème de son exposé n'est pas du tout évident. Il aurait dû le ____________ dès le début.
12 Je ne veux plus en entendre parler. ___________ !
13 Qu'est-ce qu'ils sont devenus? ___________ une heure que nous les attendons.
14 J'espère que tu ne m'en voudras pas si je te ___________ que tu t'es trompé de direction.
15 Ne ____________ pas! Ce n'est pas ta faute.
16 Il _____________ et m'a cédé sa place.
17 Elle a du mal à _______________ tous les changements qui ont eu lieu depuis la mort de son mari.
18 Cette robe ne lui va pas. Elle _________ mal.
19 Dès leur entrée ___________ un grand silence.
20 En flânant dans le vieux quartier de la ville hier, je _________________ une statue intéressante.
21 Je lui ai demandé de _________ la chaudière. Nous grelottons.
22 Cet enfant n'arrive pas à ___________ tranquille.

EXERCISE 5. Fill in the blanks with the most appropriate verbal expressions that you have studied in this chapter. Pay particular attention to the use of object pronouns with the verb **faire** followed by an infinitive.

> Pierre voudrait (1) ____________ (to give up) le piano. On ne va jamais (2) _________ (make him into) un musicien. Il (3)____________ (has done his best), mais il (4) ________________ (has got to the point of) n'en pouvoir plus. Il en (5) ______________ (has had enough of it / is fed up of it). (6) __________ (for) cinq ans qu'il essaie de (7) ______________ (to get used to) l'idée qu'il doit travailler le piano tous les jours juste pour (8)________________ (to please) ses parents. Il faudra (9)____________ (to make them understand) son point de vue. Son professeur a réussi à (10) ________________ (make him practise), mais elle n'a pas réussi à (11) _______________ (make him like) la musique. (12)____________ (That's why) il n'en peut plus. Qui plus est, s'il continue il devra (13)________________ (begin to) étudier la théorie de la musique et il (14)____________ (isn't keen on it). Dans une telle situation il faut (15) _______________ (act quickly) et cesser de (16) __________ (pretending to) s'intéresser à quelque chose qui ne lui plaît pas du tout. (17) _________ (All in all), ça (18) ________________ (will be better) s'il avoue la vérité. Il (19) ____________ (will point out to them) qu'il préfère le sport. Après tout il (20)_________ (takes after) son père qui n'a pas l'oreille musicale.

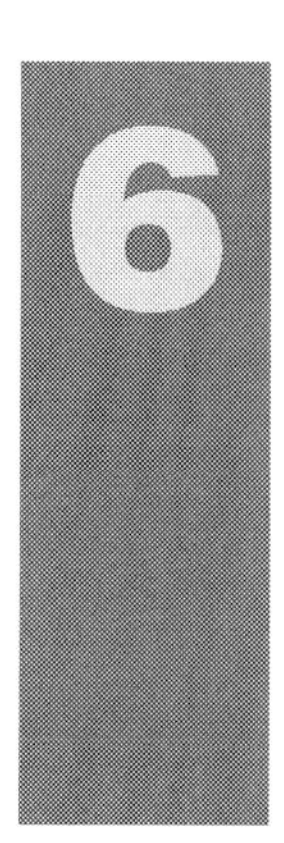

Pronominal verbs

JE NE ME SENS PAS BIEN = I DON'T FEEL WELL.
JE SENS BON = I SMELL NICE.

Pronominal verbs such as *s'en aller* and *se mettre*, which you encountered in Chapter 5, are used quite frequently in French, often with no reflexive or reciprocal meaning. In this chapter, you will learn more about the subtleties of meaning in the French of native speakers and learn to use pronominal verbs to make your own French more authentic and idiomatic.

Lexicalised pronominal verbs

Lexicalised pronominal verbs are pronominal in form, i.e. they are always accompanied by an unstressed pronoun object, *me*, *te*, *se*, *nous*, *vous*, *se*, which must agree with the subject, e.g. *je m'en suis allée* (I went away). However, in marked contrast to true reflexive verbs like *elle s'est lavée* (she washed herself) or *elles se sont vues* (they saw one another), this pronoun has no reflexive or reciprocal meaning.

1 Some of the most common lexicalised pronominal verbs are listed below.

s'abstenir de (+ noun / inf.)	to refrain from
s'accouder	to lean on one's elbows
s'accoutumer à (+ noun / inf.)	to get used to
s'accroupir	to crouch
s'adresser à quelqu'un	to address, speak to someone
s'affaiblir	to get weaker
s'affaler	to collapse
s'agenouiller	to kneel
s'allonger	to lie down
s'amuser	to have a good time
s'apercevoir de quelque chose	to notice something
s'appeler	to be called
s'approcher de quelqu'un	to approach, go up to someone
s'appuyer	to lean
s'arrêter	to stop
s'asseoir	to sit down
s'assoupir	to doze off
s'avancer vers	to move towards
se battre	to fight
se blottir contre quelqu'un	to cuddle up to someone
se briser	to break
se casser	to break
se charger de (+ noun / inf.)	to take on, assume responsibility for
se comporter	to behave
se contenter de (+ noun / inf.)	to make do with
se coucher	to go to bed; to lie down
se débrouiller	to manage
se décider à (+ inf.)	to make up one's mind to
se demander	to wonder
se dépêcher de (+ inf.)	to hurry

se dérouler	to take place; to go, proceed
se déshabiller	to undress
se diriger vers un endroit	to go towards a place
se douter de quelque chose	to suspect something
s'écarter / s'écarter d'un chemin	to part, diverge; to stray from a path
s'échapper d'un endroit	to escape from a place
s'éclaircir	to get lighter, become clearer
s'écouler	to pass by (of time)
s'écrier	to exclaim, cry out
s'écrouler	to collapse
s'effondrer	to collapse
s'effondrer en larmes	to dissolve into tears
s'éloigner d'un endroit	to move away from a place
s'emparer de quelqu'un / quelque chose	to get hold of, seize someone / something
s'en aller	to go away
s'endormir	to fall asleep
s'enfuir	to flee
s'ennuyer	to be bored
s'enquérir de quelque chose	to enquire about something
s'enrhumer	to catch a cold
s'étonner de quelque chose	to be surprised at something
s'évader d'un endroit	to escape from a place
s'évanouir	to faint
se fâcher	to get angry
se fatiguer	to get tired
se fermer	to close
se fier à quelqu'un / quelque chose	to trust someone / something
se figurer	to imagine
s'habiller	to get dressed; dress up
s'habituer à (+ noun / inf.)	to get used to
s'imaginer	to imagine
s'intéresser à quelque chose	to be interested in something
se lever	to get up
se méfier de quelqu'un / quelque chose	to mistrust someone / something
se mêler; se mêler à (+ noun); se mêler de (+ noun)	to mix, mingle; to join in; to meddle in

se mettre à (+ inf.)	to begin to
se moquer de quelqu'un	to make fun of, laugh at someone
se noyer	to drown
s'obscurcir	to get darker
s'occuper de (+ noun / inf.)	to look after; to see to
se passer	to happen
se passer de quelqu'un / quelque chose	to do without someone, to go without something
se permettre quelque chose; se permettre de faire quelque chose	to afford something; to afford to do something, to take the liberty of doing something
se plaindre de quelque chose	to complain about something
se porter	to feel, be
se presser de (+ inf.)	to hurry
se promener	to go for a walk
se rappeler	to remember
se raviser	to change one's mind
se réfugier	to take refuge
se rendre; se rendre à un endroit	to surrender; to go to a place
se repentir de (+ noun / past inf.)	to repent of, regret
se retourner	to turn around
se réveiller	to wake up
se sauver	to escape, run away
se sentir	to feel
se servir de (+ noun)	to use
se soucier de (+ noun / inf.)	to care about
se souvenir de (+ noun / past inf.)	to remember
se taire	to keep quiet
se tenir droit	to stand straight
se tromper	to be mistaken, wrong
se trouver	to be (found)
tant s'en faut; peu s'en faut	far from it; very nearly

2 Some of these lexicalised pronominal verbs only ever occur in the pronominal form, e.g. *s'écrier* (to exclaim). Others occur in both the non-pronominal and the pronominal form, each with a different meaning, e.g. *décider de* (to decide) and *se décider à* (to make up one's mind). In this case, the pronominal form has a stronger force. The same distinction of force operates between *refuser de* and *se refuser à* and between *résoudre de* (to resolve, decide) and *se résoudre à* (to make up one's mind).

You need to take particular care in cases such as those illustrated below, because the meaning of the pronominal form is different from that of the non-pronominal form, e.g. *se rendre à* (to go to), as opposed to *rendre* (to give back).

The particular meanings of *s'en aller*, *se donner*, *se faire*, se *mettre*, *se prendre* and *se tenir* have already been illustrated in Chapter 5, so they are not repeated here.

Verb	Pronominal form
apercevoir (to see, catch sight of) J'ai aperçu une lumière au loin. (I saw a light in the distance.)	**s'apercevoir de** (to notice, realise) Je me suis aperçu de son trouble. (I noticed her embarrassment.)
approcher de (to get near, approach unintentionally) Elle approchait de la soixantaine. (She was getting close to sixty.)	**s'approcher de** (to go up to, approach deliberately) Il s'est approché d'elle pour lui parler. (He went up to speak to her.)
attaquer (to attack; to tackle) Je vais attaquer cette corvée ce soir. (I will tackle this chore tonight.) The pronominal form has a stronger force.	**s'attaquer à** (to attack; to tackle) Je m'attaquerai à cette corvée ce soir. (I will set about this chore tonight.)
comporter (to include) Ce livre comporte une bibliographie. (This book includes a bibliography.)	**se comporter** (to behave) Cet enfant se comporte bien. (This child behaves well.)
coucher (to sleep) Ils couchent à l'hôtel. (They are sleeping at a hotel.) J'ai couché chez ma tante hier. (I slept at my aunt's yesterday.)	**se coucher** (to go to bed; to lie down) Ils se couchent tôt. (They go to bed early.) Je me suis couchée à 9 heures. (I went to bed at 9 o'clock.)

Verb	Pronominal form
Ils couchent ensemble. (They are sleeping together.)	Elle doit se coucher sur le dos. (She has to lie on her back.)
débrouiller (to disentangle; to solve)	**se débrouiller** (to manage)
Il a fini par débrouiller le problème. (He finally solved the problem.)	Elle s'est débrouillée toute seule. (She managed all on her own.)
décider de + inf. (to decide)	**se décider à** + inf. (to make up one's mind)
J'ai décidé de prendre un jour de congé. (I've decided to take a day's leave.)	Je me suis décidé à parler. (I have made up my mind to speak.)
décider + noun (to decide on)	**se décider pour** + noun (to decide on / choose)
Le gouvernement a décidé une politique. (The government has decided on a policy.)	Je me suis décidé pour la Ford. (I have decided on / chosen the Ford.)
demander (to ask; to ask for)	**se demander** (to wonder)
J'ai demandé ce qu'il voulait. (I asked what he wanted.)	Je me suis demandé ce qu'il voulait. (I wondered what he wanted.)
dérouler (to unroll, unwind)	**se dérouler** (to take place; to go, proceed)
On a déroulé le tapis rouge. (They rolled out the red carpet.)	La réunion s'est déroulée sans problème. (The meeting went off without a hitch.)
douter de (to doubt)	**se douter de** (to suspect)
Je doutais de leur sincérité. (I had doubts about their sincerity.)	Je ne me doutais de rien. (I didn't suspect anything.)
échapper à (to escape, avoid)	**s'échapper de** (to escape from, get out of)
Il a échappé à la mort. (He escaped death.)	Il s'est échappé de prison. (He escaped from / got out of prison.)

Verb	Pronominal form
falloir: il faut (it is necessary; it takes)	**tant s'en faut** (far from it) **peu s'en faut** (very nearly)
Il en faut pour qu'elle s'énerve. (It takes a lot for her to get annoyed.)	Tant s'en faut! (Far from it!)
Il faut un peu de patience. (It takes a bit of patience.)	Il s'en est fallu de peu qu'il y arrive. (He very nearly made it.)
fermer (to close) for a habitual action	**se fermer** (to close) for a specific action
Ce magasin ferme en août. (This shop closes in August.)	Le magasin s'est fermé il y a une heure. (The shop closed an hour ago.)
figurer (to appear)	**se figurer** (to imagine)
Ce détail ne figure pas dans le rapport. (That detail does not appear in the report.)	Je me figure la tête qu'il a tirée! (I can imagine the face he pulled!)
passer, v.t. (to pass; to spend time; to cross)	**se passer** (to happen, to go)
Je lui ai passé le vin. (I passed him the wine.)	Tout s'est bien passé. (Everything went well.)
J'ai passé huit jours à Madrid. (I spent a week in Madrid.)	
Ils ont déjà passé la frontière. (They have already crossed the border.)	
passer, v.i. (to go by)	**se passer de** (to go without)
Il est passé nous voir ce matin. (He called by to see us this morning.)	Je me suis passé de sucre pour une fois. (I went without sugar for once.)
permettre (to allow / permit something)	**se permettre** (to afford something)
On se reverra dès que les circonstances le permettront. (We will meet again as soon as circumstances allow.)	Je ne peux pas me permettre ce luxe. (I can't afford this luxury.)

Verb	Pronominal form
permettre à quelqu'un de faire quelque chose (to allow someone to do something) Je leur ai permis de rester (I have allowed them to stay.)	**se permettre de faire quelque chose** (to venture to do something) Je me suis permis de leur dire la vérité. (I ventured to tell them the truth.) Je me permets de vous écrire au sujet de . . . (I am writing to you about . . .)
plaindre (to pity) C'est elle que je plains. (She's the one I pity.)	**se plaindre** (to complain) Je vais me plaindre d'elle. (I'm going to complain about her.)
porter (to carry) Sa voix porte bien. (Her voice carries well.)	**se porter** (to feel, be) Sa mère se porte bien. (Her mother is / is feeling well.)
refuser de (to refuse) Il refuse d'accepter cette solution. (He refuses to accept this solution.)	**se refuser à** (to refuse) Il se refuse à accepter cette solution. (He refuses to accept this solution.) The pronominal form has a stronger force.
rendre (to give back; to hand in) Je leur ai rendu la clef. (I gave the key back to them.) J'ai rendu mes devoirs au professeur. (I handed in my homework to the teacher.)	**se rendre** (to surrender; to go to) Cette armée ne se rendra jamais. (This army will never surrender.) Je me rends à Londres en avion. (I go to London by plane.)
rendre + adj. (to make) Ces moules m'ont rendu malade. (Those mussels made me ill.) **BE AWARE!** You must never use **faire** in place of **rendre** in such contexts.	**se rendre** + adj. (to make oneself) Il s'est rendu malade en se gavant. (He made himself ill by stuffing himself.)

Verb	Pronominal form
rendre compte de (to give an account of)	**se rendre compte de** (to realise)
Je dois rendre compte de nos délibérations. (I have to give an account of our deliberations.)	Je me suis rendu compte de mon erreur. (I realised my mistake.)
résoudre de (to resolve, decide)	**se résoudre à** (to make up one's mind)
Il a résolu d'attendre. (He decided to wait.)	Il s'est résolu à attendre. (He made up his mind to wait.)
	The pronominal form has a stronger force.
sauver (to save)	**se sauver** (to escape, run away)
Il a sauvé la vie à cet enfant. (He saved this child's life.)	Il s'est sauvé à toute vitesse. (He rushed away.)
sentir (to feel; to smell)	**se sentir** + adj. / adv. (to feel)
Je sens leur impatience. (I can feel their impatience.)	Je me sens fatiguée. (I feel tired.)
Je sens une odeur de brûlé. (I can smell burning.)	Il se sent mieux ce matin. (He feels better this morning.)
Ça sent bon! (That smells good!)	
The meaning of the non-pronominal form, **sentir** + adj., is 'to smell'.	If you want to say 'to feel' + adj. / adv., use the pronominal verb **se sentir**.
Elle s'est mis du parfum et elle sent bon. (She has put on some perfume and she smells nice.)	Elle a mal à la tête et ne se sent pas bien. (She has a headache and doesn't feel well.)
servir de (to serve as)	**se servir de** (to use)
Cette phrase servira d'exemple. (This sentence will serve as an example.)	Je me sers d'un stylo à encre pour écrire. (I use a fountain pen to write.)

Verb	Pronominal form
tromper (to deceive; be unfaithful to)	**se tromper dans / sur / de** (to be mistaken)
Ils ont trompé l'ennemi. (They deceived the enemy.)	Il s'est trompé dans son choix. (He was mistaken in his choice.)
Elle trompe son mari. (She is cheating on her husband.)	Je me suis trompé sur lui. (I made a mistake about him.)
	Elle s'est trompée de numéro. (She got the wrong number.)

3 The pronominal verb **se faire** has already appeared in Chapter 5. Mention should also be made of **se laisser**. When followed by an infinitive, both **se faire** and **se laisser** are known as 'causative expressions', because they express the notion that the subject to some extent causes something to happen to them. This may not always be an entirely deliberate intention, as in the following examples.

Il s'est fait écraser.
(He got himself run over.)

Il s'est laissé avoir.
(He let himself be duped.)

There are some useful idiomatic expressions with **se laisser** to add to your vocabulary.

Elle se laisse aller au désespoir.
(She is giving in to despair.)

Il s'est laissé aller depuis la mort de sa femme.
(He has let himself go since his wife's death.)

On abuse de toi parce que tu te laisses faire.
(People take advantage of you because you are too easy-going.)

Tu ne devrais pas te laisser faire.
(You shouldn't let yourself be pushed around.)

Il s'est laissé convaincre par le vendeur d'acheter le dernier modèle de voiture.
(He let himself be persuaded by the salesman to buy the latest model of car.)

Il s'est laissé pousser les cheveux.
(He let his hair grow.)

In the last example, the direct object is a part of the body. A definite article is used here in French in contrast to the use of a possessive adjective in English. The same applies with **se faire** and indeed with all reflexive verbs, as the following examples will show.

Je me suis fait couper les cheveux.
(I had / got my hair cut.)

Il s'est fait raser la tête.
(He had his head shaved.)

Je me suis lavé les cheveux.
(I washed my hair.)

Pronominal verbs as intransitive

1 In many cases, the distinction between the pronominal form of a verb and the non-pronominal form is grammatical, rather than lexical, as illustrated below. The pronominal form, for example, *s'arrêter* is intransitive (has no direct object), whereas the non-pronominal form *arrêter* is transitive and does have a direct object.

Transitive verb (non-pronominal)	Intransitive verb (pronominal)
Il a amélioré son français. (He has improved his French.)	Son français s'est amélioré. (His French has improved.)
J'ai arrêté la voiture. (I stopped the car.)	La voiture s'est arrêtée. (The car stopped.)
J'ai brisé le vase. (I broke the vase.)	Le vase s'est brisé en miettes. (The vase broke into pieces.)
Il concentre ses efforts là-dessus. (He is concentrating his efforts on that.)	Il se concentre sur le problème. (He is concentrating on the problem.)
Il a étonné son fils. (He surprised his son.)	Son fils s'est étonné. (His son was surprised.)
Elle a habillé son enfant en berger. (She dressed her child as a shepherd.)	Elle s'est habillée pour la soirée. (She got dressed up for the party.)
J'ai séparé les enfants. (I have separated the children.)	Les enfants se sont séparés. (The children separated.)
J'ai tourné la page. (I turned the page.)	Je me suis tournée vers lui. (I turned to him.)

Note that it is impossible to say, for example, **J'ai tourné vers lui* for 'I turned to him'. You must use the pronominal verb *Je me suis tournée vers lui*. Contrast this with: *J'ai tourné les yeux vers lui* (I turned my eyes / I looked towards him).

2 There are many verbs that follow this pattern. One particular group of ***-ir*** verbs is highlighted here, because they will help to make your French more idiomatic. It is, for example, preferable to use *s'enrichir* (to become richer) rather than the literal rendering, *devenir plus riche*.

Transitive verb (non-pronominal)	Intransitive verb (pronominal)
Cette maladie affaiblit mes forces. (This illness is sapping my strength.)	L'euro s'affaiblit face à la livre. (The euro is getting weaker against the pound.)
Ces conquêtes ont agrandi l'Empire. (These conquests extended the Empire.)	Cette ville s'est beaucoup agrandie récemment. (This town has got a lot bigger recently.)
Les frais de scolarité les appauvrissent. (Tuition fees are impoverishing them.)	Au fil des années ils s'appauvrissent. (As the years go by, they are getting poorer.)
Son mariage l'a enrichi. (His marriage made him richer.)	Votre vocabulaire s'est bien enrichi. (Your vocabulary has become much richer.)
Il devrait éclaircir ce point. (He ought to clarify this point.)	Le ciel va bientôt s'éclaircir. (The sky will soon clear / get lighter.)
Ces arbres obscurcissaient la maison. (Those trees were making the house dark.)	Peu à peu le ciel s'obscurcissait. (Gradually the sky was getting darker.)
Elle élargit son vocabulaire. (She is widening her vocabulary.)	Les différences entre eux s'élargissent. (The differences between them are widening.)
Il raccourcit son texte de quelques lignes. (He is shortening his text by a few lines.)	Les jours se raccourcissent en automne. (The days get shorter in autumn.)

In all these cases, the pronominal verb is intransitive and the non-pronominal is transitive.

3 There are usually some exceptions to any general rule and it is worth noting **reculer** and **terminer**, whose ordinary form may be used both transitively and intransitively and is interchangeable with the pronominal form in intransitive constructions.

Transitive / intransitive verb (non-pronominal)	Intransitive verb (pronominal)
J'ai reculé la pendule d'une heure. (Transitive) (I put the clock back an hour.)	No equivalent
J'ai reculé de quelques mètres. (Intransitive) (I moved back a few metres.)	Je me suis reculé de quelques mètres. (I moved back a few metres.)
J'ai terminé ma dissertation. (Transitive) (I have finished my essay.)	No equivalent
La séance termine à minuit. (Intransitive) (The show ends at midnight.)	La séance se termine à minuit. (The show ends at midnight.)

Pronominal verbs to translate an English passive

1 A pronominal verb is often used in French where we would use a passive in English. You have already seen one example, *Cela ne se fait pas* (It is not done / It is not the done thing), in Chapter 5.

2 However, this construction only works if the subject is a thing, not a person, as in the following examples.

La vieille ville se visite à pied.
(The old town can be visited on foot.)

Ce vin se boit frais.
(This wine is drunk chilled.)

Ces pommes se vendent à 5 euros le kilo. Elles se vendent bien.
(These apples are being sold at 5 euros per kilo. They are selling well.)

La ville s'est métamorphosée.
(The town has been completely transformed.)

3 Note that if an agent (introduced by **par**) is expressed, you cannot use this construction. You must use the passive instead.

Paris a été métamorphosé par le baron Haussmann.
(Paris was transformed by Baron Haussmann.)

4 The pronominal verbs **se voir** and **s'entendre** followed by an infinitive offer a useful way of translating an English passive construction like 'she was told that'.

Elle s'est vu / elle s'est entendu dire que l'hôtel était complet.
(She was told that the hotel had no vacancies.)

Note that there is no agreement between the past participle and the preceding object pronoun with **se voir** and **s'entendre**; see **Points to remember** below.

It is impossible to translate such a construction literally into French using a passive.

An utterance such as **elle a été dit que* . . . is unacceptable. To understand why, you need to study the active construction with this verb. In English we tell someone something, but say something to someone. The French construction is always *dire quelque chose à quelqu'un*.

La réceptionniste a dit à la cliente que l'hôtel était complet.
(The receptionist told the client that the hotel had no vacancies.)

In French, it is only the direct object of an active construction that can become the subject of a passive construction, hence a literal translation of 'she was told' is impossible. The simplest and most common solution is to use the indefinite pronoun **on** as the subject of an active construction:

On lui a dit que l'hôtel était complet.
(She was told that the hotel had no vacancies.)

On lui a demandé de partir.
(She was asked to leave.)

However, this solution is not viable if the agent is expressed, hence the usefulness of the construction with **se voir / s'entendre** + infinitive.

Elle s'est vu / elle s'est entendu dire par la réceptionniste que l'hôtel était complet.
(She was told by the receptionist that the hotel had no vacancies.)

5 Other 'double object' verbs in English like 'to give' or 'to show' pose the same problem. In English, we can take an active construction and make either the direct or the indirect object into the subject of a passive. However, in French, it is only the direct object of the active sentence that can become the subject of a passive construction. For example:

Ils m'ont montré la photographie.
(They showed me the photograph = They showed the photograph to me.)

La photographie m'a été montrée. (acceptable utterance)
(The photograph was shown to me.)

* J'ai été montré la photographie. (**unacceptable utterance**)
(I was shown the photograph.)

Since it is only the direct object of *montrer* that can become the subject of a passive construction, the only possible interpretation of *'J'ai été montré'* would be that I myself was shown, like an exhibit, to other people.

The usual solution to this translation problem is to use **on** as the indefinite subject of an active verb.

On m'a montré la photographie.
(I was shown the photograph.)

The construction **se voir / s'entendre** followed by an infinitive is a useful alternative if a specific agent is expressed, as in the example below.

Elle s'est vu offrir des fleurs par ses collègues.
(She was given flowers by her colleagues.)

However, the simplest solution in such a case is to turn the sentence around and make the agent, *ses collègues*, the subject of an active construction in French.

Ses collègues lui ont offert des fleurs.
(Her colleagues gave her flowers.)

6 There are a number of French verbs that take both a direct and an indirect object.

The most common are:

apprendre	quelque chose	à quelqu'un	to teach somebody something
conseiller	"	"	to advise somebody (to do) something
défendre	"	"	to forbid somebody (to do) something
demander	"	"	to ask
dire	"	"	to tell
donner	"	"	to give
enseigner	"	"	to show; to teach
montrer	"	"	to show
offrir	"	"	to offer; to give
pardonner	"	"	to forgive
permettre	"	"	to allow
prêter	"	"	to lend
promettre	"	"	to promise
refuser	"	"	to refuse
vendre	"	"	to sell

Remember the possibility of using **se voir / s'entendre** followed by the infinitive of one of these verbs to translate an English passive. For example:

Il s'est vu / il s'est entendu refuser l'accès du bâtiment.
(He was refused entry to the building.)

State as opposed to action

1 Pronominal verbs like *s'asseoir* (to sit down) sometimes cause problems when there is a need to distinguish between a state and an action.

Action	State
Elle s'asseyait quand il y a eu un coup de feu. (She was in the process of sitting down when there was a gunshot.)	Elle était déjà assise quand il y a eu un coup de feu. (She was already sitting when there was a gunshot.)
Elle s'est assise à côté de lui. (She sat down beside him.)	Elle est assise à côté de lui. (She is sitting beside him.)
Elle s'était assise devant lui. (She had sat down in front of him.)	Elle était assise devant lui. (She was sitting in front of him.)

The crucial thing to note is that if you want to express a state, such as 'she was sitting / seated', you must **not** use a pronominal form. What you need here is the imperfect tense of *être* and the past participle *assis*. If you made the mistake of using the pronominal verb *elle s'asseyait*, you would be expressing an action in the imperfect tense, 'she was in the process of sitting down' or 'she used to sit down' in certain circumstances. If you used the pronominal verb form *elle s'était assise*, you would still be expressing an action, but in the pluperfect tense, 'she had sat down'. In this case, the object pronoun *s'* before the verb makes all the difference between an action and a state. With it you have an action, without it a state.

Mnemonic device
Perhaps the main problem for native English speakers comes from the use of a present participle in English: 'he was sitting'. If you paraphrase this into a past participle of state, 'he was seated', the correct rendering in French becomes more obvious.

2 There are many verbs that work like this in French. They include the following.

Elle était accroupie dans le coin.
(She was crouching in the corner.)

Elle était accoudée à la table.
(She was leaning with her elbows on the table.)

Elle était agenouillée devant l'autel.
(She was kneeling at the altar.)

Elle était allongée sur le lit.
(She was lying down on the bed.)

Elle était blottie contre sa mère.
(She was snuggling up against her mother.)

Elle était pendue à son bras.
(She was clinging onto his arm.)

Points to remember

Before you begin the exercises, remember the following points of grammar.

1 Pronominal verbs are listed in this chapter, as in the dictionary, in the infinitive form, e.g. *s'en aller.* Remember to replace *se / s'* with the appropriate pronoun to match the subject, e.g. *nous nous en sommes allés* (we went away).

2 All pronominal verbs are conjugated with *être* in compound tenses. Note the difference between the non-pronominal form conjugated with *avoir*, and the pronominal form conjugated with *être*, in the following examples.

J'ai rendu ma dissertation.
(I have handed in my essay.)

Je me suis rendue à Paris.
(I went to Paris.)

3 The rules for the agreement of the past participle are summarised below. You will find more detailed information in the reference grammars listed in the bibliography.

a. With lexicalised pronominal verbs, the past participle agrees with the subject. In these cases, the preceding object pronoun has no reflexive or reciprocal meaning; it has nothing to do with the subject doing something to him / herself, for example:

Elle s'est abstenue de tout commentaire.
(She refrained from any comment.)

b. This is very different from true reflexive or reciprocal verbs where the past participle agrees with the reflexive pronoun if it is the direct object, but not if it is the indirect object. Note the difference between the following.

Elles se sont vues.
(They saw one another.)

Elles se sont parlé.
(They spoke to one another.)

c. A complication arises with true reflexive verbs like *se laver* if there is a direct object following the verb. In such cases, the reflexive pronoun becomes an indirect object and the past participle does not agree with it. Contrast the following.

Elle s'est lavée.
(She washed herself.)

Elle s'est lavé les cheveux.
(She washed her hair.)

d. There is no agreement between the past participle and the preceding object pronoun with **se faire** and **se laisser** or with **se voir** and **s'entendre**.

Elle s'est fait arrêter.
(She got herself arrested.)

Elle s'est laissé faire.
(She let herself be pushed around.)

Elle s'est vu décerner le premier prix.
(She was awarded the first prize.)

Elle s'est entendu dire qu'elle avait réussi son permis de conduire.
(She was told that she had passed her driving test.)

4 All moods (indicative, subjunctive and imperative) and all tenses are possible with pronominal, as with non-pronominal, verbs.

5 Be particularly careful with the conjugation of regular ***-ir*** verbs. Remember that in the plural of the present tense and throughout the imperfect tense, an ***-iss-*** infix is required, e.g. *ils s'enrichissent* (they are getting richer) and *il s'enrichissait* (he was getting richer).

Remember also that the third-person singular of the present tense ends in ***-it*** and the past participle ends in ***-i***. Contrast the following.

La ville s'agrandit.
(The town is getting bigger.)

La ville s'est agrandie.
(The town has got bigger.)

Note that in this example, the past participle ends in *-ie*, because it agrees with the feminine subject *la ville*. Don't make the common mistake of using this *-ie* ending for the third-person singular form of the present tense!

Exercises

EXERCISE 1. Complete the following sentences, choosing the verb that best fits the context. There is one sentence where either verb is acceptable. Can you find it?

1 Il avait l'air tellement innocent que personne ne (doutait / se doutait) de ses intentions criminelles.
2 Il ne (rend / se rend) pas compte qu'il est complètement perdu.
3 La température (approche / s'approche) du zéro.
4 Elle (plaint / se plaint) qu'elle a trop de travail.
5 Je dois (rendre / me rendre) à la bibliothèque pour faire des recherches.
6 Ce mystère commence à (éclaircir / s'éclaircir).
7 Le musée (ferme / se ferme) à midi.
8 Il devrait (concentrer / se concentrer) sur ses études s'il ne veut pas rater son bac.
9 Son français (a beaucoup amélioré / s'est beaucoup amélioré) cette année.
10 L'idée de (coucher / se coucher) sous la tente ne me dit rien du tout.
11 Tout (a passé / s'est passé) très vite.
12 Tu vas (rendre / te rendre) malade si tu en manges.
13 Elle (débrouille / se débrouille) bien en français.
14 Personne (n'échappe à / ne s'échappe de) ses commentaires moqueurs.
15 Je ne sais pas ce qu'il prépare pour ce soir, mais ça (sent / se sent) bon.
16 Il (a laissé / s'est laissé) pousser les moustaches.
17 Il (a reculé / s'est reculé) de quelques pas pour mieux contempler la façade de la cathédrale.
18 Les yeux de l'enfant (ont agrandi / se sont agrandis) à la vue de tant de sucreries.
19 J'espère qu' ils (n'ont pas aperçu / ne se sont pas aperçus de) mon erreur.
20 Je (demande / me demande) s'ils vont jamais (décider de / se décider à) mettre la maison en vente. Cela fait deux ans qu'ils en parlent.

EXERCISE 2. Rewrite the following sentences using a pronominal verb. The examples below illustrate the two possible techniques. Choose whichever is appropriate in each case.

On lui a demandé de partir.
► Elle s'est vu / entendu demander de partir.

On ne dit pas cela.
► Cela ne se dit pas.

1 On m'a proposé un poste intéressant.
2 On classe les livres par auteur.
3 On range les assiettes dans le buffet de cuisine.
4 On m'a dit que le directeur était en réunion.
5 On vend ce produit uniquement en pharmacie.
6 On mange ce jambon cru.
7 On n'a jamais vu ça!
8 On leur a répondu qu'il ne restait plus de places.

EXERCISE 3. Rewrite the following sentences using **se faire** or **se laisser**, as shown in the example below.

L'homme politique a été bousculé par les manifestants.
► L'homme politique s'est fait bousculer par les manifestants.

1 Le chanteur a été hué par le public.
2 J'ai été persuadée de louer l'appartement.
3 Notre équipe a été battue par 3 à zéro.
4 Le professeur a été harcelé de questions.
5 Il a été trompé par sa femme.
6 J'ai peur d'être attaqué par surprise.
7 Les voleurs ont été arrêtés par les policiers.
8 Vous risquez d'être pris dans une bagarre.
9 Tu as été eu par cet escroc.
10 J'ai été interpellé par un chahuteur.

EXERCISE 4. Complete the following sentences by choosing the most appropriate verb.

1 (Tiens / Tiens-toi) tranquille et (arrête / arrête-toi) tes bêtises.
2 Elle (a écarté / s'est écarté) les bras pour l'étreindre.
3 Tu (as trompé / t'es trompé). Son nom (écrit / s'écrit) avec deux 'b'.
4 Il (intéresse / s'intéresse) à tous les sports.
5 Elle (a effondré / s'est effondrée) en larmes.
6 Dès qu'elle l'a vu, elle (est assise / s'est assise) à côté de lui.
7 Il (mêle / se mêle) toujours de ce qui ne le regarde pas.
8 Cette phrase ne (figure / se figure) plus dans le contrat.
9 Je ne sais pas comment les événements vont (dérouler / se dérouler).
10 J'ai du mal à le comprendre maintenant; sa voix (a beaucoup affaibli / s'est beaucoup affaiblie).
11 Elle (a cassé / s'est cassé) la jambe.

12 Qui paie ses dettes (enrichit / s'enrichit).
13 On ne peut pas nier que ce sont des arguments qui (portent / se portent).
14 Il (a tourné / s'est tourné) les yeux vers elle.
15 Elle (s'asseyait / était assise) à tricoter.
16 En rentrant, il (est allongé / s'est allongé) sur son lit.
17 Le chien (a vite habitué / s'est vite habitué) à (coucher / se coucher) dehors.
18 Ce jeune couple a décidé de (séparer / se séparer) après six mois de mariage.
19 Ces exercices devraient (servir / se servir) d'entraînement.
20 Je (sens / me sens) peu disposé à les aider.

EXERCISE 5. Fill the gaps in the following sentences by choosing one of the options given in brackets.

1 Elle s'est décidée (à / pour) la Citroën.
2 Je ne peux pas me résoudre (à / de) le renvoyer.
3 Je me permets (à / de) vous écrire pour vous demander un conseil.
4 On peut très bien se passer (de / sans) voiture.
5 Nous nous refusons (à / de) faire ce qu'il exige.
6 Il s'est trompé (dans / de / sur) leurs intentions.
7 Elle s'est trompée (dans / de / sur) son choix.
8 Il n'échappe pas (à / de) l'influence de son père.
9 Je vais m'attaquer (à / blank) cette tâche ce soir.
10 On ne s'est aperçu (de / blank) rien.

EXERCISE 6. In each but two of the following sentences, there is a single mistake, either with the form of the verb or with the ending of the past participle. Make the necessary corrections and identify the two sentences that are completely correct.

1 La livre s'affaiblie face au dollar.
2 La ville s'est agrandie considérablement ces dernières années.
3 Elle s'est lavée les mains.
4 Ils se sont écrits de longues lettres.
5 Les doubles fenêtres affaiblient le bruit de la rue.
6 Ils se sont faits avoir par cet escroc.
7 Ils se sont abstenus de fumer.
8 Les feuillages obscurçaient le jardin.
9 Ils se sont rencontré hier.
10 Elle s'est entendue dire qu'elle avait raté l'examen.

EXERCISE 7. Fill in the blanks using pronominal verbs wherever possible, but watch out for the four cases where non-pronominal forms are needed.

Même de nos jours, les femmes ne sont pas toujours traitées en égales – (1) ____________ (far from it)! Néanmoins la vie de la femme moyenne (2) ______________ (has been completely transformed) depuis les deux guerres mondiales. Pendant les deux guerres les femmes ont dû (3) ____________ (to take on) responsabilités qui jusque-là avaient été réservées aux hommes et elles (4)________________ (managed very well). Il était évident dans les années cinquante que quand une femme exerçait une activité rémunérée elle (5)______________ (enriched) toute la famille. Grâce à elle la famille pouvait (6) ______________ (afford) d'acheter des biens de consommation et leur niveau de vie (7) ____________ (improved). Toutefois la femme risquait de (8) ___________ (getting tired) en menant de front son travail à l'extérieur et l'entretien de la maison. Si une femme voulait (9) ___________ (to feel) moins impuissante, (10) ___________ (it was necessary) qu'elle ait accès à l'éducation et aux professions. Elle pourrait donc (11) ______________ (escape / avoid the) danger de (12) ________ (being) coincée dans un travail qui ne lui permettait pas d' (13) ________________ (to widen) ses horizons. De nos jours il n'est plus question pour une femme de (14) ____________ (to go without) une vie de famille pour pouvoir (15) ___________ (to concentrate) sur sa carrière. Les deux choses peuvent (16) ___________ (be reconciled) pourvu qu'on (17) _____________ (makes up one's mind) ne pas (18) _______________ (to be pushed around) au travail. C'est en (19)____________ (respecting oneself) qu'on (20)_________________ (commands respect).

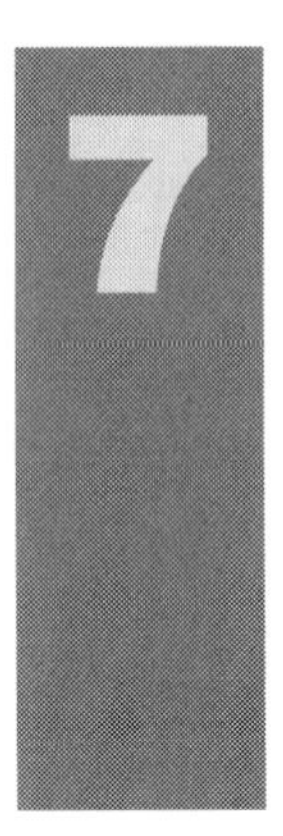

7 Problem pairs and other misused expressions

This chapter illustrates the differences between pairs and groups of words that non-native speakers of French sometimes find difficult to remember. It also highlights some French expressions that have more than one meaning and discusses common expressions that are sometimes misused by learners of French.

Problem verbs

Savoir and *connaître* (to know)

These verbs cannot normally be used interchangeably. Their particular meanings are illustrated below.

1 **Savoir** means 'to know a fact or a reason', 'to have a good command of a discipline', e.g. a language, or 'to know / be aware that . . . '

Savez-vous l'indicatif téléphonique de Bruxelles?
(Do you know the dialling code for Brussels?)

Je sais pourquoi elle est toujours en retard.
(I know why she is always late.)

Il sait bien le japonais.
(He has a good knowledge of Japanese.)

Nous savions qu'elle cachait la vérité.
(We knew / were aware that she was hiding the truth.)

BEWARE! Note that if you want to say 'to know that . . . ' you can only use **savoir**.

2 **Savoir de** means 'to have information about something or someone'.

Savoir sur is also used for 'to have information about someone'.

Je ne sais rien de leurs origines. Elle en sait plus que moi.
(I don't know anything about their background. She knows more than I do.)

Ils ne savent rien de / sur moi.
(They don't know anything about me.)

3 Followed by an infinitive, **savoir** means 'to know how to' or 'to be able to do something'.

In the following examples, where 'know how' or skill is involved, it would be incorrect to use **pouvoir**.

Savez-vous conduire?
(Can you drive?)

Il ne sait pas nager.
(He can't swim.)

Ce professeur sait bien expliquer.
(This teacher is very good at explaining things.)

Note the contrast between the use of **savoir** (to know how to) and **pouvoir** (to be able / unable to do something in particular circumstances) in the following sentence.

Je sais jouer du piano, mais je ne peux pas jouer aujourd'hui, parce que je me suis foulé le poignet.
(I can play the piano, but I cannot play today, because I have sprained my wrist.)

4 Note the use of the following tenses of **savoir**.

a. The imperfect refers to an ongoing state, while the *passé composé* or past historic refers to a punctual action. The former means 'knew / was aware' or 'was able to', whereas the latter means 'to find something out' or 'to manage to do something' at a particular point in time.

Elle savait déjà que le musée était fermé.
(She already knew that the museum was closed.)

Quand as-tu su que le musée était fermé?
(When did you find out that the museum was closed?)

Elle savait enjôler les clients.
(She was able / knew how to charm clients.)

Elle sut si bien enjôler ce client qu'il finit par signer le contrat.
(She managed to charm this client into signing the contract.)

b. The conditional can be used as an alternative to **pouvoir** in negative constructions formed with *ne* alone.

Je ne saurais vous dire comment cela s'est passé.
(I really can't tell you how it happened.)

Il ne saurait être question de divulguer l'identité de notre informateur.
(There can be no question of divulging the identity of our informer.)

5 Useful expressions with **savoir**

Est-ce que je sais, moi! (How should I know?)

je ne sais quel . . . (some . . . or other)

Ils sont allés voir je ne sais quel film.
(They've gone to see some film or other.)

je ne sais qui (somebody or other)

Ils ont fait appel à je ne sais qui.

(They called somebody or other.)

que je sache / pour autant que je sache . . . (as far as I know . . .)

Ils doivent partir demain pour autant que je sache.
(They are due to leave tomorrow as far as I know.)

à savoir (that is to say, namely)

La réunion aura lieu dans huit jours, à savoir le 20 avril.
(The meeting will take place in a week, that is to say on 20th April.)

faire savoir (see Chapter 5) (to let know, to tell)

6 **Connaître** means 'to be familiar / acquainted with' people, places, works of art, literature, etc.

Je connais leurs parents.
(I know their parents.)

Il connaît bien ce coin de France.
(He knows this part of France well.)

Je connais tous les romans de Flaubert.
(I know all of Flaubert's novels.)

7 **Connaître** also means 'to know' in the sense of 'to experience' or 'to feel'.

Il ne connaît pas la honte.
(He knows no shame.)

Elle connaît des hauts et des bas.
(She has / experiences her ups and downs.)

Elle a connu la pauvreté.
(She has known / experienced poverty.)

8 The imperfect tense of **connaître** refers to an ongoing state, while the *passé composé* or past historic refers to a punctual action. The former means 'knew', whereas the latter means 'met' someone for the first time.

Elle connaissait sa femme de vue.
(She knew his wife by sight.)

Elle a connu sa femme il y a deux ans.
(She met his wife two years ago.)

9 Useful expressions with **connaître**

On connaît la chanson / la musique!	We've heard it all before! It's the same old story!
s'y connaître en	to know all about, to be an expert in

Il s'y connaît en cinéma d'art et d'essai.
(He knows all about arthouse cinema.)

être connu	to be well known

Cette actrice est très connue en France.
(This actress is very well known in France.)

Partir, sortir, s'en aller, laisser, oublier and *quitter* (to leave)

All these verbs can mean 'to leave', but they are not normally interchangeable. Their particular meanings are illustrated below.

1 **Partir** means 'to leave', 'to go away' or 'to depart'.

Mnemonic device
Remember the meaning by thinking of **partir** = depart.

Ils sont partis il y a une heure.
(They left / went away an hour ago.)

Le train à destination de Lille va partir.
(The train for Lille is about to leave / depart.)

Notre train part de Paris à midi.
(Our train leaves Paris at midday.)

Partir cannot take a direct object. If you want to say 'to leave' + a place, use **partir + de**, as in the sentence above.

2 **Sortir** means 'to leave', 'to go out' or 'to come out'.

Mnemonic device
Remember the meaning by thinking of the noun **sortie** (way out).

Elle est sortie de la pièce sans rien dire.
(She left the room without saying anything.)

Elle est sortie faire des courses.
(She has gone out shopping.)

Elle est enfin sortie de sa chambre.
(She finally came out of her bedroom.)

Sortir can also mean 'to go out with someone'.

Elle sort avec le fils de leurs voisins.
(She is going out with their neighbours' son.)

Sortir can be used with a direct object, but only when it means 'to take out', 'to bring out' or 'to put out'.

Je vais sortir la poubelle.
(I am going to put the bin out.)

If you want to say 'to leave' a place, use **sortir + de**.

Ils sont sortis du restaurant il y a une demi-heure.
(They left the restaurant half an hour ago.)

3 **S'en aller** means 'to leave' or 'to go away'. See also Chapter 5.

Il faut que je m'en aille.
(I must leave.)

4 **Laisser** means 'to leave' a person or a thing.

J'ai laissé les clés au gardien.
(I left the keys with the caretaker.)

J'ai laissé les enfants chez ma mère.
(I've left the children at my mother's.)

If you accidentally leave something behind, you can use **oublier** (to leave, to forget).

J'ai oublié mon parapluie au bureau.
(I've left my umbrella behind at the office.)

5 **Quitter** means 'to leave' a place or a person. It can mean leaving something or someone for good.

> **Mnemonic device**
> Remember the meaning by thinking of **quitter** = to quit.

Je quitte la maison à 7 heures et demie.
(I leave the house at 7.30 a.m.)

Il a quitté l'école à 16 ans.
(He left school at 16.)

Elle a quitté l'enseignement.
(She has left teaching.)

Elle a quitté son mari l'année dernière.
(She left her husband last year.)

Habiter and *vivre* (to live)

1 **Habiter** means 'to live' or 'to dwell', and is used with names of places.

Ils habitent à Londres. Leur fils habite en France.
(They live in London. Their son lives in France.)

Habiter can be used without a preposition.

Ils habitent Londres. Leur fils habite la France.
(They live in London. Their son lives in France.)

Ils habitent cet appartement / cette maison / ce village depuis dix ans.
(They have lived in this flat / house / village for ten years.)

2 **Vivre** means 'to live', 'to be alive' or 'to live through something'.

Ils vivent dans le luxe.
(They live a life of luxury.)

Leur grand-mère vit toujours.
(Their grandmother is still alive.)

Comment a-t-il vécu le divorce?
(How did he live through / cope with the divorce?)

***Revenir*, *retourner* and *rentrer* (to return)**

1 **Revenir** means 'to come back' or 'to return'.

> **Mnemonic device**
> **Revenir** is a compound of **venir** (to come), so it means 'to come back'.

Le médecin est venu hier et il a dit qu'il reviendrait demain.
(The doctor came yesterday and he said he would come back tomorrow.)

Sa femme lui est revenue.
(His wife came back / returned to him.)

Note the idiomatic expressions:

Ça me revient!
(Now it's coming back to me! / Now I remember!)

Ça m'est revenu tout à coup!
(It came back to me all of a sudden!)

2 **Retourner** means 'to go back' or 'to return'.

Nos invités sont retournés en Espagne.
(Our guests have gone back / returned to Spain.)

3 **Rentrer** means 'to get back', 'to go back', 'to return' or 'to go home'. Remember that it is a compound of **entrer** (to go inside), and it can mean 'to go back inside' or 'to go home'.

Il est rentré hier de son voyage d'affaires.
(He got back yesterday from his business trip.)

Les enfants rentrent en classe demain.
(The children go back to school tomorrow.)

Il est minuit. Je dois rentrer.
(It's midnight. I must go home.)

Demander, poser une question and *inviter* (to ask)

1 The usual word for 'to ask' is **demander.**

J'aimerais te demander quelque chose.
(I'd like to ask you something.)

On m'a demandé d'attendre.
(I was asked to wait.)

2 However, for 'to ask a question', **demander** will not do. You need to use **poser une question**.

J'aimerais te poser une question.
(I would like to ask you a question.)

Je me suis posé la même question.
(I asked myself the same question.)

3 If 'ask' means 'invite', use **inviter**.

J'ai invité nos voisins à dîner.
(I've asked / invited our neighbours to dinner.)

Il l'a invitée à sortir au cinéma.
(He has asked her out to the cinema.)

Exercises

EXERCISE 1. Complete the following sentences by choosing the verbs that best fit the context.

1 Il prétend tout (connaître / savoir), mais en réalité il ne (connaît / sait) rien d'eux.
2 Quand (saviez-vous / avez-vous su) qu'ils se sont séparés?
3 Elle sort avec (je ne connais / je ne sais) quel cinéaste. Pour autant que je (connaisse / sache) elle (le connaissait / l'a connu) à la faculté.
4 Combien de langues (connaissez-vous / savez-vous)? Moi, je (peux / sais) parler français et espagnol.
5 D'habitude il a du mal à se faire comprendre en français, mais cette fois la réceptionniste à l'hôtel (savait / a su) le comprendre et tout s'est bien passé.
6 Il n'a jamais (connu / su) un tel échec et il ne (connaît / sait) pas ce qu'il va dire à ses parents.
7 On (connaît / sait) la chanson! Il se laisse faire tout le temps, parce qu'il ne (peut / sait) pas dire non.

8 En principe (je m'y connais / j'en sais) en littérature, mais je ne (sais / saurais) vous expliquer cette allusion.
9 Vous y trouverez trois bâtiments intéressants, à (connaître / savoir) une église médiévale, un château et un hospice.
10 Ce musicien est mieux (connu / su) en Europe qu'aux États-Unis.
11 Elle est (partie / sortie) à New York pour ne plus jamais (rentrer / revenir).
12 Il est (parti / sorti) du restaurant pour fumer. Il (retournera / reviendra) nous rejoindre dans quelques minutes.
13 Il a (laissé / quitté) le monde des affaires pour (rentrer / retourner) à l'université.
14 Il est mort à l'âge de trente-cinq ans, (laissant / quittant) une veuve et deux enfants.
15 Je dois (rentrer / revenir) chez moi. J'ai (oublié / quitté) le dossier dans le salon.
16 Ils (habitent / vivent) dans la pauvreté, mais ils ne veulent pas (laisser / quitter) le pays pour chercher fortune ailleurs.
17 J'ai (laissé / sorti) la poubelle ce matin avant de (partir / sortir) au travail.
18 Il est (parti / sorti) travailler en Amérique. Je ne (connais / sais) pas comment ses parents qui (habitent / vivent) Paris ont (connu / vécu) cette séparation.
19 Elle nous a (demandé / posé) une question difficile. Moi, je ne (connaissais / savais) pas quoi dire, mais mon mari (a connu / a su) trouver une réponse.
20 Ils se contentent de très peu et (habitent / vivent) sans se (demander / poser) de questions.

Problem nouns

If you want to talk about time in French, there are several words to choose between, each with its own particular range of meaning.

La fois, le moment, le temps, l'heure, l'époque, le délai (time)

1 **La fois** is used for 'occasion'.

On se voit deux ou trois fois par mois.
(We see one another two or three times a month.)

C'est la dernière fois que je te le dis.
(It's the last time that I'm telling you.)

Je me souviens si bien de la fois où on s'est perdu dans la forêt.
(I remember so well the time we got lost in the forest.)

Ne parlez pas tous à la fois!
(Don't all speak at once / at the same time!)

Je leur ai demandé encore une fois de baisser le volume.
(I asked them once again to turn down the volume.)

2 **Le moment** is used to refer to 'a specific point in time'.

En ce moment je ne saurais vous le dire.
(At the moment / Just now I can't tell you.)

À ce moment-là on a sonné à la porte.
(At that moment there was a ring at the door.)

Il est arrivé au bon moment pour me dépanner.
(He arrived at just the right time to help me out.)

3 **Le temps** is used for time as a general phenomenon, for a length of time and for a particular moment in time.

Le temps passe vite.
(Time flies.)

Je n'ai pas le temps de lire tous ces documents.
(I don't have time to read all these papers.)

Elle est arrivée juste à temps.
(She arrived just in time.)

Il est arrivé en même temps qu'elle.
(He arrived at the same time as she did.)

It is also used to refer to a period of time, often in the past.

Au / Du temps des Romains, les bains publics jouaient un rôle important dans la vie sociale.
(In the time of the Romans, bathhouses played an important part in social life.)

C'était au / du temps où il était directeur.
(It was at the time when he was manager.)

Dans le temps nous n'avions pas de voiture.
(In those days we didn't have a car.)

En temps de guerre tout est différent.
(In wartime everything is different.)

4 **L'heure** (f.) is used for time relating to the clock.

Quelle heure est-il?
(What time is it?)

J'ai noté l'heure de mon rendez-vous chez le dentiste.
(I've made a note of the time of my dental appointment.)

Vous trouverez les heures d'ouverture de la bibliothèque sur le site web.
(You will find the opening times of the library on the web site.)

Le train est arrivé à l'heure.
(The train arrived on time.)

It is also used to refer to a period of time.

À l'heure actuelle nous n'avons pas les moyens de voyager.
(At the present time we don't have the means to travel.)

Nous vivons à l'heure des satellites.
(We live in the satellite era / age.)

5 **L'époque** (f.) is used for a period of time.

Je me souviens de l'époque où il était complètement inconnu.
(I remember the time when he was completely unknown.)

L'Académie française a été fondée à l'époque de Louis XIV.
(The French Academy was founded in the time of Louis XIV.)

Un Chien andalou est un film de l'époque surréaliste.
(*Un Chien andalou* is a film from the surrealist period.)

6 **Le délai** is used for 'a period of time allowed for doing something'. It can also mean 'a deadline' or 'an extension of the original time limit'. See Chapter 3.

Il a écrit l'article dans le délai prescrit.
(He wrote the article within the allotted time.)

L'étudiant a obtenu un délai pour rendre son mémoire.
(The student got extra time / an extension for handing in her dissertation.)

An, année (year) and related words

There are two words in French, **un an** and **une année**, for 'year', and it is important to distinguish between them.

1 As a general rule, the masculine word is used after cardinal numbers and the feminine word after ordinal numbers and indefinites.

Ils ont passé deux ans en France.
(They spent two years in France.)

Elle est en troisième année.
(She is in third year.)

Dans quelques années il prendra sa retraite.
(In a few years he will retire.)

However, you will find exceptions, such as the following.

Ils ont eu trois années difficiles au début de leur mariage.
(They had three difficult years at the beginning of their marriage.)

Ces deux dernières années elle a beaucoup vieilli.
(In the last two years she has aged a lot.)

The use of **année** in the examples above emphasises the length of time or the events that have taken place within it.

2 More generally, an emphasis on the length of time or the events that have taken place within it determines the use of **une journée** rather than **un jour** for 'day', **une matinée** rather than **un matin** for 'morning' and **une soirée** rather than **un soir** for 'evening'.

Il a travaillé pendant toute la journée / matinée / soirée.
(He worked all day / morning / evening.)

Mnemonic device
In order to remember this point, bear in mind the following well-known expressions. The masculine word is used as a greeting; the feminine word is used to emphasise the whole duration of the day or evening and to wish someone a pleasant time throughout it.

Bonjour. (Good morning, hello.)	Bonne journée. (Have a nice day.)
Bonsoir. (Good evening.)	Bonne soirée. (Have a good evening / night out.)

3 It has to be said, however, that often the use of the masculine or feminine word is purely a matter of convention, as in the following set phrases.

en début de journée / matinée / soirée	at the beginning of the day / morning / evening
en fin de journée / matinée / soirée	at the end of the day / morning / evening
les années 80	the eighties
l'année scolaire / universitaire	the school / academic year

Le parti, la partie and *la part*

The three words **le parti, la partie** and **la part** look similar, but you need to choose carefully between them according to meaning.

1 **Le parti** means a 'political party'. It can also mean an 'option' or 'side', and a 'match' (in marriage).

Il a la carte du Parti socialiste.
(He is a card-carrying member of the Socialist Party.)

J'hésite entre deux partis.
(I'm hesitating between two options.)

Le professeur a pris parti pour les étudiants.
(The teacher took the side of the students.)

C'est un beau parti.
(He is an eligible bachelor.)

2 **La partie** means 'part' of a whole. It is also used for a game of sport.

Nous avons étudié la première partie du livre en classe.
(We studied the first part of the book in class.)

La majeure partie des gens se méfient des hommes politiques.
(Most people do not trust politicians.)

Nous allons faire une partie de tennis.
(We're going to have a game of tennis.)

Note the expression **faire partie de** (to be a part of).

Elle fait partie de la famille.
(She is part of / one of the family.)

3 **La part** means 'portion', 'part' or 'share'.

J'ai coupé le gâteau en huit parts égales.
(I cut the cake into eight equal portions.)

Cette somme représente une grande part de mon revenu.
(This sum represents a large part of my income.)

Il fait sa part de ménage.
(He does his share of the housework.)

La part also means 'side' and is used in several set phrases.

Il s'est fait attaquer de toutes parts.
(He was attacked from all sides.)

Il y a un esprit de compromis de part et d'autre.
(There is a spirit of compromise on both sides.)

Pour ma part, je n'y vois pas d'inconvénient.
(For my part, I have no objection.)

D'une part je perds courage, d'autre part je veux mener ce projet à bien.
(On the one hand I am losing heart, on the other I want to see this project through.)

Occupations

Some names for occupations can be a source of confusion.

1 **Un / une photographe** is a photographer.
Une photographie is a photograph.

2 Some nouns referring to occupation end in a similar way to their English equivalents. However, there are some notable exceptions, so it is always a good idea to check in the dictionary.

For example, the French for an archaeologist, a geologist and a sociologist is **un / une archéologue**, **un / une géologue** and **un / une sociologue.** The forms *archéologiste, *géologiste and *sociologiste do not exist.

Note also that the French for a physicist is **un physicien** (see Chapter 3). The form *physiciste does not exist.

However, sometimes there are two options in French, for example an anthropologist is either **un / une anthropologiste** or **un / une anthropologue**.

3 The most common problem has already been mentioned in Chapter 3. The French word for a scientist is **un / une scientifique**. Although **un / une scientiste** does exist, it is a false friend. It means a follower of scientism.

Exercises

EXERCISE 2. Choose the most appropriate noun or expression to fill the blanks.

1 La Norvège ne fait pas (parti / partie) de l'Union Européenne.
2 Nous avons attendu jusqu'au dernier (moment / temps), mais elle n'a pas téléphoné. Ce n'est pas (le premier temps / la première fois) qu'elle nous a fait tourner en bourrique.
3 (À ce moment / En ce moment) cette étudiante est très assidue, mais (à l'heure / dans le temps) elle ne respectait jamais les (délais / heures).
4 Nous sommes arrivés à Paris en début de (matin / matinée) de sorte que nous avons eu (le moment / le temps) de visiter le Louvre avant de déjeuner.
5 (À l'heure actuelle / Au temps actuel) il fait ses études ici en Écosse, mais à la fin de (l'an / l'année) universitaire il retournera en France.
6 J'ai passé (tout le jour / toute la journée) à réviser le texte de mon article. Enfin j'ai décidé de rayer toute la première (part / partie) et de rédiger une nouvelle entrée en matière.
7 Les (partis / parties) de l'opposition s'attaquent au ministre. Ce dernier, se voyant assailli (de toutes parts / de toutes parties), ne sait plus où donner de la tête.
8 Elle est arrivée à l'aéroport juste (à la fois / à temps) pour s'enregistrer.
9 Nous étudions le mouvement des suffragettes dans les (ans / années) vingt. À cette (époque / heure) les femmes étaient prêtes à se battre pour la cause.
10 Elle se plaint de son co-locataire parce qu'il ne fait jamais sa (part / partie) de ménage.
11 Cette église date (de l'époque victorienne / du temps victorien).
12 Est-ce que tu veux une (part / partie) du gâteau?
13 Son père est (scientifique / scientiste) tandis que sa mère est (sociologiste / sociologue).
14 En nous voyant à l'entrée du cinéma il nous a souhaité (Bonsoir / une bonne soirée).
15 D'une (part / partie) je comprends leur refus de participer (au soir / à la soirée), d'autre (part / partie) je pense qu'ils devraient se montrer plus obligeants.

Meilleur and *mieux*; *y* and *en*

1 Sometimes students find it difficult to choose between the adjective **meilleur** (better / best) and the adverb **mieux** (better / best).

As a general rule, it is easier to distinguish between the adjective **bon** and the adverb **bien**, probably because a distinction is made in English between the adjective 'good' and the adverb 'well'. Unfortunately, **meilleur** and **mieux** both translate into English as 'better' or 'best'.

If you are hesitating between the adjective **meilleur** and the adverb **mieux**, ask yourself whether you would have used the adjective **bon** or the adverb **bien** in the same context. The examples below illustrate the point.

C'est un bon écrivain. C'est un meilleur écrivain que son frère. C'est le meilleur écrivain du groupe.
(He is a good writer. He is a better writer than his brother. He is the best writer in the group.)

Elle chante bien. Elle chante mieux que sa sœur.
(She sings well. She sings better than her sister.)

Ça sent bon. Ça sent meilleur.
(That smells good. That smells better.)

Je me sens bien. Je me sens mieux. Je me sens le mieux du monde.
(I feel well. I feel better. I feel the best in the world = absolutely fine.)

See Chapter 6 for the use of **sentir bon** (to smell good) and **se sentir bien** (to feel well).

Cet immeuble est bien conçu. Cet immeuble est mieux conçu que le nôtre. Cet immeuble est le mieux conçu de tous.
(This building is well designed. This building is better designed than ours. This building is the best designed of all.)

Note the following phrases.

garder le meilleur pour la fin	to keep the best bit until the end
pour le meilleur et pour le pire	for better or for worse
aller de mieux en mieux	to be getting stronger / better all the time
de mieux en mieux!	that's absolutely great! (ironic)
à qui mieux mieux	each one more than the other

Ils criaient à qui mieux mieux.
(They were all shouting, each one louder than the other.)

j'aime mieux + infinitive	I would rather
changer en mieux	to change for the better
faire de son mieux	to do one's best
Tout est pour le mieux (dans le meilleur des mondes)	All is for the best (in the best of all possible worlds)

2 You may sometimes find it difficult to choose between the pronouns **y** and **en**.

Mnemonic device
Remember that **y** replaces **à**, **dans**, **en**, **sur** + noun, or **à** + infinitive.
En replaces **de** + noun or infinitive.

Elle est partie en France. (She has gone off to France.)	Elle y est partie. (She has gone off there.)
Je pense aux vacances. (I'm thinking about the holidays.)	J'y pense. (I'm thinking about them.)
Je pense à partir. (I'm thinking about / of leaving.)	J'y pense. (I'm thinking about it.)
Que pensez-vous de leur appartement? (What do you think of their flat?)	Qu'en pensez-vous? (What do you think of it?)
Elle a peur de voyager en avion. (She is afraid of flying.)	Elle en a peur. (She is afraid of it.)

See Chapter 8 for the use of **penser à** and **penser de**.

Exercises

EXERCISE 3a. Complete the sentences by filling in the blanks with **meilleur** or **mieux** as appropriate.

1 Elle n'est pas tout à fait guérie, mais elle va de ______ en ______.
2 Je n'ai jamais bu de ________ vin.
3 Je me suis approché de la fenêtre pour _______ voir ce qui se passait.
4 Ils se sont mariés pour le ________ et pour le pire.
5 Ils proféraient des injures à qui ________ ________.
6 Elle est _______ payée que son mari, et on a une _______ opinion d'elle.

7 Tu ne vas pas me dire que la voiture est tombée en panne. De ______ en _____ !

8 J'ai fait de mon ________ pour leur préparer un _______ dîner que l'autre soir.

9 Il est vrai qu'elle a changé en _______.

10 Je trouve ce film bien ________ que le roman dont il est tiré.

EXERCISE 3b. Complete the sentences by filling in the blanks with **y** or **en** as appropriate.

1 Je n'ai pas encore commencé ma dissertation, mais je vais m'_____ mettre demain.

2 Cela fait des années que je n'ai pas vu ce film, mais je m'___ souviens très bien.

3 Qu'est-ce que tu penses de la situation? Moi, je n'__ pense rien du tout.

4 Tant que j'___ pense, je te rappelle que c'est l'anniversaire de grand-papa demain.

5 Essaie de trouver le temps de lui parler. Il ____ a bien besoin.

6 Il vient d'acheter une nouvelle voiture et il _____ est ravi.

7 On m'a demandé d'aller le chercher à la gare, mais je n'____ ai pas le temps.

8 Il aime beaucoup la musique, mais elle ne s'___ intéresse pas du tout.

9 Si vous avez le temps d'__ jeter un coup d'œil, je vous ____ serais reconnaissant.

10 Je lui ai demandé si elle voulait aller au cinéma, mais elle n'___ avait pas envie.

Common expressions with more than one meaning

1 The verb **arriver** can mean 'to arrive', 'to reach', 'to manage to' or 'to happen'.

Ils sont arrivés en retard.
(They arrived late.)

Ils sont arrivés à un accord.
(They reached an agreement.)

Ils sont arrivés à trouver l'adresse.
(They managed to find the address.)

On ne sait jamais ce qui peut arriver.
(You never know what may happen.)

Il n'arrive jamais rien ici.
(Nothing ever happens here.)

On se reverra quoi qu'il arrive.
(We'll meet again whatever happens.)

Note the crucial difference in meaning between the following.

Qui est-ce qui est arrivé?
(**Who** has arrived?)

Qu'est-ce qui est arrivé?
(**What** has happened?)

2 The verb **attendre** can mean 'to wait', 'to wait for' or 'to expect'.

Nous attendons les enfants.
(We are waiting for the children.)

Sa jeune femme attend un enfant.
(His young wife is expecting a child.)

J'attendais mieux de ce nouveau traitement.
(I was expecting more of this new treatment.)

On attendait mieux d'elle.
(They were expecting more of her.)

Note also the pronominal verb **s'attendre à**, meaning 'to expect'.

Je m'attendais à les voir hier.
(I was expecting to see them yesterday.)

Je m'attends à ce qu'ils partent demain.
(I'm expecting them to leave tomorrow.)

Note that if the subject is the same in both halves of the sentence, as in the first example above, an infinitive is used after **s'attendre à**. However, if there is a change of subject, as in the second example, you need to use **à ce que** + subjunctive.

3 The adverbs **ici** and **là** can refer to place, meaning 'here' and 'there' respectively, but they can also refer to time, meaning 'now' and 'then', as illustrated in the examples below.

Jusqu'ici je n'ai pas eu le temps de penser aux vacances.
(Until now I haven't had time to think about the holidays.)

On en parlera d'ici peu.
(We'll speak about it in a little while from now = shortly.)

Je reviendrai te voir demain. D'ici là, repose-toi bien.
(I'll come back to see you tomorrow. Between now and then = meanwhile, have a good rest.)

Il sera de retour d'ici trois jours.
(He'll be back three days from now.)

D'ici à ce qu'elle change d'avis, il n'y a pas loin.
(It won't be long before she changes her mind.)

Et là tout à coup j'ai entendu un cri.
(And then, all of a sudden, I heard a scream.)

À quelque temps de là j'ai entendu un bruit de pas.
(Some time later I heard footsteps.)

D'ici là on a le temps de décider.
(Between now and then we have time to decide.)

Il faut que j'en parle à mes parents; jusque-là je ne peux pas accepter.
(I need to talk to my parents about it; until then / in the meantime I can't accept.)

4 The relative pronoun **où**, which often refers to place (where, in which), can also refer to time (when), as illustrated below.

À l'époque où ils habitaient aux États-Unis leur fils était en internat en Angleterre.
(At the time when they lived in the USA, their son was at boarding school in England.)

Au moment où le train partait son portable a sonné.
(Just as the train was leaving her mobile rang.)

The relative pronoun can be omitted in English, but not in French.

Le jour où il est arrivé à Paris il pleuvait à verse.
(On the day he arrived in Paris it was pouring with rain.)

Note that it is not possible to use **quand** as a relative pronoun referring back to *époque*, *moment*, *jour*, etc. The correct relative pronoun in such cases is **où**.

À l'époque où je le connaissais, il avait les cheveux longs.
(In the days / At the time when I knew him, he had long hair.)

Le jour où il sera à l'heure, je n'en reviendrai pas!
(The day he's on time, I will be amazed!)

However, if you want to say 'one day when', you need **un jour que**.

Exercises

EXERCISE 4. Fill in the blanks with the most appropriate expressions from the box below.

> d'ici (× 2); d'ici là; d'ici peu; jusqu'ici; jusque-là; là; où; qu'est-ce qui; qui est-ce qui; quoi qu'il arrive

1 ________ à ce qu'il décide de démissionner, il n'y a pas loin.
2 Le matin _____ je l'ai rencontrée elle avait l'air distrait.
3 _______ elle n'a pas commis la moindre erreur.
4 ________ vous aurez de mes nouvelles, je vous le promets.
5 À quelques jours de ___ il est mort.
6 On en parlera la semaine prochaine, __________ ne faites rien. _________, vous pourrez y réfléchir à tête reposée.
7 J'ai entendu une explosion. ___________ est arrivé?
8 Il ne l'abandonnera jamais ___________.
9 J'aurai les résultats _____ deux jours.
10 _______ se serait attendu à ce qu'elle gagne?

Misused expressions

1 **Il s'agit de** can only be used impersonally. In general terms, it means 'it is a question / a matter of' or 'it is about'. Native speakers of English must remember not to use this expression with a specific subject. Hence, if you want to translate 'This film is about . . . ', it is not acceptable to say **Ce film s'agit de* . . . The correct version is: **Dans ce film il s'agit de . . .**

Remember that **il s'agit de** is always singular, as you will see in the example below.

Dans tous ces articles il s'agit du féminisme.
(All these articles are about feminism.)

Note also the following idiomatic uses of **il s'agit de**.

De quoi s'agit-il?
(What is it about?)

Mais il ne s'agit pas de ça!
(But that's not the point!)

Quand il s'agit de faire la vaisselle, elle n'est jamais là!
(When there's washing up to be done, she is never around!)

The expression can be used in different tenses, as shown below.

Au cours de la réunion il s'est agi des réclamations des ouvriers.
(During the meeting there was discussion of the workers' complaints.)

Il tenait à ce qu'elle se repose, parce qu'il s'agissait de sa santé.
(He was anxious for her to rest, because her health was at stake.)

D'après les média, il s'agirait d'un attentat.
(According to the media, it would appear to be an act of terrorism.)

You will also find the present participle **s'agissant de**, meaning 'as regards'.

S'agissant des soins médicaux, vous n'avez pas à vous inquiéter.
(As far as medical care is concerned, you do not need to worry.)

In all the examples above, **il s'agit de** is followed by a noun or pronoun, but it can also be used with an infinitive. It then expresses necessity.

Il s'agit de partir tout de suite.
(We / You must leave straight away.)

Il s'agirait de nous remettre au travail sans délai.
(We'd better get back to work immediately.)

In the negative, it means 'there can be no question of'.

Il ne s'agit pas de se mettre en grève.
(There can be no question of going on strike.)

2 The verb **manquer** is treacherous for native speakers of English. When followed by **à** + person or thing, it means 'to be missed by someone'. Remember that in French, the grammatical subject is the person or thing who is missed and not the person who is missing the other. The classic example is shown below. It means 'I miss you' and not 'You miss me'.

Tu me manques.
(I miss you.)

Compare and contrast the following:

Sandrine manque à son fiancé. Elle lui manque.
(Her fiancé misses Sandrine. He misses her.)

Son fiancé manque à Sandrine. Il lui manque.
(Sandrine misses her fiancé. She misses him.)

If you want to say that someone is short of something, use **manquer de**.

Nous manquons d'argent.
(We are short of money.)

Alternatively, you can use the impersonal verb **il manque**. Like **il s'agit de**, it is always singular.

Il manque 1 000 euros dans la caisse.
(1,000 euros are missing from the till.)

By using an indirect object pronoun with this impersonal verb, you can say that someone is short of something.

Il leur manque 1 000 euros. Il nous manque 2 000 euros.
(They are short of 1,000 euros. We are short of 2,000 euros.)

3 If you want to say you like something or someone, you can use **plaire**, but remember that its literal meaning is 'to please', so it is constructed in a different way from **aimer** (to like / love). Compare the following examples.

Il aime la musique.
(He likes music.)

La musique lui plaît.
(Music pleases him / He likes music.)

Elle aime les livres.
(She likes books.)

Les livres lui plaisent.
(Books please her / She likes books.)

Nous avons aimé le film.
(We liked the film.)

Le film nous a plu.
(The film pleased us / We liked the film.)

The grammatical subject of **plaire** is the thing or person that pleases; hence the verb is plural in the second example above with books.

In these examples, the music, the books and the film are pleasing to somebody, so this person becomes the indirect object of the verb. Always remember to use the appropriate indirect object pronoun, or to use **à** + noun with **plaire**.

Elle plaît aux jeunes hommes.
(Young men like her / find her attractive.)

Elle leur plaît.
(They like her / find her attractive.)

4 **Beaucoup** gives rise to two main problems.

First, note the distinction between **beaucoup de / d'** and **beaucoup des**.

Like most expressions of quantity, e.g. *assez de*, *peu de* and *trop de*, **beaucoup** is usually followed by **de / d'** + noun.

Beaucoup d'étudiants manquent d'argent.
(Many students are short of money.)

You only need to use the definite article before the noun if you are referring to a specific group. In such a case, **beaucoup + de + les** results in **beaucoup des**, as in the example below.

Beaucoup des étudiants à qui j'ai parlé manquaient d'argent.
(Many of the students to whom I spoke were short of money.)

Second, note that **beaucoup** is never preceded by any qualifying expression such as *assez*, *aussi*, *si* or *très.*

If you want to say 'as many / as much', 'so many / so much', 'quite a lot' and 'an awful lot', see below.

On y voit **autant de** femmes **que** d'hommes.
(You see *as many* women *as* men there.)

Il n'a pas **autant d'**argent **qu'**elle.
(He doesn't have *as much* money *as* she does.)

Nous avons **tant** / **tellement de** choses à leur dire.
(We have *so much* / *so many* things to say to them.)

Cela m'inquiète **tellement**.
(It worries me *so much*.)

Ils ont **beaucoup** voyagé.
(They have travelled *quite a lot*.)

Ils ont **pas mal** bossé.
(They have worked *quite a lot*.)

Ils ont **pas mal d'**amis.
(They have *quite a lot of* friends.)

Note that the expression **pas mal** / **pas mal de** is characteristic of informal language. It should not be used in careful speech or writing.

Il a perdu **une bonne part de** sa fortune.
(He has lost *quite a lot of* his fortune.)

Cela arrive **très souvent**.
(That happens *quite a lot*.)

Ils ont **énormément de** problèmes.
(They have *an awful lot of* problems.)

Exercises

EXERCISE 5a. Rewrite the following sentences, using the verbs indicated in brackets.

1 Il aime son nouveau rôle de représentant du parti. (plaire)
2 Cet ouvrage traite des origines du mouvement féministe. (s'agir)
3 Ils regrettent que les enfants ne soient pas là. (manquer)
4 Mais on ne parle pas de ça! (s'agir)
5 Elle n'a pas d'humour. (manquer)
6 Elle aime les truffes au chocolat. (plaire)
7 En ce qui concerne la santé (s'agir), mieux vaut prévenir que guérir.
8 Elle a besoin de 1 000 euros pour payer son loyer. (manquer)
9 Il lui a conseillé de bien réfléchir, parce que son bonheur était en jeu. (s'agir)
10 Il est hors de question d'accepter cette proposition. (s'agir)
11 Il regrette que sa femme soit partie. (manquer)
12 De quoi a-t-on parlé? (s'agir)
13 Je regrette que tu ne sois pas là. (manquer)
14 De quoi allez-vous traiter dans votre nouveau livre? (s'agir)
15 Ils ont aimé les cadeaux. (plaire)
16 Nous devons répondre sans délai. (s'agir)

EXERCISE 5b. Complete the following sentences by choosing between **beaucoup de** and **beaucoup des** as appropriate.

1 Ils ont beaucoup (d' / des) amis.
2 Les enfants ont mangé beaucoup (de / des) bonbons que Mamie leur avait offerts.
3 Beaucoup (de / des) gens sont du même avis que vous.
4 J'ai visité beaucoup (d' / des) églises romanes en France.
5 Beaucoup (d' / des) églises que j'ai visitées sont connues dans le monde entier.

EXERCISE 5c. Complete the blanks in the following sentences.

1 Comment peut-elle manger (as much)?
2 Ils ont (quite a lot of) fric. (Note that **le fric** is a colloquial word for money.)
3 Il y a (so many) enregistrements de cette symphonie que je ne sais pas lequel choisir.
4 Je n'ai pas (as much) énergie que vous.
5 Il lui arrive de voyager à l'étranger (quite a lot).
6 J'ai (an awful lot of) respect pour eux
7 On n'y a jamais vu (so many) monde.

8 Ils ont consacré (quite a lot of) leur budget à l'aménagement de la cuisine.
9 Son comportement m'énerve (so much) que je ne vais plus l'inviter chez moi.
10 Nous avons si peu de temps et (so many) projets à discuter.

EXERCISE 6. Fill in the blanks with the most appropriate expressions that you have studied in this chapter.

Hélène est une étudiante en quatrième (1) ________ (year) qui prépare son examen oral d'anglais. Elle a décidé de faire son exposé sur le système d'enseignement supérieur en Grande-Bretagne. Elle le (2) __________ (knows) assez bien parce qu'elle a passé cinq (3) ________ (years) là-bas quand son père, qui est (4) __________ (a scientist), travaillait à l'université de Londres. Tout de même, il en (5) ________ (knows) plus qu'elle, donc elle (6) __________ (went back) à la maison familiale le weekend dernier pour lui (7) _________ (ask questions) sur son expérience et pour lui (8) ________ (ask) ce qu'il (9) _____________ (thought about it). Il lui a répondu que (10) __________ (on the one hand) il avait gardé de bons souvenirs (11) __________ (of the time) qu'il avait passé à Londres, mais (12) __________ (on the other hand) il a conclu que le système éducatif français est (13) ________ (better) que le système britannique surtout du point de vue financier. (14) ___________ (What he likes) surtout en France, c'est que les frais de scolarité ne sont pas excessifs. Par contre en Grande-Bretagne, (15) _________ (many students) doivent souscrire un prêt pour subvenir à leurs besoins. Il est vrai que (16) __________ (many of the students) qu'il (17) __________ (knew) personnellement travaillaient pour gagner de l'argent, mais par suite ils perdaient (18) _________ (quite a lot of the time) qu'ils auraient pu consacrer à leurs études.

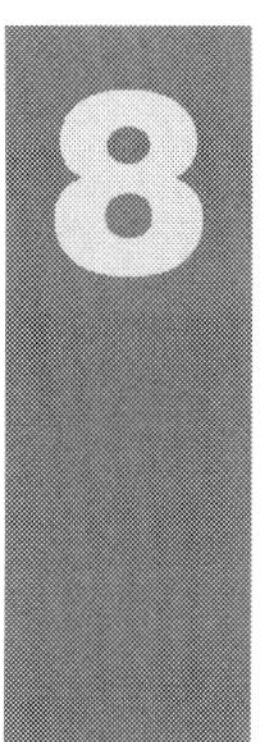

Use of prepositions

The correct use of prepositions is a good indication of your mastery of French. It is an area where English learners are particularly prone to make mistakes, because usage is so idiomatic and frequently different from English. Native speakers know instinctively which preposition to use and when not to use

one at all. This chapter draws your attention to the most significant points of difference between English and French, and provides a variety of exercises to practise and test what you have learnt.

Prepositions used in expressions of place

In English, we use prepositions to distinguish between movement to a place and location at or in it. In French, no such distinction is made. Instead prepositional usage varies according to whether a town, country, region or island is involved, and according to the gender of the country or region.

1 **À** is used before the name of a town, e.g.

Nous allons **à** Paris demain. Nos cousins nous rejoindront **à** Paris.
(We are going *to* Paris tomorrow. Our cousins will meet up with us *in* Paris.)

If the name of the town, e.g. *Le Havre*, includes the definite article *le*, *à* combines with it to give *au*, e.g.

L'action du film *Quai des brumes* se déroule **au** Havre.
(The action of the film *Quai des brumes* takes place *in* Le Havre.)

2 **À + definite article** is used before the masculine name of a country, e.g.

Je vais **au** Maroc cet été.
(I'm going *to* Morocco this summer.)

Il passe trois mois **au** Maroc.
(He is spending three months *in* Morocco.)

Aux is used before plural names of countries and groups of islands, e.g.

Nos cousins vont **aux** États-Unis.
(Our cousins are going *to* the United States.)

Elle a élu domicile **aux** Antilles.
(She has taken up residence *in* the West Indies.)

3 **À alone** is used before the feminine names of some islands that are also countries, e.g.

Elle habite **à** Chypre. Il va **à** Malte.
(She lives *in* Cyprus. He is going *to* Malta.)

À + la is used before the feminine names of some small (usually non-European) islands, e.g.

Elle va **à la** Martinique. Ils font leurs études **à la** Réunion.
(She is going *to* Martinique. They are studying *in* Réunion.)

4 **En** is used before the feminine name of a country or region or a large island that is not also a country, e.g.

Nous allons **en** Suisse l'année prochaine après avoir passé quatre ans à l'université **en** Écosse.
(We're going *to* Switzerland next year after having spent four years at university *in* Scotland.)

Cet été nous allons passer les vacances **en** Toscane et **en** Sicile.
(This summer we're going to spend the holidays *in* Tuscany and *in* Sicily.)

En is also used before the masculine singular name of a country, region or province beginning with a vowel, e.g.

Ils vont **en** Israël cet automne.
(They are going *to* Israel this autumn.)

Ils habitent **en** Anjou / **en** Ontario.
(They live *in* Anjou / *in* Ontario.)

5 Most countries / regions ending in -**e** are feminine, but there are exceptions, e.g. *le Mexique* (Mexico).

Note the difference in French between Mexico City and the country Mexico:

Mexico est la capitale **du Mexique**.
(*Mexico City* is the capital of *Mexico*.)

6 Use of **dans**

Dans is used for movement to and location in geographical areas such as mountains, e.g. *dans les Alpes*; French departments of masculine gender, e.g. *dans le Pas-de-Calais*; as well as American states and English counties of masculine gender, e.g. *dans le Texas*, *dans le Kent*.

It is also used for location in towns and countries modified by adjectives, quantifiers or adjectival phrases, e.g.

dans le vieux Londres	*in* old London
dans toute l'Espagne	*in* all Spain
dans le Brésil des années 80	*in* the Brazil of the 1980s

More generally, **dans** is used to indicate location inside somewhere, e.g.

Les clefs sont **dans** le tiroir.
(The keys are *in* the drawer.)

Note particularly the expression *Je suis dans le train*, where in English we would say 'I am on (= inside) the train'. A literal rendering into French with *Je suis sur le train* would conjure up an image of someone literally on the roof of the train, as you see in the cartoon at the beginning of the chapter.

7 When 'in' is the equivalent of 'at', **à** tends to be used in French, rather than **dans**, e.g.

Il est **à** l'école. Sa petite sœur est **à** la maison.
(He is *at* school. His little sister is *at* home.)

Contrast the examples above with the following:

J'ai laissé mon passeport quelque part **dans** la maison.
(I've left my passport somewhere *in* the house.)

L'assassin est déjà **dans** l'école.
(The murderer is already *inside* the school.)

8 Use of **de**

De, meaning 'from', is used to indicate geographical origin or movement away from a place, e.g.

Elle est **de** Paris.
(She is *from* Paris.)

If the name of the town, e.g. *Le Havre*, includes the definite article *le*, *de* combines with it to give d*u*, e.g.

Il est **du** Havre.
(He is *from* Le Havre.)

Before the masculine name of a country or region, use **de + definite article**, e.g.

Il est **du** Japon; elle est **des** États-Unis.
(He is *from* Japan; she is *from* the United States.)

Before the feminine name of a country, region or island, use **de** alone, e.g.

Cet écrivain du Moyen Âge s'appelait Marie; elle était **de** France.
(This medieval writer was called Marie; she was *from* France.)

Before the masculine singular name of a country or region beginning with a vowel, use **d'** alone, e.g.

> Ils attendent un vol en provenance **d'**Israël
> (They are waiting for a flight *from* Israel)

There is one exception to note:

> Il vient **de l'**Inde.
> (He comes *from* India.)

For more information about the usage of prepositions with names of countries and islands, see Appendix 1 at the end of the book. See also Chapter 1 for the gender of place names.

Exercises

EXERCISE 1. Complete the following sentences with the appropriate prepositions or preposition + article and make any necessary changes.

1 Elle a passé trois mois ____ Afrique cet été et l'année prochaine elle voudrait aller ____ Amérique latine.
2 ____ France de nos jours il n'est pas facile de trouver un stage.
3 Il vient ____ Le Havre. Elle est ____ Mexico.
4 Les écoliers ont fait leurs devoirs ____ le bus.
5 C'est un archéologue qui fait des fouilles ____ Chypre. L'année dernière il a travaillé ____ Corse.
6 Sa petite-fille est ____ l'université____ États-Unis.
7 Nos cousins sont en vacances ____ le Cantal tandis que leurs parents sont ____ les Pyrénées.
8 Son mari vient ____ Mexique, mais elle est ____ (Guyane).
9 Les policiers avaient essayé de boucler la rue, mais les manifestants étaient déjà ____ l'école.
10 Elle est allée ____ Pérou pour voir la vallée sacrée. Sa cousine est allée ____ Israël pour étudier l'archéologie.

Prepositions used in expressions of time

1 There are three different ways to translate 'for' + time into French, depending on context.

Depuis + present tense is used for an action that began in the past, but is still continuing at present, e.g.

J'apprends l'italien **depuis** six mois.
(I have been learning Italian *for* six months and am still learning it.)

Depuis + imperfect tense is used for an action that had begun some time previously, but was still continuing at a particular point of time in the past, e.g.

J'apprenais l'italien **depuis** six mois quand on m'a demandé de traduire cet article.
(I had been learning Italian *for* six months when I was asked to translate this article.)

Pendant is used for actual periods of time and can refer to the past or future, e.g.

Elle a travaillé à Pau **pendant** trois mois.
(She worked in Pau *for* three months.)

Je vais travailler en Écosse **pendant** deux ans.
(I am going to work in Scotland *for* two years.)

Pour is used for intention, usually referring to the future, e.g.

Nous sommes là **pour** huit jours.
(We are here *for* a week.)

Je vais à Paris **pour** quinze jours.
(I'm going to Paris *for* a fortnight.)

However, with the future of the verb *être*, use **pendant**, e.g.

Nous serons à Rome **pendant** trois semaines.
(We will be in Rome *for* three weeks.)

Note that you should not use any preposition with the verb *rester*, e.g.

Je pense rester un an à Madrid.
(I'm thinking of staying *for* a year in Madrid.)

Je suis restée trente ans à Aberdeen.
(I have stayed *for* thirty years in Aberdeen.)

2 'in' + time

Distinguish between:

Dans + an expression of time, which is used for a deadline, the time after which something will occur, e.g.

Je dois rendre mon mémoire **dans** deux jours.
(I have to hand in my dissertation *in* two days' time from now.)

En + an expression of time, which is used for the duration of time taken to complete a task, e.g.

Je l'ai écrit **en** deux jours.
(I wrote it *in* two days.)

Mnemonic device
Remember that **dans** begins with 'd' for a deadline.

Note the idiomatic expression: **sous peu** (in a little while, before long).

3 Use of prepositions in other common expressions of time

Note and learn the following useful expressions:

à ce moment-là	then (referring to past or future time)
en ce moment	now, at the present moment
à temps	in time
dans le temps	in those days; at some time in the past
de temps en temps	from time to time
de mon / leur temps	in my / their day or time
en ce temps-là	at that time, in those days
en même temps que	at the same time as
en temps de guerre	in wartime
en temps de paix	in peacetime

Remember that 'in the morning / evening' is **le matin** and **le soir** with no preposition.

La réunion est **le matin** / **le soir**.
(The meeting is *in the morning* / *evening*.)

See also Chapter 7 on problem nouns (time).

Exercises

EXERCISE 2a. Complete the following sentences with the appropriate preposition: **depuis**, **pendant**, **pour**, **dans**, **en**, **sous**, or leave a blank if appropriate.

1 _____ combien de temps travaillez-vous ici?
2 On se reverra _____ peu.
3 Je t'ai attendu _____ des heures.
4 Nous sommes restés _____ un mois en Espagne.
5 Il sera absent _____ trois jours.
6 Elle sera de retour _____ une heure.
7 ____ un moment tout a été fini.
8 Elle le connaissait _____ longtemps, mais elle ne savait pas où il habitait.
9 Il va à Rome cet été _____ huit jours.
10 Elle va rester _____ un an à Paris.

EXERCISE 2b. Complete the following sentences with expressions of time chosen from the list at the end of the section above.

1 _________ (Then) il y aura bien des plaintes.
2 _________ (In their day), ils étaient sportifs.
3 Elle est arrivée _________ (at the same time) que lui.
4 Je suis très fatiguée _________ (at the moment).
5 _______ (In those days) on n'avait pas l'électricité.
6 Ils se revoient _______ (from time to time).
7 Cela se fait surtout _______ (in wartime).

Prepositions used in expressions of manner

1 de + façon / manière to translate 'in a certain way'

Note that in French, **de** is used with **façon** and **manière** where in English we would say 'in a certain way', e.g.

Il parle **d'**une façon désagréable.
(He speaks *in* an unpleasant way.)

You need therefore to use **la façon / manière dont** to translate 'the way that' or 'the way in which', e.g.

La façon / manière **dont** il parle me déplaît.
(I don't like the way *that* / *in which* he talks.)

Note the expression: **d'une manière ou d'une autre** (in one way or another).

2 Use of **de** where English would often use 'in' or 'with'

With movement, **de** is often used in French where in English we would say 'in' or 'with', e.g.

Il a avalé le whisky **d'**un trait.
(He swallowed the whisky *in* one gulp.)

Il a écarté les branches **de** son bras.
(He moved the branches aside *with* his arm.)

3 Ways of travelling

À is the most common preposition used for natural movements, e.g.

à pied (on foot)

à quatre pattes (on all fours)

au pas (at a crawl)

En is most commonly used for travel by vehicle, e.g.

en voiture (by car)

en bus (by bus)

en train (by train)

However, in the last case, **par le train** is also common.

À may be used as an alternative to **en** for bikes and motorbikes, which you sit astride, so just as you say **à cheval** (on horseback), you can say: **à vélo** and **à moto**, as an alternative to **en vélo** and **en moto,** respectively.

Prepositions used in expressions of measurement

1 Distances

Note the following use of prepositions and contrast it to the English usage:

J'habite **à** dix kilomètres **de** l'université.
(I live 10 kilometres *(away) from* the university.)

Mnemonic device
Remember that in French you have to put **à** (for **away**) before the distance.

2 Measurements

De is used in the following ways to give measurements. There is no corresponding preposition in English.

Cette tour a 35 mètres **de** haut.
Cette tour est haute **de** 35 mètres.
(This tower is 35 metres high.)

Une tour haute **de** 35 mètres . . .
(A 35-metre high tower . . .)

3 Comparatives and superlatives

Remember that **de** is often used in comparisons to express the **difference** between the things / people being compared. There is no corresponding preposition in English, e.g.

Ce sac est **de** 50 euros moins cher que l'autre.
(This bag is 50 euros cheaper than the other.)

After superlative expressions, use **de** to translate 'in', e.g.

C'est le plus grand joueur **du** (contraction of **de + le**) monde entier.
(He's the greatest player *in* the whole world.)

Exercises

EXERCISE 3. Complete the following sentences with the appropriate preposition, preposition + article, or pronoun.

1 La façon ___ elle se comporte ne cesse de me surprendre.
2 Elle est arrivée ___ moto.
3 Elle est plus grande que son mari ___ plusieurs centimètres.
4 Nous habitons ___ 500 kilomètres ___ nos parents.
5 Cette statue est haute ____ 3 mètres.
6 Je suis sûr que tu y arriveras ____ une manière ou _____ autre.
7 Il y a un embouteillage et nous roulons ____ pas.
8 Je préfère voyager _____ train.
9 Il l'a saluée ____ la main.
10 Cet élève est le plus doué _____ la classe.

Common translation problems from English to French

In each case, the examples illustrate how the translation will vary depending on the context.

1 about / concerning

un livre **sur** l'Afrique post-coloniale
(a book *about* post-colonial Africa)

It would also be possible to use one of the following:

au sujet de; à propos de; concernant

If you want to say 'to speak about', use **parler de.**

For **about,** meaning 'approximately', see **around** below.

2 according to

D'après / **Selon** lui, les prix vont augmenter.
(*According to* him, prices are going to go up.)

J'ai fait les calculs **suivant** ses instructions.
(I made the calculations *according to* his instructions.)

3 across / through

Elle l'a vu **de l'autre côté de** la salle.
(She saw him *across* = *on the other side of* the room.)

Il a parlé de ses voyages **à travers** l'Europe.
(He spoke about his travels *across* Europe.)

Il a couru **à travers** les champs.
(He ran *across* the fields.)

In the example above, distance is implied, but if the space crossed is limited, e.g. a road or river, verbs of movement cannot normally be used with **à travers**. See the final section of this chapter for the translation of 'to swim across the river'.

Je sentais le froid **à travers** mes gants.
(I could feel the cold *through* my gloves.)

Le coupable est passé **au travers des** mailles du filet de la police.
(The culprit slipped *right through* the police net.)

L'arbre est tombé **en travers du** chemin.
(The tree fell *right across* the path).

4 among

Le chômage **chez** les jeunes suscite des inquiétudes.
(Unemployment *among* young people is giving cause for concern.)

The primary meaning of **chez** is 'at the house' or 'at the business premises' of someone, e.g.

Je vais **chez** le dentiste ce matin.
(I am going **to** the dentist's this morning.)

However, it is also used to translate 'among', as in the first example above, as well as 'about', 'with' or 'in the works of', e.g.

Ce que j'aime **chez** lui, c'est l'humour.
(What I like *about* him is his sense of humour.)

C'est une habitude **chez** lui.
(It's a habit *with* him / of his.)

C'est un thème récurrent **chez** Flaubert.
(It's a recurrent theme *in the works of* Flaubert.)

Other ways to translate 'among' are as follows:

J'essaie de le trouver **parmi** la foule.
(I'm trying to find him *among / amongst* the crowd.)

On est **entre** amis.
(We are *among* friends.)

J'ai déjà parlé à plusieurs **d'entre** vous.
(I've already spoken to several *among / of* you.)

Deux **d'entre** eux / elles sont parti(e)s tout de suite.
(Two *of* them left straight away.)

In the two examples immediately above, **d'entre** is used before a personal pronoun to select some people from a group.

5 around / about (approximately)

Elle avait **vers** 18 ans.
Elle avait 18 ans **environ**.
Elle avait **autour de** 18 ans.
Elle avait **dans les** 18 ans. (informal)
(She was *around / about / approximately* 18 years old.)

Note that **environ** is the odd one out of these prepositions, because it follows the expression that it qualifies.

6 as

Il s'est déguisé **en** moine.
(He disguised himself *as* a monk.)

En tant que secrétaire de l'Association des parents d'élèves et des professeurs, je vous écris pour . . .
(*As / In my capacity as* the secretary of the PTA, I am writing to . . .)

Elle travaille **comme** interprète.
(She is working *as* an interpreter.)

Note that in French, there is no need for an indefinite or definite article after these prepositions. This is in contrast to English usage, 'as a(n) / the . . . '.

7 because of

Nous sommes restés à la maison **à cause de** la pluie.
(We stayed at home *because of* the rain.)

Contrast the example above with the following:

Nous sommes restés à la maison **parce qu**'il pleuvait.
(We stayed at home *because* it was raining.)

If you want to say 'because of', use the preposition **à cause de**, not the conjunction **parce que / qu'**, which introduces a clause with subject and verb.

Mnemonic device
à cause DE (because **OF**)

8 before

Elle arrivera **avant** midi.
(She will arrive *before* midday.)

Le paysage s'étendait **devant** eux.
(The landscape stretched out *before* them.)

Il a comparu **devant** le tribunal.
(He appeared *before* the court.)

Ils se sont fait voler **sous** nos propres yeux.
(They were robbed *before* our very eyes.)

Note that **avant** is used for time, **devant** is used for position and **sous** is used idiomatically in the expression **sous mes / ses propres yeux** (before my / his / her very eyes).

9 by

Il a été attaqué **par** des voleurs.
(He was attacked *by* thieves.)

Il était respecté **de** tous ses collègues.
(He was respected *by* all his colleagues.)

In a passive construction, the agent is normally introduced by **par**, but **de** is preferred if the verb expresses an ongoing state.

10 from

The usual way of translating 'from' with place or time is **de**.

Ils voyagent **de** Londres à Paris.
(They are travelling *from* London to Paris.)

Nous travaillons **de** 9 heures à midi.
(We are working *from* 9 o'clock to midday.)

However, the prepositions **dès** and **à partir de** are also useful with expressions of place and time.

dès Édimbourg	*from* Edinburgh *onwards*
dès le depart / le début	*right from* the start
dès le moment où	*from* the moment when
dès maintenant	*from* now on
dès leur arrivée	*from* the time of their arrival, as soon as they arrive
à partir du carrefour	*from* the crossroads
à partir de 17 heures	*from* 5 o'clock
à partir de là	*from* then on

À partir de also translates the idea of 'from', meaning 'on the basis of'.

À partir de ces résultats, il a soutenu que . . .
(*From / on the basis* of these results, he argued that . . .)

11 in

Note the following idiomatic expressions.

La clef est **sur** la porte.
(The key is *in* the door.)

Il est sorti **sous** la pluie.
(He went out *in* the rain.)

Il a présenté les données **sous** forme de tableau.
(He presented the data **in** tabular form.)

12 on

Remember that no preposition is used for **on** + a particular day or date, e.g.

Je t'appellerai jeudi. Mon examen est le 7 juin.
(I will call you *on* Thursday. My exam is *on* 7th June.)

However, to translate an expression such as 'on a fine autumn day', use **par**.

Ils ont déménagé **par** une belle journée d'automne.
(They moved house *on* a fine autumn day.)

Note the following examples of figurative usage.

Je l'ai entendu **à** la radio. Je l'ai vu **à** la télévision.
(I heard it *on* the radio. I saw it *on* television.)

Je vous appelle **de la part de** M. Duval.
(I'm calling you *on behalf of* Mr Duval.)

13 out of

To express position and also movement away from, use **hors de,** e.g.

Hors de la maison, elle se sent libre.
(*Out of* the house she feels free.)

Hors d'ici!
(Get *out of* here!)

With some verbs, it is possible to use **de** alone for movement away from, e.g.

Sortez **d'**ici!
(Get *out of* here!)

Note the difference between French and English usage in expressions such as the following:

Qui a bu **dans** ce verre?
(Who has been drinking *out of* this glass?)

J'ai découpé cette annonce **dans** le journal.
(I've cut this advert *out of* the paper.)

Prenez une serviette **dans** le placard.
(Take a towel *out of* the cupboard.)

In the examples above, the preposition **dans** is used in French to indicate the original position of things, whereas in English, 'out of' expresses the direction of the movement that has taken or is about to take place.

When used figuratively, 'out of' is sometimes rendered by **hors de**, e.g.

C'est tout à fait **hors de** question.
(That's absolutely *out of* the question.)

Je suis **hors d**'haleine.
(I am *out of* breath.)

However, **par** introduces a motive force, and **sur** is used with numbers, e.g.

Elle l'a dit **par** amour / compassion.
(She said it *out of* love / compassion.)

On lui a mis douze **sur** vingt.
(He was given the mark of twelve *out of* twenty.)

Mnemonic device
Think of how you might write 'twelve out of twenty' in figures. Twelve would be on the line and twenty beneath it, hence the use of **sur** in French.

14 towards

For movement towards, use **vers**, e.g.

Il s'est dirigé **vers** la sortie.
(He made his way *towards* the exit.)

For attitude towards, use **envers**, e.g.

Il a changé d'attitude **envers** elle.
(He has changed his attitude *towards* her.)

15 until

To translate 'until', use **jusqu'à**, e.g.

J'attendrai **jusqu'à** midi.
(I will wait *until* midday.)

However, if you want to say 'not . . . until', use one of the following instead:

Je ne le saurai **que** vendredi.
Je ne le saurai pas **avant** vendredi.
(I will *not* know *until* Friday.)

16 with

In some contexts, the literal translation **avec** is used, e.g.

Venez **avec** moi. Parlez **avec** elle.
(Come *with* me. Speak *with* her.)

However, **de** is used in cases such as the following:

Elle a rougi **de** honte.
(She blushed *with* shame.)

Je te remercie **de** tout mon cœur.
(I thank you *with* all my heart.)

La route est bordée **d'**arbres.
(The road is lined *with* trees.)

In descriptive phrases, note the use of **à + definite article**, contracted where appropriate to **au, aux.**

Un homme **à la** barbe rousse
(A man with a red beard)
La fille **aux** cheveux de lin
(The girl with flaxen hair)

Exercises

EXERCISE 4. Complete the following sentences with the appropriate preposition, preposition + article, or leave blank where appropriate.

1 Je lui ai mis 15 _______ (out of) vingt.
2 Elle habite ___________ (across) la rue.
3 Ça ne sera pas prêt ________ (until) la semaine prochaine.
4 C'est une obsession ________ (with) elle! Elle tient à voyager _______ (across) le monde.
5 ________ (In) quelle forme vas-tu présenter les données?
6 Il a écrit un livre _______ (about) le cinéma français. (Note: use a single word)
7 Je ne le connais qu' __________ (through) ses écrits.
8 (As the) secrétaire de la société littéraire je suis chargée de rédiger le compte rendu des réunions.

9 (Right from) le début je savais que cela ne marcherait pas.
10 Il a laissé la clé (in) la porte.
11 As-tu vu l'homme (with) cheveux roux?
12 Elle a pris une casserole (out of) le placard.
13 Ils sont arrivés ______ (around) minuit. Plusieurs _____ (among) eux étaient ivres morts.
14 On l'a amené ________ (before) le juge.
15 Nous l'avons entendu ___ (on) la radio ___(on) vendredi soir.
16 Il l'a aidée ______ (out of) compassion. En plus il avait des engagements ______ (towards) elle.
17 _______là (From then on), tout a basculé.
18 Ce n'est pas ________ (because of) toi qu'il s'en va.
19 ________ (From / On the basis of) cet exemple il nous a persuadés qu'il avait raison.
20 ____ (Get out of) ici ! Sinon, je me ferai houspiller (by) mes collègues.

French verbs with two different usages

1 Croire (to believe)

Distinguish carefully between the following:

Croire + direct object means 'to believe' a fact or a person, e.g.

Il faut le voir pour le croire.
(It has to be seen to be believed.)

Je veux bien vous croire, mais . . .
(I'd like to believe you, but . . .)

Croire + à or croire + en means 'to believe in', in the sense of 'having confidence or faith in', e.g.

Croyez-vous à l'amour ?
(Do you believe in love?)

Je crois en Dieu.
(I believe in God.)

Il faut croire en soi.
(You have to believe in yourself.)

2 Penser (to think)

This verb is somewhat treacherous for an English speaker, because 'to think of' has two meanings and each is translated into French in a different way.

Penser à means 'to have something or someone in mind', e.g.

À quoi peut-il bien penser?
(What can he be thinking of?)

Elle pense aux enfants tout le temps.
(She is thinking about the children the whole time.)

Penser de means 'to have an opinion about something or someone', e.g.

Que pensez-vous de cette idée?
(What do you think about this idea?)

Il m'a demandé ce que je pensais de sa cravate?
(He asked me what I thought about his tie.)

Mnemonic device
Remember that **penser à** means 'to turn your thoughts *to*', whereas **penser de** means 'to have an opinion of'.

3 Jouer (to play)

Jouer + à + definite article (contracted before a masculine noun to **au, aux**) + **sport, game**, e.g.

Il joue au football. Elle préfère jouer aux échecs.
(He plays football. She prefers playing chess.)

Jouer + de + definite article (contracted before a masculine singular noun beginning with a consonant or aspirate 'h' to **du) + musical instrument**, e.g.

Il joue du violon. Elle joue du hautbois. Leur cousin joue de la clarinette.
(He plays the violin. She plays the oboe. Their cousin plays the clarinet.)

4 Manquer (to miss, mess up; to be short of; to fail in; to miss)

With a direct object, manquer means 'to miss' or 'mess up', e.g.

Le footballeur a manqué le but.
(The footballer missed the goal.)

Je ne sais quoi faire, j'ai tout manqué.
(I don't know what to do, I've made a mess of everything.)

With de, manquer means 'to be short of' or 'to be lacking in', e.g.

Nous manquons d'argent.
(We are short of money.)

With à + noun, manquer means 'to fail in' or 'not to respect', e.g.

Elle a manqué à son devoir.
(She failed in her duty.)

Elle a manqué à sa parole.
(She broke her word.)

With à + person or with an indirect object pronoun, it means 'to be away / absent' from someone and therefore 'to be missed' by them, e.g.

Aurélie manque à son fiancé.
(Aurélie is away from her fiancé and therefore he misses her.)

Elle lui manque.
(She is away from him and therefore he misses her.)

See also Chapter 7 on misused expressions (**manquer**).

Exercises

EXERCISE 5. Complete the following sentences with the appropriate preposition, preposition + article, or leave a blank where appropriate.

1 Tu penses déjà ___ la rentrée?
2 Les Romains ont cru ___ la victoire.
3 Il manque ____ expérience.
4 Savez-vous jouer ___ tennis?
5 Ils ne croient pas ____ Dieu.
6 Qu'est-ce que tu penses ____ l'université?
7 Elle a manqué _____ sa vie.
8 Je voudrais apprendre à jouer ____ violoncelle.
9 Les enfants manquent _____ leur père quand il est en voyage d'affaires.
10 Je ne crois pas _____ ce qu'on m'a raconté.

Different constructions in English and French after a verb

1 Verbs that take a direct object in French

Be careful not to suppose that because an English verb takes a preposition before a noun, the French verb will necessarily behave in the same way. For example, although the English verb 'to look' takes 'at' before a noun, the French verb **regarder** does not usually require a preposition, e.g.

Nous regardons un film à la télévision.
(We are looking *at* a film on TV.)

Note, however, that you will sometimes find **regarder + à**, but it means 'to watch' in the sense of 'to think about / pay attention to', e.g.

Il ne regarde pas **à** la dépense; c'est la qualité qui compte pour lui.
(He doesn't think *about* expense; quality is what counts as far as he is concerned.)

Learn the expression: **à y regarder de plus près** (on closer examination).

Other English verbs to beware of include the following. In each case, the French translation equivalent takes a direct object (with no preposition before it).

approuver une décision	to approve **of** a decision
attendre le bus	to wait **for** the bus
chercher un dossier	to look **for** a file
demander un service	to ask **for** a favour
écouter la radio	to listen **to** the radio
espérer quelque chose	to hope **for** something
opérer quelqu'un	to operate **on** someone
payer un repas	to pay **for** a meal
remplir un formulaire	to fill **in** a form
viser les jeunes	to aim **at** young people
voter quelque chose	to vote **for** something

Note: Remember to use direct object pronouns in French with all these verbs, e.g.

Avez-vous trouvé mon dossier? Je ne **l'**ai pas encore cherché.
(Have you found my file? I haven't looked *for it* yet.)

2 Verbs that take **à + noun** in French

On the other hand, sometimes a French verb takes **à** before a noun whereas its English translation equivalent takes a direct object.

Some of the most common examples are:

aller à	to suit
assister à	to attend
convenir à	to suit
nuire à	to harm
obéir à	to obey
désobéir à	to disobey
plaire à	to please
déplaire à	to displease
renoncer à	to renounce, give up
répondre à	to answer
résister à	to resist
ressembler à	to resemble, look like
réussir à un examen	to pass an exam
survivre à	to survive
téléphoner à	to telephone

3 There are also a number of verbs, like **demander**, that take the construction: **demander quelque chose à quelqu'un** (to ask someone something).

Other common examples include:

apprendre quelque chose à quelqu'un	to teach someone something
conseiller quelque chose à quelqu'un	to give some advice to someone
défendre quelque chose à quelqu'un	to forbid someone something
dire quelque chose à quelqu'un	to tell someone something
donner quelque chose à quelqu'un	to give someone something
enseigner quelque chose à quelqu'un	to teach someone something
montrer quelque chose à quelqu'un	to show someone something
offrir quelque chose à quelqu'un	to give / offer someone something
pardonner quelque chose à quelqu'un	to forgive someone for something

permettre quelque chose à quelqu'un	to allow someone something
prêter quelque chose à quelqu'un	to lend someone something
promettre quelque chose à quelqu'un	to promise someone something
refuser quelque chose à quelqu'un	to refuse someone something
vendre quelque chose à quelqu'un	to sell someone something

Mnemonic device
There are two ways to remember how to construct these French verbs. With some of them, you can rephrase the English, e.g. 'I gave my mother a present' as 'I gave a present TO my mother'.

For the rest, remember the acrononyms: TAT (Teach, Advise, Tell) and FAF (Forbid, Allow, Forgive).

4 Verbs that take **de** + **noun** in French

In some cases, a French verb takes **de** before a noun whereas its English translation equivalent takes a direct object. Some of the most common examples are:

s'apercevoir de	to notice
s'approcher de	to approach
avoir besoin de	to need
avoir envie de	to want
changer de	to change one thing for another of the same kind
disposer de	to have at one's disposal
douter de	to doubt
hériter de	to inherit
jouir de	to enjoy
manquer de	to lack
se méfier de	to distrust
se servir de	to use
se souvenir de	to remember

Note the expression: **à n'en pas douter** (undoubtedly, without a doubt).

Remember to use appropriate pronouns, such as **dont** and **en**, to reflect usage with **de**, e.g.

L'ordinateur **dont** il se sert est détraqué.
(The computer *which* he is using is on the blink.)

A-t-il terminé sa dissertation ? J'**en** doute.
(Has he finished his essay? I doubt *it*.)

There are some other French verbs that also take **de + noun**. Their English translation equivalents take a variety of different prepositions, such as 'on', 'for' and 'at', e.g.

dépendre de	to depend on
remercier de	to thank for
rire de	to laugh at
vivre de	to live on

5 Verbs that take other prepositions in French

There are many verbs in French that take a different preposition from their English translation equivalent. They include:

consister en	to consist of
entrer dans	to enter + direct object
se fâcher contre	to get angry with

If in doubt, check in the French half of the dictionary to see which preposition to use.

Exercises

EXERCISE 6a. Complete the following sentences with the appropriate preposition from **à**, **de / d'**, **contre**, **dans** and **en**, or leave a blank if appropriate.

1 Il dépend ___ toi de te présenter à l'heure.
2 Il faut écouter ____ ce qu'elle dit!
3 Je refuse de me fâcher _____ lui.
4 Cette mauvaise note va nuire ___ ses chances de réussite.
5 Je ne me souviens pas ____ son nom.
6 J'ai demandé ___ ma mère de venir me chercher à l'aéroport.
7 Je n'ai jamais douté ___ ton talent.
8 Je voudrais payer __ un verre à mes invités.
9 Il est très ambitieux, mais je ne sais pas s'il vise ___ une carrière précise.

10 Elle ne ressemble pas ______ l'image que j'en avais.
11 On ne manque ___ rien ici.
12 L'examen consiste _____ deux épreuves.
13 N'en parlons plus, changeons ______ sujet!
14 L'Italie jouit ____ un heureux climat.
15 On entre ______ la ville par une avenue bordée d'arbres.
16 L'Assemblée a voté _____ la loi sur les crédits agricoles.
17 Elle a hérité ______ une grosse fortune.
18 Il ne pourra jamais résister ____ cette tentation.
19 Il ne s'est aperçu ______ rien.
20 Cette date ne convient pas _____ mon collègue.

EXERCISE 6b. Complete the following sentences with the appropriate personal or relative pronoun, paying attention to the construction used with each verb and making any necessary changes.

1 Mes parents m'ont demandé de ______ téléphoner ce soir.
2 Je brûle d'impatience de savoir mes résultats. Je ____ attends depuis trois semaines.
3 J'ai trouvé toutes les informations ____ j'avais besoin pour remplir le formulaire de déclaration des revenus.
4 Elle prétend avoir tout fait, mais je _____ doute.
5 Les enfants ont fait appel à leur mère et elle ____ a permis de sortir.
6 Cet enfant est chahuteur en classe, mais ses parents ______ pardonnent tout.
7 À _____ regarder de plus près, on voit que c'est un faux.
8 Christine est quelqu'un ______ on se souvient.
9 Le chirurgien est venu voir le malade _____ il avait opéré la veille.
10 C'est exactement ce _____ j'avais envie.
11 Il m'a demandé mon avis et je ______ ai conseillé de ne pas se fier à eux.
12 Les enfants m'ont demandé de ______ apprendre à nager.

Translation of English phrasal verbs into French

1 One verb in French to translate an English phrasal verb (verb + preposition)

Prepositions are often used in English to form so-called 'phrasal verbs', made up of a verb + preposition, e.g. 'to go out', 'to put out', 'to throw out'. These verbs are most commonly translated into French by one verb with no preposition. You will find many examples in a good bilingual dictionary by reading through the entry on the English verb in question, e.g. 'to put' with its subsections, 'to put aside', 'to put back', etc.

to go out – **sortir**

Nous **sortons** tous les soirs.
(We *go out* every evening.)

Elle **sort** avec Jean-Paul.
(She *is going out* with Jean-Paul.)

Contrast the emphatic use of 'outside', as opposed to 'inside' in:

Allez jouer **dehors**!
(Go and play *outside*!)

to put out – **sortir** + direct object or **éteindre** + direct object

N'oubliez pas de **sortir** la poubelle demain matin.
(Don't forget to *put* the bin *out* tomorrow morning.)

Les pompiers ont réussi à **éteindre** les flammes.
(The firefighters managed to *put out* the flames.)

to throw out – **jeter** + direct object

Il faut **jeter** toutes ces affaires à la poubelle.
(You must *throw* all those things *out*.)

2 How to translate an English phrasal verb of movement

To translate an English phrasal verb of movement, e.g. 'He ran up the stairs', into French, you need to specify first of all the direction of the movement with a verb and then to indicate the manner of the movement with an adverbial phrase or a gerund, e.g.

Elle **a monté** l'escalier **en courant**.
(She *ran up* the stairs.)

Ils ont **traversé** le fleuve **à la nage**.
(They *swam across* the river.)

Sometimes a verb alone is sufficient, e.g.

Elle a **traversé** la rue.
(She *walked across* the road.)

Ils **ont franchi** le mur.
(They *got over* the wall.)

Exercises

EXERCISE 7a. Complete the following sentences with a single French verb from the box below and translate it into English with an appropriate phrasal verb. Use the dictionary to help you if necessary and be aware that the translation will depend on the context. For example, the verb **éteindre** can mean 'to put out' a fire or 'to switch off' a light or a television.

> descendre, éteindre (× 2), étendre, franchir, jeter, monter, se passer, poser, prendre, rapporter, rapprocher, remettre (× 2), rentrer, sortir

1 Avant de parler, il a _____ son verre sur la table.
2 J'ai oublié de _______ la poubelle ce matin.
3 Peux-tu ______ du lait en rentrant ?
4 Le porteur va ______ tous les bagages au rez-de-chaussée.
5 Je parle au téléphone. Tu peux _________ la radio?
6 Je ne trouve pas le journal d'hier. Tu ne l'as pas _____?
7 Comment va-t-on _______ le piano au deuxième étage?
8 Il ne ________ jamais les livres à leur place.
9 Il fait beau et je vais en profiter pour _______ le linge.
10 Je devrais téléphoner à la banque mais je ______ toujours ça à plus tard.
11 Je lui ai demandé d'________ sa cigarette.
12 Quel vacarme! Qu'est-ce qui _____ là-haut?
13 Je vais ______ le linge, il va pleuvoir.
14 Elle nous _________ toujours un cadeau de ses voyages.
15 Ce club _______ des gens d'horizons très différents.
16 Elle vient de ________ un cap difficile.

EXERCISE 7b. Complete the following sentences. In each case, you will need to combine one of the verbs from list A (in the appropriate *passé composé* form) with a gerund or adverbial expression from list B. Note that the verbs **descendre**, **monter, sortir**, which are usually conjugated with **être,** take the auxiliary **avoir** when they have a direct object, e.g. *Il a descendu la colline en courant.* (He ran down the hill).

List A	**List B**
s'approcher	à la nage
avancer	à skis
descendre (× 2)	à tâtons
s'éloigner	d'un pas désinvolte
monter	en boitant
sortir	en courant (× 2)
traverser	en rampant

1 Le bébé ____________ l'escalier _________.
(The baby crawled up the stairs.)
2 Le vieillard __________ les marches ___________.
(The old man limped down the steps.)
3 Nous __________ dans la caverne ___________.
(We felt our way forward into the cave.)
4 La jeune femme _________ la rue _________.
(The young woman ran across the street.)
5 Il ________ de nous _________.
(He swam away from us.)
6 Il a __________ la pente _________.
(He skied down the slope.)
7 Elle __________ de lui _________ pour essayer de le gêner devant les autres.
(She waltzed up to him to try to embarrass him in front of the others.)
8 Il ________ de la salle ________ pour essayer de rattraper l'enfant.
(He raced out of the room to try to catch up with the child.)

EXERCISE 8. Fill in the blanks in the following text with the appropriate words, paying particular attention to the use of prepositions.

Christine prépare une licence (1) ___________ (in) français (2) ___ (at) l'université d'Édimbourg (3) __________ (in) Écosse. (4) __________ (At the moment) elle pense (5) _____ (about) l'année prochaine qu'elle va passer (6) __________ (in) un pays francophone. Plutôt que de travailler (7) ___________ (as a) assistante de langue ou de (8) _______ (look for) un stage en entreprise, elle a décidé de participer au programme Erasmus qui facilite la mobilité d'études (9) __________ (across) l'Europe. Elle ne saura pas (10) _____ (until) la fin du mois si elle va (11) _______ (to) Réunion, qu'elle a choisie en premier, ou si elle devra se contenter de rester (12) ________ (in) Europe. De toute façon, la décision ne dépend pas (13) ________ (on) elle. Elle a (14) ___________ (filled in) les formulaires qu'on (15) _______ (her) a demandé de remplir et il faut attendre la décision des professeurs. Entre-temps elle fait des recherches sur Internet (16) _________ (about) les cours qu'elle pourrait suivre soit (17)___________ (in) Réunion, soit (18) ________ (in) Rennes. Elle aime bien Édimbourg et (19) ______________ (she will miss the town), mais elle ne restera que (20) ___________ (for) deux semestres à l'étranger et c'est une occasion à ne pas manquer.

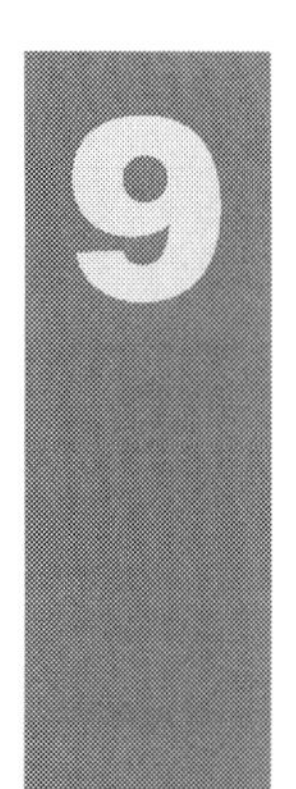

Spelling and more

If you want your written French to look professional, you need to pay attention to spelling, the use of accents, elision and capital letters. This chapter draws your attention to common problems and highlights key differences between written English and written French. The exercises will enable you to practise the French conventions.

Spelling of lookalike words

Particular care is needed with near lookalike words. These have been grouped below into patterns so that they are easier to remember. The examples are given by way of illustration and are not exhaustive.

1 A single consonant in French where there is a double consonant in English:

> une adresse (an address), agressif (aggressive), apaiser (to appease), un comité (a committee), exagérer (to exaggerate), le trafic (traffic; trafficking)

2 A double consonant in French where there is a single consonant in English:

> le développement (development), développer (to develop), l'hommage (homage), l'impressionnisme (impressionism), conditionnel (conditional), professionnel (professional), sensationnel (sensational), traditionnel (traditional)

Be particularly on your guard for French words with a double 'n'.

3 A different vowel in French:

> un exemple (an example), indépendant (independent), la médecine (medicine), naturel (natural), responsable (responsible), une tendance (a tendency)

4 The French word does not contain a letter that is present in the English word:

> l'alcool (alcohol), un garde (a guard), le langage (language), un objet (an object; a purpose), pratique (practical), le rythme (rhythm)

Note that in French, 'gu' is used before the vowel 'a' only to produce the sound [gw], e.g. le Guatémala (Guatemala).

5 There are one or more letters in the French word that do not appear in the English word:

> l'environnement (environment), le gouvernement (government)

6 The French word ends in **–f**, but the English word ends in **-ve**:

> un adhésif (an adhesive), un explétif (an expletive), un impératif (an imperative), un infinitif (an infinitive), un laxatif (a laxative), un objectif (an objective), le subjonctif (the subjunctive)

The most common mistake is with un *objectif* (an objective).

Watch out for some notable exceptions to this pattern, e.g. *une alternative* (an alternative), *une directive* (a directive).

Watch out also for adjectives whose feminine form ends in **–ve**, but whose masculine form ends in **–f**, and avoid the common mistake of using **–ve** for both.

l'aspect positif (the good side), une attitude positive (a positive attitude)

7 Avoid the temptation to make a French word look different from its English equivalent if in fact it is exactly the same.

le public (the public), en public (in public)

The word *publique* does exist, but it is the feminine form of the adjective *public*. Note the difference between *un hôpital public* (a state-run hospital) and *la dette publique* (the national debt).

8 Remember the link between *beaucoup* and the adjective *beau*, and avoid the common misspelling **beacoup*.

Exercises

EXERCISE 1. In each but one of the following sentences, there is a single spelling mistake. Correct the mistakes and identify the sentence that is completely correct.

1. Nous avons pour objective de porter cette affaire à la connaissance du public.
2. Les professionnels de la santé devraient apprendre le language des sourds-muets.
3. L'alcool est responsible de nombreux accidents.
4. Nous avons eu beacoup de mal à apaiser les militants.
5. Pour ce qui est de cela il faut vous addresser au comité d'entreprise.
6. À l'exemple de sa mère, elle tient à son indépendence.
7. Il a une tendance naturelle à la paresse.
8. Il ne faut pas sous-estimer l'importance de la médicine traditionnelle.
9. Elle a parlé de lui en termes très positives, rendant hommage à ses nombreuses réussites.
10. Il est parti au Guatémala sans laisser d'addresse.

Use of accents

This section focuses on common problems with the acute, grave and circumflex accents and the cedilla, treated in that order.

1 Never use an acute accent on 'e' if it is followed by 's' + another consonant, or by 'x'. For example, the verbs *espérer* (to hope) and *expédier* (to send) do not have an acute accent on their first 'e'.

2 Be careful with verbs ending in -**éer**, e.g. *créer* (to create), *maugréer contre* (to grumble about). They are perfectly regular, though the succession of vowels in the past participle may look surprising.

> Elle a maugréé contre son patron.
> (She grumbled about her boss.)

In the example above, it is perfectly correct to have two 'e's with an acute accent in succession; the first is part of the stem of the verb, the second is the regular ending of the past participle. If you do not write an acute accent on the ending of the past participle, you will end up with the present tense form instead, e.g. *elle maugrée* (she is grumbling), instead of *elle a maugréé* (she grumbled).

It is even possible to have three 'e's in succession, e.g.

> Elle ne veut pas quitter la clientèle qu'elle a créée.
> (She doesn't want to leave the practice she has built up.)

In this example, the third 'e' marks the agreement with the feminine singular preceding direct object, la clientèle (the practice).

3 There is no grave accent on 'a' in the demonstrative pronouns **ça** and **cela**. Note the difference in meaning between **ça** (that) and **çà** with a grave accent, as used in the expression **çà et là** (here and there).

4 Remember to use a grave accent to distinguish the preposition **à** (to, at, in) from **a**, the third-person singular present tense verb form of *avoir* (to have), for example:

> Elle **a** passé deux mois **à** Paris.
> (She has spent two months in Paris.)

5 Remember also to use a grave accent to distinguish **où** (where) from **ou** (or), for example:

> **Où** est-il allé? Il se moque de nous, **ou** quoi?
> (Where has he gone? Is he making fun of us or what?)

6 Remember to use a circumflex accent to distinguish **dû**, the past participle of *devoir* (to have to), from **du** (the contraction of **de** + **le**), for example:

> Il a **dû** oublier l'heure **du** rendez-vous.
> (He must have forgotten the time of the appointment.)

7 Take care with verbs ending in **-aître**, e.g. *connaître* (to know), *paraître* (to seem). You need a circumflex on the 'i' only when it is followed immediately by 't'. This occurs in the third-person singular of the present tense, e.g. *il connaît*, *il paraît*, in the infinitive, and throughout the future and conditional (which take the infinitive minus the final **-e** as their stem), e.g. *je connaîtrai*, *il paraîtra*, *je connaîtrais*, *il paraîtrait*.

8 Remember to use a cedilla under 'c' before 'a', 'o' or 'u', to indicate a soft 'c', e.g. *ça* (that) in contrast to *car* (for) with a hard 'c'.

Mnemonic device
Think of the three vowels in the name, ADOLPHUS.

There is no need for a cedilla before 'e' or 'i', because 'c' is always soft before these two vowels, hence the difference between *ça* with a cedilla and *cela* without.

9 You will frequently see accents omitted on capital letters, particularly the grave accent on capital 'A', but you must never omit a cedilla, where needed, on a capital 'C'. The title of the magazine *Ça m'intéresse* should serve as a useful reminder.

Spelling changes and use of accents in some -er verb forms

The stems of some **-er** verbs change their sound and their written form when they are followed by a mute **-e**. This happens throughout the singular and in the third-person plural of the present tense of the indicative and subjunctive and throughout the future and conditional tenses.

1 Most verbs ending in **-eler** or -**eter** double the final consonant of the stem, e.g.

appeler: j'appelle, tu appelles, il appelle, ils appellent; j'appellerai; j'appellerais

but nous appelons, vous appelez

jeter: je jette, tu jettes, il jette, ils jettent; je jetterai; je jetterais

but nous jetons, vous jetez

2 As a variant on the above, some verbs change the '**e**' of the stem to **è**, e.g.

acheter: j'achète, tu achètes, il achète, ils achètent; j'achèterai; j'achèterais

but nous achetons, vous achetez

Some verbs ending in **-ener** behave likewise, e.g.

mener: je mène, tu mènes, il mène, ils mènent; je mènerai; je mènerais

but nous menons, vous menez

3 The acute accent changes to a grave in verbs ending in **-é** + consonant + **er**, e.g.

céder: je cède, tu cèdes, il cède, ils cèdent

but nous cédons, vous cédez

espérer: j'espère, tu espères, il espère, ils espèrent

but nous espérons, vous espérez

In the future and conditional tenses, however, an acute accent remains, e.g.

je céderai, je céderais; j'espérerai; j'espérerais

4 Finally there is a spelling change to note in verbs ending in –**cer** and **-ger**. When a 'c' or 'g' is followed by the vowel 'o', or 'a', a cedilla is used to preserve the soft sound of the 'c' and an 'e' is written after the 'g'. This occurs in the first-person plural of the present tense and throughout the imperfect tense, e.g.

nous commençons, nous mangeons; je commençais, je mangeais

Exercises

EXERCISE 2. In each but one of the following sentences, a single accent has been omitted or used incorrectly. Make the necessary corrections and identify the one sentence that is completely correct.

1 Ou avez-vous trouvé cette explication bizarre?
2 Ça m'étonne!
3 Il a a peine touché à son assiette.
4 Des vêtements étaient éparpillés ça et là dans la chambre.
5 Son livre paraitra aux éditions Hachette.
6 Il a du accepter leur décision sans maugréer.
7 As-tu vu cet article qui a paru dans le dernier numéro de *Ca m'intéresse*?
8 Ce romancier a crée des personnages extraordinaires.
9 Où on va se promener, ou on reste à la maison, mais décide-toi!
10 Nous nous connaîssons de longue date.

EXERCISE 3a. Complete the sentences below with the present tense form of the verb indicated, paying particular attention to spelling and the use of accents.

1 Il ne ___________ (jeter) jamais rien.
2 L'égoïsme _________ (mener) le monde.
3 Nous ___________ (commencer) à en avoir marre.
4 Ils ____________ (espérer) faire mieux demain.
5 Je t' __________ (appeler) ce soir.
6 Nous ne __________ (manger) jamais au restaurant.
7 Cela ne s'__________ (acheter) pas.

EXERCISE 3b. Complete the sentences below with the future tense form of the verb indicated, paying particular attention to spelling and the use of accents.

1 Si je trouve des abricots au marché, j'en _________ (acheter).
2 Tu as beau essayer de le persuader, il ne _________ (céder) jamais.
3 Si tu ne fais pas attention, il se __________ (jeter) à l'eau.
4 Si tu ne vas pas mieux demain, j'__________ (appeler) le médecin.
5 Cinquante euros, ça ne nous _________ (mener) pas loin!

Elision and word division

The key point here is the difference between a mute and an aspirate 'h' in French, though these terms are misleading, because there is no 'h' sound at all in spoken French. However, there is a small group of words beginning with a so-called aspirate 'h', which behave as if they began with a consonant, whereas those that begin with a mute (or inaspirate) 'h' behave as if the 'h' were not there and they began with a vowel.

1 **Before a noun or an adjective beginning with a vowel or a mute 'h', there is elision**. The definite articles *le* and *la* elide to *l'*, the partitive articles *du* and *de la* become *de l'*, and *de* elides to *d'*. Before a verb beginning with a vowel or a mute 'h', *je* contracts to *j'*, and *me, te, se, ce, le, la, de, ne, que* also contract before a word beginning with a vowel or a mute 'h'.

l'amour (m.)	love
l'aube (f.)	dawn
l'hiver (m.)	winter
l'horrible objet (m.)	the hideous object
l'harmonie (f.)	harmony
faire de l'humour (m.)	to make jokes
de l'huile (f.)	some oil
l'escalier d'honneur (m.)	the main staircase
je l'adore	I love him / her
j'habite	I live

2 **Before an aspirate 'h', by contrast, there is no elision.**

le handicap	disability, handicap
le hérisson	hedgehog
le Haut Moyen Âge	the early Middle Ages
la haine	hatred
la haute Égypte	Upper Egypt
faire du hors-piste	to go off-piste skiing
de la honte	shame
plein de hauteur	haughty
je hais le mensonge	I hate lies
je le hais	I hate him / her

Mnemonic device
To help you remember that there is no elision before an aspirate 'h', bear in mind the title of the film ***La Haine,*** the place names **Le Havre** and **La Haye** and the phrase **Ce n'est pas le fait du hasard si** . . . (It is no accident that . . .).

3 There are only a few dozen words in French that begin with an aspirate 'h'. Many of them were borrowed in the early medieval period from the Germanic speech of the Franks, or in more recent times from English. In addition to the words listed above, they include:

la hache (axe), le hall (entrance hall, lobby), le hameau (hamlet), handicapé (disabled), le hareng (herring), le haricot (bean), la harpe (harp), la hâte (haste), la hausse (rise), le hautbois (oboe), la hauteur (height), le héros (hero), le hibou (owl), la hiérarchie (hierarchy), le homard (lobster), la Hollande (Holland), la Hongrie (Hungary), la honte (shame), le huit (eight); the adjective hippie (hippy); the verbs harceler (to pester, harass) and heurter (to hit, strike).

4 The best thing to do is simply to learn these words, and if in doubt to check in a dictionary. A good dictionary will indicate an aspirate 'h' by putting ['] at the beginning of the phonetic transcription of the word. There is one idiosyncrasy to note. Although **le héros** begins with an aspirate 'h', the related words **l'héroïne** and **l'héroïsme** do not.

5 The main focus in this section is on elision, but it should also be noted that in speech there is no liaison before a word beginning with an aspirate 'h', so the final consonant of the plural articles *les* and *des* is not pronounced [z], as it would be if the word began with a vowel or a mute 'h'. The most common error is with *des / les héros* (heroes). This should not sound the same as *des / les zéros* (zeroes / noughts). Remember also that there is no liaison in *les Halles* (covered market; well-known metro station in Paris).

6 **Si elides before il(s) to s'il(s), but there is no elision before elle(s)**. Contrast the following:

S'il décide de partir . . .
(If he decides to leave . . .)

Si elle décide de partir . . .
(If she decides to leave . . .)

7 **Remember that que elides to qu' before a vowel, but qui does not.** Contrast the following examples where **qu'** is the object of the verb in the relative clause and **qui** is the subject:

Le train **qu'**il va prendre est en retard.
(The train which he is going to catch is late.)

Le train **qui** entre en gare va à Dijon.
(The train coming into the station is going to Dijon.)

8 Note the difference between the pronouns **quelqu'un** (someone) and **chacun** (each one), and do not make the common mistake of writing *chaqu'un. The asterisk indicates that such a form does not exist.

9 Remember that **quelque chose** (something) is written as two words in French, but **quelquefois** (sometimes) is written as one.

Exercises

EXERCISE 4. Choose the correct form in each case.

1 C'est (l' / le) hasard qui les a réunis.
2 Travailler si tard dans la nuit, c'est (de l' / du) héroïsme!
3 Il faut couper le tissu dans le sens de (l' / la) hauteur.
4 Elle ne cesse de (l' / le) harceler de questions.
5 C'est une femme (d' / de) haute taille.
6 Ils ont monté l'escalier (d' / de) honneur.
7 On se verra tout à (l' / la) heure dans (l' / le) hall (de l' /du) hôtel.
8 Je me demande (s' elle / si elle) aura le courage de leur parler et (s'ils / si ils) l'écouteront.
9 Ce (qu' / que / qui) est affreux, c'est que tout ce (qu' / que / qui) il dit est faux.
10 (Chacun / Chaqu'un) a ses défauts. Je me demande (quelque fois / quelquefois) pourquoi elle se croit parfaite.

Capital letters

Capital letters are used in French at the beginning of a sentence and for proper names, e.g. *Amélie* and *Dijon*, but elsewhere they are used less widely than in English.

1 Note the following instances where lowercase letters are used in French, but capital letters are the norm in English.

- Days of the week and months of the year, e.g. lundi (Monday), septembre (September)
- The words for road, street, square, etc. in place names, e.g. la rue de Vincennes, la place de la République, as opposed to Regent Street and Trafalgar Square in English
- Geographical terms forming part of a proper name, e.g. la mer Méditerranée (the Mediterranean Sea), l'océan Pacifique (the Pacific Ocean)
- Titles of individuals, e.g. le docteur Dumas (Doctor Dumas), le général Pétain (General Pétain), la reine Élisabeth (Queen Elizabeth) and even monsieur / madame / mademoiselle Dumas (Mr / Mrs / Miss) Dumas, except in direct address or in a letterhead or when abbreviated to M., Mme, Mlle
- Languages, e.g. l'anglais (English), le français (French)

2 Adjectives describing nationality, geographical origin or religious affiliation begin with a lowercase letter in French, e.g.

> un écrivain français (a French writer), un pays méditerranéen
> (a Mediterranean country), un prêtre catholique (a Catholic priest)

Nouns indicating religious affiliation behave likewise, e.g.

> Ce sont des catholiques.
> (They are Catholics.)

However, nouns indicating nationality or geographical origin take a capital letter in French, as they do in English. Compare and contrast the following examples:

> Il est espagnol.
> (He is Spanish.)

> Les Espagnols me font sourire.
> (The Spanish make me smile.)

> Je n'aime pas les Parisiens, mais j'aime la région parisienne.
> (I don't like the Parisians, but I do like the Paris region.)

3 Names of institutions, organisations, major historical events, etc. have fewer capitals than in English. As a general rule, the main noun and any adjectives preceding it are capitalised, but the following adjectives and any subordinate nouns are not, e.g.

la Bourse (the Stock Exchange), la Révolution française (the French Revolution), le Moyen Âge (the Middle Ages), la Grande Guerre (the Great War), la Sécurité sociale (Social Security), la Chambre des communes (the House of Commons)

Exceptions include *la Comédie-Française* (the oldest national theatre company with premises in Paris) and the names of government departments, e.g. *le ministère des Affaires Étrangères* (the Foreign Office).

There is now a growing tendency to follow the Anglo-American pattern of using capitals for all nouns, so you will sometimes find *l'Organisation Mondiale de la Santé* (the World Health Organization), rather than the more traditional *l'Organisation mondiale de la santé*.

4 You will find a variety of practices in French when citing the titles of books, films, etc., but in general there are fewer capital letters than in English. One common convention in French is to capitalise the first noun and any words that precede it, but not the words that follow it, e.g. *Les Petits Enfants du siècle*, *La Femme rompue*, *Les Fleurs du mal*, *Les Quatre Cents Coups, Voyage au bout de la nuit*.

Exercises

EXERCISE 5. Choose the correct form in each case.

1 Son père est d'origine (espagnole / Espagnole), mais il a acquis la nationalité (française / Française) l'année dernière.
2 La (reine / Reine) Élisabeth n'a pas le droit d'entrer dans (la Chambre des communes / la Chambre des Communes).
3 Nous l'avons croisé (rue de Rivoli / Rue de Rivoli), près de la (place de la Concorde / Place de la Concorde).
4 Nous avons traversé (l'océan Atlantique / l'Océan Atlantique) pour la première fois cet (été / Été).
5 Les immigrés (maghrébins / Maghrébins) se concentrent dans la région (parisienne / Parisienne).
6 Ce sont des (catholiques / Catholiques). Leur petite fille va faire sa première communion (dimanche / Dimanche).
7 Le (général de Gaulle / Général de Gaulle) a prononcé un discours important le 18 (juin / Juin) 1940.
8 Cette église date de la fin du (moyen Âge / Moyen Âge).
9 La (Sécurité sociale / Sécurité Sociale) ne rembourse pas certains médicaments.
10 J'ai enfin trouvé un DVD de (*À Bout de souffle* / *À Bout de Souffle*) qui est sous-titré en (anglais / Anglais).

Presentation of numbers

French usage of the comma and full stop with numbers is strikingly different from English usage. If you want your written French to look authentic, it is important to get this right.

Where English uses a comma in a large number to separate thousands from millions and hundreds from thousands, French normally uses a typographical space. It is also possible to use a full stop.

English	French
1,000,000	1 000 000 or 1.000.000
500,000	500 000 or 500.000

However, note that no punctuation is used in either language with year dates, e.g.

l'an 2018 (the year 2018).

Where English uses a full stop (decimal point) to separate whole numbers from decimals, French uses a comma.

English	French
15.75	15,75
0. 25%	0, 25%
£4.75	4,75 EUR / 4,75€ / €4,75

Exercises

EXERCISE 6. Add the missing punctuation to the numbers in the following sentences.

1 Nous vous accordons une remise de 2 5% sur votre commande. Votre facture est donc ramenée de 520000€ à 518700€.
2 En règlement de votre facture du 25 mai 2020, veuilllez trouver ci-joint un chèque bancaire d'un montant de 1500€.
3 J'ai eu une augmentation de 0 5%, tandis que le taux d'inflation est de 1 3%.
4 Au total, fin mars 2020, le nombre de demandeurs d'emploi en France s'établit à 5290500. Ce nombre est en hausse de 0 5% sur un mois (+28000) et de 6 7% sur un an (+334200).

EXERCISE 7. Complete the text of the following letter by choosing between the alternatives given in brackets.

Amiens, le 17/10/2020
Aurélie DUPONT
Directrice du CIO Amiens Nord
Aux
Invités de (l'espace / l'éspace)
'Europe-International'

(OBJECT / OBJET): Invitation au Forum 'du lycéen à l'étudiant'

À l'occasion de la vingt-septième édition du Forum 'du lycéen à l'étudiant' de l'Académie d'Amiens, j'ai (l'honneur / le honneur) et le plaisir de vous inviter (a / à) participer à (l'espace / l'éspace) 'Europe-International' que j'organise. Je serais très heureuse de vous accueillir parmi nous cette année. (L'objectif / L'objective) de (l'espace / l'éspace) est de réunir des (professionels / professionnels) de l'orientation des différents pays de l'Union (européenne / Européenne), et internationaux, ainsi que des partenaires du réseau Euroguidance.

Le Forum se déroulera les (jeudi / Jeudi) 08, (vendredi / Vendredi) 09 et samedi / Samedi) 10 (janvier / Janvier) de 9 h à 17h au Centre des Expositions de Mégacité, (avenue / Avenue) de l'Hippodrome à Amiens. Cette manifestation (s'adresse / s'addresse) principalement aux élèves scolarisés en première et terminale de lycée, et aux étudiants de L'Université Picardie Jules Verne, ainsi (que / qu') aux parents d'élèves.

Lors des entretiens individuels que vous (menerez / mènerez), vous aurez (a / à) informer les futurs étudiants sur principalement:

- les poursuites d'études supérieures, la réglementation des (echanges / échanges) universitaires
- les aides financières possibles pour étudier dans un pays (européen / Européen) et à l'étranger ou pour y (effectuer / éffectuer) un stage (professionel / professionnel) ou un séjour de (perfectionement / perfectionnement) linguistique
- les conditions de travail et les possibilités d'emploi, les conditions de vie dans le pays visé

Par ailleurs, de brefs (exposés / éxposés) sur ces principaux thèmes seront proposés à de petits groupes de jeunes pendant la durée de la manifestation. Si vous êtes volontaire pour ce type d'intervention je vous prie de m'en informer sur la fiche ci-jointe, vous y trouverez l'intitulé (exact / éxact) des thèmes proposés.

Je vous (rappele / rappelle) que vos déplacements, ainsi que (l'hébergement / le hébergement) et les repas sont pris en charge.

Les modalités (practiques / pratiques) de votre séjour à Amiens vous seront envoyées fin (décembre / Décembre).

Comptant vivement sur votre participation, si possible, les trois jours de la manifestation, je reste à votre entière disposition pour tout renseignement complémentaire.

Bien cordialement,
Aurélie DUPONT

Appendix 1

Use of prepositions with names of countries and islands

Europe

to/in	from	English name
en Albanie (f.)	d'Albanie	Albania
en Allemagne (f.)	d'Allemagne	Germany
en Andorre (f.)	d'Andorre	Andorra (principality)
en Angleterre (f.)	d'Angleterre	England
en Autriche (f.)	d'Autriche	Austria
aux (îles) Baléares (f.)	des Baléares	the Balearic Islands
à Majorque (f.)	de Majorque	Majorca
à Minorque (f.)	de Minorque	Minorca
en Belgique (f.)	de Belgique	Belgium
en Bosnie-Herzégovine (f.)	de Bosnie-Herzégovine	Bosnia-Herzegovina
en Bulgarie (f.)	de Bulgarie	Bulgaria
à Chypre (f.)	de Chypre	Cyprus
en Corse (f.)	de Corse	Corsica
en Crète (f.)	de Crète	Crete
en Croatie (f.)	de Croatie	Croatia
au Danemark (m.)	du Danemark	Denmark
en Écosse (f.)	d'Écosse	Scotland
en Éire (f.)	d'Éire	Eire
en République (f.) d'Irlande	de la République d'Irlande	the Republic of Ireland
en Espagne (f.)	d'Espagne	Spain
au pays basque (m.)	du pays basque	the Basque country
en Estonie (f.)	d'Estonie	Estonia

en Finlande (f.)	de Finlande	Finland
en France (f.)	de France	France
au Pays de Galles (m.)	du Pays de Galles	Wales
en Grande-Bretagne (f.)	de Grande-Bretagne	Great Britain
en Grèce (f.)	de Grèce	Greece
au Grœnland (m.)	du Grœnland	Greenland
en Hollande (f.)	de Hollande (aspirate 'h')	Holland
aux Pays Bas (m.)	des Pays Bas	the Netherlands
en Hongrie (f.)	de Hongrie (aspirate 'h')	Hungary
en Irlande (f.) du Nord	d'Irlande du Nord	Northern Ireland
en Italie (f.)	d'Italie	Italy
au Vatican (m.)	du Vatican	the Vatican
en Lettonie (f.)	de Lettonie	Latvia
en Lithuanie (f.)	de Lithuanie	Lithuania
au Luxembourg (m.)	du Luxembourg	Luxembourg (Grand-Duchy)
à Malte (f.)	de Malte	Malta
en Norvège (f.)	de Norvège	Norway
en Pologne (f.)	de Pologne	Poland
au Portugal (m.)	du Portugal	Portugal
en République (f.) tchèque	de la République tchèque	the Czech Republic
au Royaume Uni (m.)	du Royaume Uni	United Kingdom
en Roumanie (f.)	de Roumanie	Romania
en Russie (f.)	de Russie	Russia
en Union Soviétique (f.)	de l'Union Soviétique	the Soviet Union
en URSS (f.)	de l'URSS	USSR
en Sardaigne (f.)	de Sardaigne	Sardinia
en Serbie (f.)	de Serbie	Serbia
en Sicile (f.)	de Sicile	Sicily
en Slovaquie (f.)	de Slovaquie	Slovakia
en Suède (f.)	de Suède	Sweden
en Suisse (f.)	de Suisse	Switzerland
en Turquie (f.)	de Turquie	Turkey
en Ukraine (f.)	d'Ukraine	Ukraine

Middle East

to/in	from	English name
en Arabie saoudite (f.)	d'Arabie saoudite	Saudi Arabia
en Irak (m.)	d'Irak	Iraq

en Iran (m.)	d'Iran	Iran
en Israël (m.)	d'Israël	Israel
en Jordanie (f.)	de Jordanie	Jordan
au Liban (m.)	du Liban	Lebanon
au Moyen-Orient (m.)	du Moyen-Orient	the Middle East
au Proche-Orient (m.)	du Proche-Orient	the Near East
en Syrie (f.)	de Syrie	Syria
au Yémen (m.)	du Yémen	Yemen

Africa

to/in	from	English name
en Afrique (f.) du Sud	d'Afrique du Sud	South Africa
en Algérie (f.)	d'Algérie	Algeria
en Angola (m.)	d'Angola	Angola
au Bénin (m.)	du Bénin	Benin
au Burkina Faso (m.)	du Burkina Faso	Burkina Faso
au Cameroun (m.)	du Cameroun	Cameroon
au Congo (m.)	du Congo	the Congo
en Côte (f.) d'Ivoire	de la Côte d'Ivoire	the Ivory Coast
en Égypte (f.)	d'Égypte	Egypt
en Éthiopie (f.)	d'Éthiopie	Ethiopia
au Gabon (m.)	du Gabon	Gabon
au Ghana (m.)	du Ghana	Ghana
au Kenya (m.)	du Kenya	Kenya
au Libéria (m.)	du Libéria	Liberia
en Libye (f.)	de Libye	Libya
à Madagascar (f.)	de Madagascar	Madagascar
au Maghreb (m.)	du Maghreb	the Maghreb (Morocco, Algeria and Tunisia)
au Malawi (m.)	du Malawi	Malawi
au Mali (m.)	du Mali	Mali
au Maroc (m.)	du Maroc	Morocco
à (l'île) Maurice (f.)	de (l'île) Maurice	Mauritius
en Mauritanie (f.)	de Mauritanie	Mauritania
au Mozambique (m.)	du Mozambique	Mozambique
en Namibie (f.)	de Namibie	Namibia
au Niger (m.)	du Niger	the Niger
au Nigéria (m.)	du Nigéria	Nigeria
en Ouganda (m.)	d'Ouganda	Uganda

en République centrafricaine (f.)	de la République centrafricaine	Central African Republic
à la Réunion (f.)	de la Réunion	Reunion
au Sénégal (m.)	du Sénégal	Senegal
en Sierra Leone (f.)	de Sierra Leone	Sierra Leone
en Somalie (f.)	de Somalie	Somalia
au Soudan (m.)	du Soudan	Sudan
en Tanzanie (f.)	de Tanzanie	Tanzania
au Tchad (m.)	du Tchad	Chad
au Togo (m.)	du Togo	Togo
en Tunisie (f.)	de Tunisie	Tunisia
en Zambie (f.)	de Zambie	Zambia
au Zimbabwe (m.)	du Zimbabwe	Zimbabwe

Asia and Australasia

to/in	from	English name
en Afghanistan (m.)	d'Afghanistan	Afghanistan
en Australie (f.)	d'Australie	Australia
au Bangladesh (m.)	du Bangladesh	Bangladesh
en Birmanie (f.)	de Birmanie	Burma
au Cambodge (m.)	du Cambodge	Cambodia
en Chine (f.)	de Chine	China
en Corée (f.) du Nord	de Corée du Nord	North Korea
en Corée (f.) du Sud	de Corée du Sud	South Korea
en Inde (f.)	**de l'Inde (*exception*)**	India
en Indonésie (f.)	d'Indonésie	Indonesia
au Japon (m.)	du Japon	Japan
au Laos (m.)	du Laos	Laos
en Malaisie (f.)	de Malaisie	Malaysia
au Myanmar (m.)	du Myanmar	Myanmar
au Népal (m.)	du Népal	Nepal
en Nouvelle-Calédonie (f.)	de Nouvelle-Calédonie	New Caledonia
en Nouvelle Zélande (f.)	de Nouvelle-Zélande	New Zealand
au Pakistan (m.)	du Pakistan	Pakistan
aux Philippines (f.)	des Philippines	the Philippines
à Sri Lanka (m.)	de Sri Lanka	Sri Lanka
en Tasmanie (f.)	de Tasmanie	Tasmania
en Thaïlande (f.)	de Thaïlande	Thailand
au Tibet (m.)	du Tibet	Tibet
au Vietnam (m.)	du Vietnam	Vietnam

North America

to/in	from	English name
au Canada (m.)	du Canada	Canada
au Québec (m.)	du Québec	Quebec
aux États-Unis (m.)	des États-Unis	United States
aux USA (in speech)	des USA	USA

Central America

to/in	from	English name
aux Antilles (f.)	des Antilles	West Indies
au Costa Rica (m.)	du Costa Rica	Costa Rica
à Cuba (f.)	de Cuba	Cuba
en Guadeloupe (f.)	de la Guadeloupe	Guadeloupe
au Guatémala (m.)	du Guatémala	Guatemala
en Haïti (m.)	d'Haïti	Haiti
au Honduras (m.)	du Honduras (aspirate 'h')	Honduras
à la Jamaïque (f.)	de la Jamaïque	Jamaica
à la Martinique (f.)	de la Martinique	Martinique
au Mexique (m.)	du Mexique	Mexico
au Nicaragua (m.)	du Nicaragua	Nicaragua
au Panama (m.)	du Panama	Panama
à Porto Rico (f.)	de Porto Rico	Puerto Rico
en République dominicaine (f.)	de la République dominicaine	the Dominican Republic
au Salvador (m.)	du Salvador	El Salvador

South America

to/in	from	English name
en Argentine (f.)	d'Argentine	Argentina
en Bolivie (f.)	de Bolivie	Bolivia
au Brésil (m.)	du Brésil	Brazil
au Chili (m.)	du Chili	Chile
en Colombie (f.)	de Colombie	Colombia
en Équateur (m.)	d'Équateur	Ecuador
en Guyane (f.)	de Guyane	Guyana
au Paraguay (m.)	du Paraguay	Paraguay
au Pérou (m.)	du Pérou	Peru
en Uruguay (m.)	d'Uruguay	Uruguay
au Vénézuela (m.)	du Vénézuela	Venezuela

Appendix 2
Answer key to exercises

Chapter 1

EXERCISE 1

1. un; Quel / 2. premières; du / 3. officielle; du / 4. Ce; de la; du / 5. conservées; du; de la / 6. La; le / 7. une; bleue; mon / 8. l'un; la; allemande / 9. La; du; pertinente / 10. le; du; un; attentif / 11. Le; de la / 12. la; du; la; Le premier; supérieur / 13. un; aucun / 14. Le; humain / 15. Un; animé; la / 16. ce; une vieille / 17. la; du; une / 18. du; de la / 19. blancs; réguliers / 20. Le; un

EXERCISE 2

1. une image / 2. le Mexique / 3. une espèce / 4. un concombre / 5. le silence / 6. le Rhône / 7. une jument / 8. une photo / 9. un domaine / 10. le choix / 11. un murmure / 12. une pizza / 13. la couleur / 14. la misère / 15. un bastion / 16. la peau / 17. un stade / 18. une loi / 19. une clé / 20. un musée

EXERCISE 3

1. une crêpe; la poêle / 2. le même moule / 3. du chèvre; un crème / 4. la critique / 5. Le manœuvre; la manœuvre; sa droite / 6. un espace / 7. Le mode / 8. au poste / 9. une mémoire / 10. son physique / 11. la mort / 12. le vase / 13. une somme; droit / 14. Un voile / 15. un tour / 16. la Manche / 17. Le rose / 18. la livre / 19. la page / 20. à la merci; à la solde

EXERCISE 4

1. bon / 2. motivés / 3. Seules certaines gens / 4. Tous les gens / 5. interrogées / 6. Quel / 7. une vraie œuvre / 8. l'œuvre sculpté / 9. tombé / 10. Joyeux; Joyeuses

EXERCISE 5

1. les chapeaux / 2. les mois / 3. les travaux / 4. les pneus / 5. des choux / 6. des maux de tête / 7. des yeux / 8. Messieurs / 9. des bals / 10. des baux / 11. des vœux / 12. des trous / 13. des ciels de Turner / 14. des chevaux / 15. des cheveux

EXERCISE 6

1. un timbre-poste; des timbres-poste / 2. une pause-café; des pauses-cafés / 3. un chef-d'œuvre; des chefs-d'œuvre / 4. un tête-â-tête; des tête-à-tête / 5. une demi-heure; des demi-heures / 6. un pare-brise; des pare-brise / 7. un soutien-gorge; des soutiens-gorge / 8. Un tire-bouchon; des tire-bouchons / 9. un faire-part; des faire-part / 10. un grand-parent; des grands-parents

EXERCISE 7

1. des progrès; linguistique / 2. des recherches / 3. du raisin / 4. vacances / 5. son pantalon; l'escalier / 6. des connaissances approfondies; physique / 7. applaudissements / 8. Pléchot / 9. arrive; est / 10. les informations

EXERCISE 8

1. scolaires; longues / 2. Toutes; occupées / 3. mêmes / 4. Même; douteux / 5. fournis; inexacts / 6. Tous; interviewés; même / 7. aucun; importants / 8. Seule / 9. continuels; aînés; pleine / 10. ensemble

EXERCISE 9

1. lectrice / 2. des recherches / 3. des renseignements / des informations / 4. la région / 5. les alentours / 6. sont / 7. pittoresques / 8. un centre / 9. l'industrie pétrolière / 10. le logement / 11. un studio / 12. du centre-ville / 13. un appartement / 14. le choix / 15. limité / 16. ce stade / 17. le problème / 18. une avance / 19. son salaire / 20. verser des arrhes

Chapter 2

EXERCISE 1

1. aveuglée / 2. crient / 3. se tourmente / 4. atteint / 5. de transformer / 6. équilibrer / 7. me débarrasser / 8. enivrer / 9. pondu / 10. remarqué / 11. remplacé / 12. faire semblant / 13. reprendre / 14. reste / 15. reporter / 16. ne supporte pas / 17. usé / 18. exigent / 19. atténuantes / 20. passer / 21. convenu / 22. importuner

EXERCISE 2

1. Ils ont confronté trois textes différents.
2. Les soucis l'ont usé.
3. J'ai assisté à un incident regrettable.
4. Des avions évoluaient dans le ciel pendant le meeting aérien.
5. Il ne pourra jamais réaliser tous ses projets.
6. Cet enfant m'excède avec ses petites manies.
7. J'ignore où ils habitent.

8. Le directeur doit contrôler la fiabilité du texte.
9. Nous avons commandé une caisse de vin.
10. Cet attentat l'a conforté dans l'idée d'être journaliste.
11. L'humidité a altéré la décoration de la chambre.
12. L'accusé a crié son innocence.
13. Si vous disposez d'une voiture, vous pourrez y aller.
14. Ces longues heures de travail l'avaient exténué.
15. Elle avait été intoxiquée par des champignons vénéneux.
16. Il a réussi à son examen de rattrapage.
17. Elle a moins d'expérience qu'on ne le prétend.
18. On nous a demandé de replacer les chaises dans la salle de classe.
19. Il faut considérer les conséquences avant d'agir.
20. Il ressent de la colère contre elle.

EXERCISE 3

1. te reposer / 2. blindé / 3. exige / 4. en veux / 5. griser / 6. balancer / 7. achevée / 8. désaltère / 9. agréer / 10. signalé / 11. usé / 12. m'abuse / 13. se servir de / 14. réalisé / 15. remarqué / 16. contrôler / 17. remplacer / 18. prétend / 19. replacer / 20. fait remarquer

EXERCISE 4

1. passer / 2. reporter / 3. te rends compte / 4. atténuantes / 5. se laisser abuser / 6. réussi / 7. se remettre / 8. pleurait à chaudes larmes / 9. importuner / 10. m'en veut / 11. excède / 12. s'achève / 13. me reposer / 14. je m'en balance / 15. dispose / 16. changer / 17. me tourmenter

Chapter 3

EXERCISE 1

1. évidence / 2. succès / 3. tromperies / 4. la misère / 5. le changement / 6. un avertissement / 7. un délai / 8. disgrâce / 9. ivresse / 10. d'injures / 11. halles / 12. question / 13. nombreux dérangements / 14. du chagrin / 15. capacités / 16. un mémoire 17. un cours / 18. convenances personnelles / 19. à l'ordre du jour / 20. plainte

EXERCISE 2

1. n / 2. e / 3. h / 4. i / 5. m / 6. r / 7. q / 8. p / 9. f / 10. g / 11. t / 12. j / 13. k / 14. o / 15. d / 16. a / 17. s / 18. b / 19. c / 20. l

EXERCISE 3

1. l'altération / 2. une casserole / 3. caution / 4. convenance / 5. retard / 6. les témoignages / 7. une inconvenance / 8. cours / 9. ingénuité / 10. délai / 11. affluence / 12 l'agonie / 13. une annonce / 14. la cave / 15. commodité

EXERCISE 4

1. petite monnaie / 2. ta punition / 3. une étape / 4. la peine / 5. locataire / 6. misère / 7. une licence / 8. loyers . . . élevés / 9. procès / 10. lieu / 11. studio / 12. un vers / 13. audience / 14. motoristes / 15. préjugés / 16. train / 17. physicien / 18. de la scène / 19. troubles / 20. location

EXERCISE 5

1. d / 2. e / 3. b / 4. l / 5. s / 6. c / 7. a / 8. k / 9. f / 10. n / 11. m / 12. t / 13. o / 14. g / 15. r / 16. j / 17. p / 18. h / 19. q / 20. i

EXERCISE 6

1. librairies / 2. office / 3. figure / 4. pièce / 5. bibliothèque / 6. occasion / 7. formation / 8. essence / 9. préjugés / 10. trouble / 11. scientifique / 12. parent / 13. patron / 14. préjudice / 15. pétrole

EXERCISE 7

1. licence / 2. stage / 3. librairie / 4. bibliothèque / 5. rétribution / 6. expérience / 7. occasion / 8. formation / 9. permis / 10. conducteur / 11. train / 12. son mémoire / 13. argent / 14. studio / 15. pensionnaires / 16. locataire / 17. peine / 18. issue / 19. occasion / 20. congrès

Chapter 4

EXERCISE 1

1. En fait / 2. anciens / 3. intéressants / 4. courtois / 5. active / 6. abusive / 7. universitaires / 8. abusive / 9. actuelle / 10. qu'elle a entraînés / 11. honteux / 12. satisfaite / 13. sans cesse / 14. finalement / 15. précieux / 16. tout à l'heure / 17. raisonnables / 18. impolie / 19. séduisant / 20. d'importantes / 21. robustes / 22. efficacement / 23. méticuleuse / 24. détaillée / 25. occupée / 26. lamentables / 27. sympathique / 28. inutilisable

EXERCISE 2

1. Ce sont des pouvoirs abusifs
2. Elle est présentement en vacances.
3. Aussi a-t-il résolu de ne jamais revenir.
4. Elle portait une robe disgracieuse.
5. Vous pourrez éventuellement vous en servir.
6. Quelle idée géniale!
7. Les portes s'ouvriront incessamment.
8. Elle a perdu une importante somme d'argent.
9. Ce sont des objets précieux.
10. Cette marque est très prisée.
11. C'est un artiste académique.
12. Ce remède est efficace.
13. En fait elle écrit très mal.
14. Il y a différentes explications.

15. Elle a épousé un brave garçon.
16. Cela représente une réduction conséquente.
17. Elle a de larges connaissances.
18. Il est très pétulant.
19. Son salaire est inférieur au tien.
20. Il mène une vie scandaleuse.

EXERCISE 3a

1. L'Ancien Testament / 2. une situation intéressante / 3. une vie large / 4. sensible au froid / 5. douée / 6. amusants / 7. la fonction publique / 8. devient effectif / 9. les grandes tailles / 10. L'opinion générale

EXERCISE 3b

1. exactement / 2. incessamment / 3. effectivement / 4. éventuellement / 5. actuellement / 6. largement / 7. tout à l'heure / 8. sensiblement / 9. aussi / 10. en fait

EXERCISE 4

1. différentes / 2. géniale / 3. terrible / 4. romanes / 5. sans cesse / 6. efficace / 7. aussi / 8. douée pour les études / 9. luxueux / 10. supérieur / 11. largement / 12. éventuellement / 13. intéressant / 14. rude / 15. doux / 16. cordiaux / 17. En fait / 18. différents / 19. aussi / 20. importantes

Chapter 5

EXERCISE 1

1. as; as / 2. Vas / 3. donnez; est / 4. serait or fût / 5. N'aie / 6. ont / 7. donner / 8. eu / 9. va / 10. eu / 11. donne / 12. m'est / 13. es / 14. va / 15. a / 16. être / 17. eus. / 18. Avez / 19. avoir / 20. donne

EXERCISE 2

1. il y a belle lurette / 2. À qui / 3. c'est ça / 4. en avez pour longtemps / 5. Va-t'en! / 6. ça y est / 7. Il en va / 8. il y a de quoi / 9. donne sur / 10. Il y en a / 11. donne dans / 12. Il n'y a pas de quoi / 13. j'y suis / 14. ont beau / 15. n'ont rien donné / 16. J'étais en train de / 17. il en va de même pour / 18. se donne pour; il n'en est rien / 19. cela étant / 20. se donne

EXERCISE 3

1. vient / 2. faire / 3. mettre / 4. venait / 5. fait / 6. mettre / 7. pris / 8. tenir / 9. tombez; viennent / 10. prend / 11. venir / 12. fait / 13. prend / 14. met / 15. mis; faire / 16. tombent / 17. mettre / 18. venir / 19. prend / 20. venir / 21. tient / 22. tombée

EXERCISE 4

1. Mettons / 2. ferait du bien / 3. faire venir / 4. se mettre / 5. prendre / 6. se fait / 7. vient / 8. Tiens! . . . tenu / 9. s'y prendre / 10. faire part / 11. mettre en exergue / 12. Laisse tomber / 13. Cela fait / 14. fais remarquer / 15. t'en fais / 16. s'est mis debout / 17. se faire à / 18. tombe / 19. il se fit / 20. suis tombé sur / 21. mettre en marche / 22. se tenir

EXERCISE 5

1. laisser tomber / 2. faire de lui / 3. a fait de son mieux / a fait son possible / 4. en est venu à / 5. a assez / a marre / 6. Il y a or Cela / ça fait / 7. se faire à / 8. faire plaisir à / 9. leur faire comprendre / 10. le faire travailler / 11. lui faire aimer / 12. De là vient qu' / 13. se mettre à / 14. n'y tient pas / 15. faire vite / 16. faire semblant de / 17. À tout prendre / 18. ira mieux / 19. leur fera remarquer / 20. tient de

Chapter 6

EXERCISE 1

1. se doutait / 2. se rend / 3. approche / 4. se plaint / 5. me rendre / 6. s'éclaircir / 7. ferme / 8. se concentrer / 9. s'est beaucoup amélioré / 10. coucher / 11. s'est passé / 12. te rendre / 13. se débrouille / 14. n'échappe à / 15. sent / 16. s'est laissé / 17. Either option is acceptable. / 18. se sont agrandis / 19. ne se sont pas aperçus de / 20. me demande; se décider à

EXERCISE 2

1. Je me suis vu / entendu proposer un poste intéressant.
2. Les livres se classent par auteur.
3. Les assiettes se rangent dans le buffet de cuisine.
4. Je me suis vu / entendu dire que le directeur était en réunion.
5. Ce produit se vend uniquement en pharmacie.
6. Ce jambon se mange cru.
7. Ça ne s'est jamais vu!
8. Ils se sont vu / entendu répondre qu'il ne restait plus de places.

EXERCISE 3

1. Le chanteur s'est fait huer par le public.
2. Je me suis laissé persuader de louer l'appartement.
3. Notre équipe s'est fait battre par 3 à zéro.
4. Le professeur s'est fait harceler de questions.
5. Il s'est laissé tromper par sa femme.
6. J'ai peur de me faire attaquer par surprise.
7. Les voleurs se sont fait arrêter par les policiers.
8. Vous risquez de vous faire / laisser prendre dans une bagarre.
9. Tu t'es laissé avoir par cet escroc.
10. Je me suis fait interpeller par un chahuteur.

EXERCISE 4

1. Tiens-toi; arrête / 2. a écarté / 3. t'es trompé; s'écrit / 4. s'intéresse / 5. s'est effondrée / 6. s'est assise / 7. se mêle / 8. figure / 9. se dérouler / 10. s'est beaucoup affaiblie / 11. s'est cassé / 12. s'enrichit / 13. portent / 14. a tourné / 15. était assise / 16. s'est allongé / 17. s'est vite habitué; coucher / 18. se séparer / 19. servir / 20. me sens

EXERCISE 5

1. pour / 2. à / 3. de / 4. de / 5. à / 6. sur / 7. dans / 8. à / 9. à / 10. de

EXERCISE 6

1. s'affaiblit / 2. correct! / 3. lavé / 4. écrit / 5. affaiblissent / 6. fait / 7. correct! / 8. obscurcissaient / 9. rencontrés / 10. entendu

EXERCISE 7

1. tant s'en faut / 2. s'est complètement transformée / 3. se charger de / 4. se sont très bien débrouillées / 5. enrichissait / 6. se permettre / 7. s'améliorait / 8. se fatiguer / 9. se sentir / 10. il fallait / 11. échapper au / 12. se trouver / 13. élargir / 14. se passer d' / 15. se concentrer / 16. se réconcilier / 17. se décide à OR se résolve à / 18. se laisser faire / 19. se respectant / 20. se fait respecter

Chapter 7

EXERCISE 1

1. savoir; sait / 2. avez-vous su / 3. je ne sais; sache; l'a connu / 4. savez-vous; sais / 5. a su / 6. connu; sait / 7. connaît; sait / 8. je m'y connais; saurais / 9. savoir / 10. connu / 11. partie; revenir / 12. sorti; reviendra / 13. quitté; retourner / 14. laissant / 15. rentrer; oublié / 16. vivent; quitter / 17. sorti; partir / 18. parti; sais; habitent; vécu / 19. posé; savais; a su / 20. vivent; poser

EXERCISE 2

1. partie / 2. moment; la première fois / 3. En ce moment; dans le temps; délais / 4. matinée; le temps / 5. À l'heure actuelle; l'année / 6. toute la journée; partie / 7. partis; de toutes parts / 8. à temps / 9. années; époque / 10. part / 11. de l'époque victorienne / 12. part / 13. scientifique; sociologue / 14. une bonne soirée / 15. part; à la soirée; part

EXERCISE 3a

1. mieux; mieux / 2. meilleur / 3. mieux / 4. meilleur / 5. mieux mieux / 6. mieux; meilleure / 7. mieux; mieux / 8. mieux; meilleur / 9. mieux / 10. meilleur

EXERCISE 3b

1. y / 2. en / 3. en / 4. y / 5. en / 6. en / 7. en / 8. y / 9. y; en / 10. en

EXERCISE 4

1. D'ici / 2. où / 3. Jusqu'ici / 4. D'ici peu / 5. là / 6. jusque-là; D'ici là / 7. Qu'est-ce qui / 8. quoi qu'il arrive / 9. d'ici / 10. Qui est-ce qui

EXERCISE 5a

1. Son nouveau rôle de représentant du parti lui plaît.
2. Dans cet ouvrage il s'agit des origines du mouvement féministe.
3. Les enfants leur manquent.

4. Mais il ne s'agit pas de ça!
5. Elle manque d'humour.
6. Les truffes au chocolat lui plaisent.
7. S'agissant de la santé / Quand il s'agit de la santé . . .
8. Il lui manque 1 000 euros . . .
9. . . . il s'agissait de son bonheur.
10. Il ne s'agit pas d'accepter cette proposition.
11. Sa femme lui manque.
12. De quoi s'est-il agi?
13. Tu me manques.
14. De quoi va-t-il s'agir dans votre nouveau livre?
15. Les cadeaux leur ont plu.
16. Il s'agit de répondre sans délai.

EXERCISE 5b

1. d' / 2. des / 3. de / 4. d' / 5. des

EXERCISE 5c

1. autant / 2. pas mal de / 3. tant d' / tellement d' / 4. autant d' / 5. assez souvent / 6. énormément de / 7. autant de / 8. une bonne part de / 9. tellement / 10. tant / tellement de

EXERCISE 6

1. année / 2. connaît / 3. ans / 4. scientifique / 5. sait / 6. est retournée / 7. poser des questions / 8. demander / 9. en pensait / 10. d'une part / 11. du temps / 12. d'autre part / 13. meilleur / 14. Ce qui lui plaît / 15. beaucoup d'étudiants / 16. beaucoup des étudiants / 17. connaissait / 18. une bonne part du temps

Chapter 8

EXERCISE 1

1. en; en / 2. Dans la / 3. du Havre; de / 4. dans / 5. à; en / 6. à; aux / 7. dans; dans / 8. du; de / 9. dans / 10. au; en

EXERCISE 2a

1. Depuis / 2. sous / 3. pendant / 4. no preposition / 5. pendant / 6. dans / 7. En / 8. depuis / 9. pour / 10. no preposition

EXERCISE 2b

1. À ce moment-là / 2. De leur temps / 3. en même temps / 4. en ce moment / 5. Dans le temps **or** En ce temps-là / 6. de temps en temps / 7. en temps de guerre

EXERCISE 3

1. dont / 2. à **or** en / 3. de / 4. à; de / 5. de / 6. d'; d' / 7. au / 8. en **or** par le / 9. de / 10. de

EXERCISE 4

1. sur / 2. de l'autre côté de / 3. avant / 4. chez; à travers / 5. Sous / 6. sur / 7. à travers / 8. En tant que / 9. Dès / 10. sur / 11. aux / 12. dans / 13. vers; d'entre / 14. devant / 15. à; no preposition / 16. par; envers / 17 À partir de / 18. à cause de / 19. À partir de / 20. Hors d' **or** Sors/Sortez d'; par

EXERCISE 5

1. à / 2. à / 3. d' / 4. au / 5. en / 6. de / 7. no preposition / 8. du / 9. à / 10. no preposition

EXERCISE 6a

1. de / 2. no preposition / 3. contre / 4. à / 5. de / 6. à / 7. de / 8. no preposition / 9. no preposition / 10. à / 11. de / 12. en / 13. de / 14. d' / 15. dans / 16. no preposition / 17. d' / 18. à / 19. de / 20. à

EXERCISE 6b

1. leur / 2. les / 3. dont / 4. j'en / 5. leur / 6. lui / 7. y / 8. dont / 9. qu' / 10. dont / 11. lui / 12. leur

EXERCISE 7a

1. posé (put down) / 2. sortir (take / put out) / 3. prendre (pick up) / 4. descendre (bring / take down) / 5. éteindre (switch off) / 6. jeté (thrown out) / 7. monter (bring / take / get up) / 8. remet (puts back) / 9. étendre (hang / put out) / 10. remets (put off) / 11. éteindre (put out) / 12. se passe (is going on) / 13. rentrer (bring in) / 14. rapporte (brings back) / 15. rapproche (brings together) / 16. franchir (get through)

EXERCISE 7b

1. a monté . . . en rampant / 2. a descendu . . . en boitant / 3. avons avancé . . . à tâtons / 4. a traversé . . . en courant / 5. s'est éloigné . . . à la nage / 6. a descendu . . . à skis / 7. s'est approchée . . . d'un pas désinvolte / 8. est sorti . . . en courant

EXERCISE 8

1. de / 2. à / 3. en / 4. En ce moment / 5. à / 6. dans / 7. comme / 8. chercher / 9. à travers / 10. avant / 11. à la / 12. en / 13. d' / 14. rempli / 15. lui / 16. sur / 17. à la / 18. à / la ville lui manquera / 20. no preposition

Chapter 9

EXERCISE 1

1. objectif / 2. langage / 3. responsable / 4. beaucoup / 5. adresser / 6. indépendance / 7. correct! / 8. médecine / 9. positifs / 10. adresse

EXERCISE 2

1. Où / 2. correct! / 3. à peine / 4. çà / 5. paraîtra / 6. dû / 7. *Ça* / 8. créé / 9. Ou / 10. connaissons

EXERCISE 3a

1. jette / 2. mène / 3. commençons / 4. espèrent / 5. appelle / 6. mangeons / 7. achète

EXERCISE 3b

1. achèterai / 2. cédera / 3. jettera / 4. appellerai / 5. mènera

EXERCISE 4

1. le / 2. de l' / 3. la / 4. le / 5. de / 6. d' / 7. l'; le; de l' / 8. si elle; s'ils / 9. qui; qu' / 10. Chacun; quelquefois

EXERCISE 5

1. espagnole; française / 2. reine; la Chambre des communes / 3. rue de Rivoli; place de la Concorde / 4. l'océan Atlantique; été / 5. maghrébins; parisienne / 6. catholiques; dimanche / 7. général de Gaulle; juin / 8. Moyen Âge / 9. Sécurité sociale / 10. *À Bout de souffle*; anglais

EXERCISE 6

1. 2,5%; 520 000€ (or 520.000€); 518 700€ (or 518.700€) / 2. 2020 (no punctuation); 1 500€ (or 1.500€) / 3. 0,5%; 1,3% / 4. 2020 (no punctuation); 5 290 500 (or 5.290.500); 0,5%; +28 000 (or +28.000); 6,7%; +334 200 (or +334.200)

EXERCISE 7

l'espace / OBJET / l'honneur / à / l'espace / L'objectif / l'espace / professionnels / européenne / jeudi / vendredi / samedi / janvier / avenue / s'adresse / qu' / mènerez / à / échanges / européen / effectuer / professionnel / perfectionnement / exposés / exact / rappelle / l'hébergement / pratiques / décembre

Bibliography

Adamson, Robin and others. (1999) *Le Français en faculté, cours de base*, 3rd edition, London: Hodder and Stoughton.

Batchelor, Ronald Ernest and Offord, Malcolm Hugh. (2000) *Using French: A Guide to Contemporary French Usage*, 3rd edition, Cambridge: Cambridge University Press.

Coffman Crocker, Mary E. (2009) *Schaum's Outline of French Grammar*, 5th edition, New York: McGraw-Hill.

Crowe, Ann and Weslowski, Maureen. (1993) *NTC's Dictionary of French faux pas. Common Errors of English-speakers in French and How to Avoid Them*, Indiana: National Textbook Company.

Duffy, Jean. (1992) 'Problems with prepositions', *French Studies Bulletin* 42, 4–10.

Duffy, Jean. (1999) *Using French Vocabulary*, Cambridge: Cambridge University Press.

Engel, Dulcie, Evans, George and Howells, Valerie. (1998) *A French Grammar Workbook*, Oxford: Blackwell.

Ferrar, Henry. (1982) *A French Reference Grammar*, 2nd edition, Oxford: Oxford University Press.

Hawkins, Roger and Towell, Richard. (2015) *French Grammar and Usage*, 4th edition, London: Routledge.

Hawkins, Roger, Towell, Richard and Lamy, Marie-Noëlle. (2015) *Practising French Grammar*, 4th edition, London: Routledge.

Jubb, Margaret. (2007) *Upgrade your French*, 2nd edition, London: Hodder Arnold.

Jubb, Margaret and Rouxeville, Annie. (2014) *French Grammar in Context*, 4th edition, London: Routledge.

Judge, Anne and Healey, Frederick. (1985) *A Reference Grammar of Modern French*, London: Arnold.

Kirk-Greene, Christopher Walter Edward. (1990) *NTC's Dictionary of faux amis*, Indiana: National Textbook Company.

L'Huillier, Monique. (1999) *Advanced French Grammar*, Cambridge: Cambridge University Press.

Morton, Jacqueline. (2013) *English Grammar for Students of French*, 7th edition, Ann Arbor, Michigan: Olivia and Hill Press.

Muñoz-Basols, Javier, David, Marianne and Núñez Piñeiro, Olga. (2010) *Speed Up Your Spanish. Strategies to Avoid Common Errors,* Oxford and New York: Routledge.

Price, Glanville. (2008) *A Comprehensive French Grammar*, 6th edition, Oxford: Blackwell.

Thoday, Philip and Evans, Howard. (1988) *Faux Amis and Key Words: a Dictionary-guide to French Language, Culture and Society through Lookalikes and Confusables*, London: Athlone Press.

Thomas, Adolphe Victor. (2014) *Dictionnaire des difficultés de la langue française*, Paris: Larousse.

Turk, Phil and Vandaele, Geneviève García. (2006) *Action grammaire*, 3rd edition, London: Hodder Education.

Bilingual dictionaries

Collins Robert French Dictionary (2010) 9th edition, Glasgow and Paris: HarperCollins and Dictionnaires Le Robert.

The Oxford-Hachette French Dictionary (2007) 4th edition, Oxford: Oxford University Press.

Online dictionary

www.wordreference.com/

Index

Printed in Great Britain
by Amazon